Developing Collections of
U.S. Government Publications

**FOUNDATIONS IN LIBRARY AND
INFORMATION SCIENCE, VOLUME 12**

Editor: Robert D. Stueart, *Dean, Graduate School of Library and
Information Science, Simmons College*

Foundations in
LIBRARY AND INFORMATION SCIENCE

A Series of Monographs, Texts and Treatises

Series Editor: **Robert D. Stueart**
*Dean Graduate School of Library and Information Science
Simmons College, Boston*

Developing Collections of U.S. Government Publications

by   PETER HERNON
*Graduate School of Library
and Information Science
Simmons College*

GARY R. PURCELL
*Graduate School of Library
and Information Science
University of Tennessee,
Knoxville*

 JAI PRESS INC.

Greenwich, Connecticut   *London, England*

Library of Congress Cataloging in Publication Data

Hernon, Peter.
Developing collections of U.S. government publications.

(Foundations in library and information science;
v. 12)
Bibliography: p.
Includes index
1. Libraries—Special collections—Government
publications.   2. United States—Government publications.   I. Purcell, Gary R.   II. Title.   III. Title:
Developing collections of US government publications.
IV.
Series.

Z688.G6H468   1982   015.73   82-21226
ISBN 0-89232-135-0

CONTENTS

List of Tables

Chapter 4

Chapter 5

List of Figures

Preface

In planning the special issue of *Government Publications Review* devoted to collection development (Volume 8A, 1981, Numbers 1 and 2), we identified many topics and problems in the documents field that could not be fully developed in article format. Further, a central weakness of the issue is that the articles frequently could not draw upon research findings relating to government publications. This observation is less a commentary upon the articles included in the issue than on the state of knowledge and thinking on collection development for government publications at this time.

The literature of documents librarianship has traditionally viewed collection development as selection and acquisition. Collection development, in fact, is a planning process, the dimensions of which cover more than these two activities. Developing collections of public documents involves the identification and retention of source material likely to generate the most use. Since satisfying clients' demands for lesser-needed resources becomes very costly, libraries not attempting to be institutions of record should rely upon inter-institutional cooperation for lesser-needed items. This book focuses upon collection development within institutions and does not address resource sharing, which is a topic meriting separate treatment. However, we realize that libraries will only develop functional collections of government publications, ones centering on the more heavily needed source material, when a prompt and reliable document delivery system is in place. The depository library program operated by the U.S. Government Printing Office does not currently comprise such a system.[1]

The number of staff members assigned to documents related activities is declining. Documents staff members often lack training in on-line data base searching and do not have ready access to searching facilities.[2] In addition, library budgets are not keeping pace with inflation, and the number of publications available for depository distribution increases each year. Many libraries large and small are faced with hard choices involving zero growth for documents collections. Under these circumstances, it is no wonder that many libraries regard microforms as an alternative to selection and retention in hardcopy, and that they have accepted the decision of the GPO to rely on microfiche as the primary format for depository distribution. However, if microformatted publications are substituted in quantity for hardcopy paper materials, microform collections will expand dramatically and at some point present major collection management problems.[3] Further, collection development principles such as those discussed in this book apply to government publications of all types regardless of collection format.

Depository and non-depository libraries are becoming more selective in the document titles acquired and retained. Even many regional depository libraries are discovering that they lack the space to store all the titles distributed by the GPO each year. It is evident that the library community requires research into collection development and assistance in planning functional collections. Although the book focuses on the publication program of the GPO, the issues, discussion, and model collection development policy can be applied to other publishers/distributors of government information as well as to other levels of government.

The book should be of value to practicing librarians, library educators, and library science students. It provides an overview of collection development and its application to the documents field in Chapters 1 and 2, examines selection patterns for depository libraries as represented in the GPO's automated item number file in Chapter 3, suggests an adaptation of the file for collection development purposes in Chapter 4, describes document use patterns of one client group—academic economists—in Chapter 5, and presents a model collection development policy in Chapter 6. In addition, the appendices contain several types of useful information. For example, government publication collection development policies from seven institutions are reprinted.

The authors hope that the ideas expressed herein will assist the GPO in keeping its publication and depository programs attuned to the needs of the library community and the client groups they serve. Insights into selection and use patterns reinforce the view that bibliographic control over the document output produced each year and depository distribution are not synonymous. Comprehensive bibliographic control is a worthy goal. The notion that it is a desirable goal to distribute all documents, however, is questionable, especially since many of them will receive little or no use and will be costly in terms of distribution and storage. This cost must be borne by the distributing agency of government and by the many libraries that receive items not used.

The research reported in this book should be regarded as exploratory and as building upon two other works, *Use of Government Publications by Social Scientists* and *Microforms and Government Information*.[4] It is our hope that future studies will continue the effort to identify those government bodies as well as document types and titles likely to generate the most use. Since collection development takes into account factors external to the immediate institution, researchers must also examine depository library programs and their ability to deliver documents not held in the immediate setting. Such studies involving cost/benefit and cost/effectiveness must examine the programs as a whole and look at interrelationships among the various parts. Only with such research can we move toward a national information policy covering government publications; one whereby the information resources of various levels of government become available in an interlocking network.

Peter Hernon and Gary R. Purcell

NOTES AND REFERENCES

1. For a discussion of this point see: Peter Hernon, *Microforms and Government Information* (Westport, CT: Microform Review, Inc., 1981).
2. See Charles R. McClure, "Online Government Documents Data Base Searching and Use of Microfiche Documents Online by Academic and Public Depository Librarians," *Microform Review* 10 (Fall 1981): 245-259.
3. See Hernon, *Microforms and Government Information*.
4. Ibid., and Peter Hernon, *Use of Government Publications by Social Scientists* (Norwood, N.J.: Ablex Publishing Corp., 1979).

Acknowledgments

We are indebted to many people who made this book possible. Mr. C. A. LaBarre and his staff (especially Jim Livsey, J. D. Young, and Janet L. Erickson) provided us with a copy of the automated item number file and were supportive of our efforts to use the file for collection development purposes. Mr. LaBarre also granted permission for inclusion of Appendices B and C.

A number of people offered suggestions at various stages of the project. In this regard, we wish to thank Janet L. Erickson and Charles R. McClure of the University of Oklahoma.

Sincere appreciation is expressed to library staff members from the institutions depicted in Appendix A for allowing us to reprint their collection development policies. We are grateful to James C. Baughman of Simmons College for his willingess to let us reprint and adapt from his works on collection development.

Computer analysis on the automated item number file was performed at the University of Tennessee. We are grateful to this institution for its support of this analysis.

We also wish to thank the editor of this book series, Robert D. Stueart, and the publisher, Herbert M. Johnson, for their consistently cooperative attitude and their determination to publish a book on collection development for government publications based upon research findings.

Finally, we owe a special debt to our families (Elinor, Alison and Linsay Hernon; and Carolyn, Kay Margaret, Kristen, Beth, Ronald, and Benjamin Purcell) for their support and patience during the completion of this book. Undoubtedly they were subjected to more discourses on collection development and government publications than they would have preferred.

Chapter 1

Collection Development

The professional literature of librarianship has addressed the need for quality and discrimination in the selection of items for library collections from early times. For example, at the 1876 Philadelphia conference of the American Library Association, the topic of selection evoked controversy and debate.[1] In the intervening years a substantial literature has developed that explores the multiple facets of materials selection and collection development. An examination of this literature shows evidence of key issues that can be followed through the years, and perhaps more importantly, evidence of an evolution in the underlying theory of collection development. One of the objectives of this chapter is to trace the evolution of this theory with the intent of showing how the parameters of collection development have expanded. A second objective is to characterize the theoretical foundations of collection development as currently understood. A final objective is to provide a context for the central theme of this book, by recapitulating the basic elements which comprise an operational concept of collection development.

EVOLUTION OF THE THEORY OF COLLECTION DEVELOPMENT

The connotation of the term "collection development" as used and understood in the 1980s is the result of an evolution in the thinking about the role of the library and its staff in relation to the library collection. This evolution has led to a change in the profession's view of that role, and consequently to an enlargement of the theory of collection development. The three stages in the evolution of this theory will be discussed to demonstrate how the concept has expanded.

Written statements from the 19th century through mid 20th century about the role of the library professional staff in collection development

1

tend to address certain dominant themes. Because these can be differentiated by type of library, a distinction can be made between the dominant concerns of public and academic libraries, as reflected in the literature of this period.

Central to the concern of the public library was the operation of the materials selection process. This is the process of choosing the best monograph or serial titles for purchase. The literature which dealt with the role of the public librarian in this process stressed the application of selection principles. Also indicative of this concern is the content of library school courses on book selection. Historically, these were heavily oriented toward the selection process as carried out in public and school libraries. The content of these courses thus provides some insight into the emphasis in public library materials selection. One author characterized the method of approach in these courses (and hence by inference, in libraries) as "almost wholly that of book evaluation, of the comparison of new books with old or standard and critically well recommended lists."[2] As further noted by this author, the necessity of understanding the information needs of users was essentially taken for granted in these courses, but apparently little explicit attention was given to this topic.

The dominant theme of writings concerned with academic library collections also dealt with selection, but book evaluation, although present, was subordinate to another issue. This was the question of whether the primary responsibility for selection should rest with the faculty or the library staff. An examination of the literature which addresses materials selection in academic libraries reveals that strong advocacy for a more central role in the selection process was an important theme well into the late 1960s.[3]

The common feature of this stage in the theory of collection development in academic and public libraries was the emphasis on evaluation of individual titles. The label that will be used to identify this stage in the evolutionary process is the "selection" stage of collection development. The literature was typified by a preoccupation with the identification of criteria for choices among individual books, periodicals, or other materials, and recommendations about the application of those criteria. In standard publications such as Helen Haines *Living with Books: the Art of Book Selection*, book evaluation constituted the major portion of the process.[4] The Haines book, used for years in American library schools and highly regarded by librarians in the field, no doubt had a major impact in shaping the concerns of librarians in relation to their collections.

In the post World War II period, another concept began to emerge in the literature. This was the notion of "collection building," which was broader than "selection" in that it extended the vision of the librarian's role beyond "book evaluation" to regard to entire collection as a matter of concern. However, the object of this concern was to "build" the collection, and the very use of this term carried the implicit expectation of continued growth. It was during this time that libraries experienced some spectacular gains in the levels of funding available for library materials. Also, many former teachers colleges were upgraded to the status of universities and a number of new academic institutions emerged. Large institutions worked toward building extensive research collections. This activity was augmented by the emergence of resource sharing programs such as the Farmington Plan and institutions such as the Center for Research Libraries. This collection building psychology was accompanied by a notable increase in the rate of monograph and journal publishing. Whether this influenced the library profession to move toward more vigorous collection building cannot be determined, but the increase in monograph and serial titles provided fertile ground for further expansion of library collections.[5]

The philosophy of collection building was encouraged by increased availability of ready made "collections" offered through several channels. For example, libraries that ceased to be economically viable sold their collections to institutions with a stronger financial base. Some vendors sold (and continue to sell) pre-selected collections for purchase, in paper copy originals or reprint. Several publishers began to sell pre-selected research collections in microform. The concept of the pre-selected standing order service (approval plans) fostered by vendors such as Richard Abel and others provided libraries with yet another option to build collections quickly without imposing a substantial increase in staff time required for individual book selection or evaluation.[6]

These options provided welcome relief for libraries with limited funds for expanding staff time to meet rapidly expanding materials budgets. They also gave librarians the opportunity to build collections quantitatively in a very short time, and library growth rates indicate that this did occur. In instances where federal funds were available, the funds often became available with limited time for individual choices to be made. Sometimes substantial sums of money were spent for library materials with scant attention given to the quality of the items purchased or the appropriateness of those items for the clientele served.

The collection building concept began to lose its attraction as economic circumstances changed in the middle and late 1970s. The factors which appear to have had the biggest impact on the collection building concept are the sharp increase in the cost of materials and the leveling off, or in some cases, the actual drop in funds available for the purchase of materials. At the time inflation and budget reductions took their toll, the literature began to show evidence of the emergence of yet another collection related concept, one which called for an expanded role for the librarian in relation to the collection. This is the concept of "collection development."

The term collection development is in common use now in the literature and in the vocabulary of librarianship. In this chapter the term is used in the dual role to identify the overall process and to label the current stage in the evolution of the theory. The concept described by this term enlarges the theoretical base through unifying several ideas. It is also a manifestation of greater maturity of thinking than evidenced in the past, and it provides the profession with a better conceptual tool with which to examine the process.

The expression "collection development" can be found in the literature as early as the late fifties, but used with a much narrower meaning than the term has come to hold. For example, Lane concludes a review of materials selection in academic libraries by quoting from a 1957 article which noted that ". . . librarians ought to assume responsibility for the development of the library collection."[7] However, Lane's article as well as the literature that he reviewed still dealt with the issue of whether the librarian or the faculty should have the responsibility for selecting materials for the academic library.

An indication of the larger concept of collection development is made by Haro in a paper concerned with academic book selection. He wrote that

> Most of the larger academic libraries with firmly established area studies or medium sized libraries with accelerated programs for collection development were utilizing bibliographers or subject specialists responsible for the selection of library materials.[8]

Edelman and Tatum also discuss the emergency of the subject bibliography in the 1960 as a manifestation of the attempt by large academic libraries to implement collection development programs.[9]

THEORETICAL FOUNDATIONS OF COLLECTION DEVELOPMENT

In what ways does the expanded concept of "collection development" differ from the earlier concepts labeled "selection" and "collection building"? A response to this should begin with a definition of the collection development concept. McClure states that

> Collection development is more than the selection and acquisition of materials. It is a decision making process that determines specific materials that will be obtained in terms of subject content, format and other criteria. A collection development policy is a plan that provides guidelines to the selectors as to the appropriateness of various types of materials for a particular collection. As such, it is a framework by which all

Figure 1.1. Collection Development: A Structural Approach.*

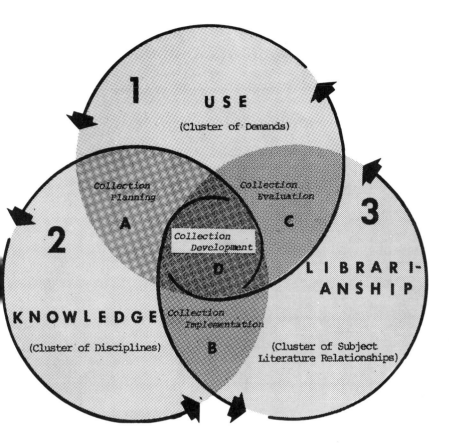

the various departments in the library work toward common collection goals and standards.[10]

The term "collection development" implies the application of a set of interrelated concepts. Baughman observes that there are three major constructs which are "integral" to collection development. These are 1) use, which represents a cluster of demands, 2) knowledge, which represents a cluster of disciplines, subjects, topics or areas of study, and 3) librarianship, which is a manifestation of a cluster of subject literature relationships.[11] His constructs are presented in a venn diagram (see Figure 1.1), which depicts overlapping areas among the constructs and leads

*This figure is reprinted from James C. Baughman, "Toward a Structural Approach to Collection Development," *College and Research libraries*, 38 (May 1977): 243, with the permission of the author and the American Library Association.

to the conceptualization of collection development as: collection plan ning + collection implementation + collection evaluation.[12]

The notion of collection development as formulated above clearly ex pands the concept of the relationship between library staff and collection as stated in earlier literature. The idea of overall collection planning i unquestionably more comprehensive than "selection" and "collection build ing." In fact, "selection" can be incorporated in Baughman's model subsumed under the concept of collection implementation. Collection development implies the idea that the entire collection, with all its com ponent formats, should be viewed as a whole in terms of the subjec content conveyed rather than as separate and distinct entities with differ ing collection development objectives.

The concept of collection development, if properly implemented, leave little room for heavy emphasis on "collection building" as practiced ir the 1960s and early 1970s. It also seems to challenge some application of standing order purchasing and its variant, profile purchasing througl approval plans. In both of these cases, it can be questioned whether lonς recognized standards for selection were followed. If Baughman's con struct is used as an explanation of the theoretical base of collection development, the result is the existence of a process that should result ir the acquistion and maintenance of vital collections that are more fully utilized than evidence shows collections to have been used previously.[13]

The concept of collection development, to be useful in an operationa way by libraries, must be described in terms of specific operational ele ments. This is to say that the process must be defined in terms of whai happens at each stage. The remainder of this chapter will deal with the collection development process by describing the operational elements.

OPERATIONAL ELEMENTS OF COLLECTION DEVELOPMENT

To gain maximum utilization of the enlarged concept of collection development, it is necessary to recognize and understand the constituen elements and their relationship to one another. In Baughman's model, three elements are identified. However, for application in an operationa context, these need to be defined with more specificity. The constituent elements of an operational definition of the collection development pro cess are addressed, to one degree or another, in a number of sources particularly texts on selection, collection building, and collection devel opment. For example, a recent two volume treatise on the subject, edited by Robert D. Stueart and George B. Miller, includes several valuable papers which deal with a wide range of collection development topics.[14] For the purposes of this chapter, G. Edward Evans's book, *Developing*

Library Collections, provides the clearest and most useful enumeration of the operational elements. In addition, Evans provides practical ideas for the implementation of this model. He describes collection development as a "dynamic, self-perpetuating cycle (which) consists of six definable elements; community analysis, policies, selection, acquisiton, weeding and evaluation."[15] The remainder of this chapter will be devoted to characterizing each of these elements, with the added intent of showing their relationship to each other and to the collection development theory as defined by Baughman.

Community Analysis

Figure 1.1 shows the overlap between use (cluster of demands) and knowledge (cluster of disciplines) to be the first aspect of collection development, collection planning. This planning phase is crucial to the success of the collection development process, for without a clear notion of where the process is going, it is not possible to determine if it is moving in the right direction.

The planning process requires two essential types of knowledge on the part of the librarian. It requires knowledge of the content and structure of the literature of various topics or subject fields. (Knowledge of the structure of subject literatures requires an understanding of the information formats preferred in different fields and the bibliographic control sources designed to provide intellectual access.) It also requires knowledge of the information requirements and demands of the community or constituency served by the library. The latter leads to the first defined element in the collection development process, community analysis.

The purpose of a community analysis is to determine the characteristics of the actual and potential users of the library and, insofar as possible, to attempt to determine current and anticipated information requirements. The object of acquiring this information is to gain an understanding of the community that can be translated into effective decision making further along in the collection development process.

Use of the term "community" is meant to include the constitutency served by any type of library, thus the "community" is library specific. For example, a community analysis for a pharmaceutical company technical library would include the research staff, mangagement and technical personnel, but because of the proprietary nature of the company would exclude persons not associated with the company. (An exception to the limitation of "community" to the specific constituency served by each library is imposed by the U.S. Government Printing Office depository system. Each depository, except for appellate court libraries, must make available documents received through the system to the general public. Thus, although the primary users served by the depository typically consist of the main constituency served by the library, all citizens can be considered potential users of a depository collection.)

As suggested above, a community analysis should identify the characteristics and information requirements of a representative sample of all constitutents of the library, including known and potential users. The "community" actually consists of several communities, each with different information requirements and interests. This is especially evident in the case of public libraries, which serve a heterogenous population represented by different ages, income, racial and ethnic groups. Also, individuals within the "community" reflect varying roles at different times. Therefore, the relevance of the collection will vary with individuals and with the same individual, depending on the roles played at a given time.[16] The dynamic nature of the user population means that the conduct of a community analysis should be an ongoing activity of the library.

A successful community analysis should show the multiplicity of subject interests of the constituency and the various roles individuals might play in their use of the collection. One means by which this can be done is to focus on sub-groups within the community. An example of this is found in Chapter 5 of this book, which is a study of academic economists, one identifiable sub-group served by academic libraries. This type of subject oriented use study could be employed with other groups served by academic libraries and adopted for use in other library settings. A composite picture would reflect areas of similarity and difference and help libraries to develop collections of the more heavily needed source material.

The process by which community analyses or use/user studies are conducted has been dealt with in greater detail elsewhere than space allows here.[17] However, three key features of a community analysis are described below. It is important for library decision makers to keep these in mind because all three have a direct impact on this process.

1. Demographic Information. A study intended to reveal the characteristics of the community served by the library must begin with an examination of basic demographic characteristics of the constituency such as age, sex, race, language groups served, and occupations represented. In academic and special libraries, subject specialization should also be studied. These data, when collected, can be compared to other characteristics of the population of the community. Because shifts in the nature of the user community will ultimately be reflected in changes in use patterns, these should be monitored on a continuing basis.

2. Identifiable Information Requirements. Knowledge of the actual or anticipated information requirements of actual and potential users is of vital importance because it is the primary basis for determining the direction of collection growth. Once the range of information requirements are known, libraries can decide which they wish to address and to which they will give priority. With limited resources, funds generally should be spent to meet the most immediate, known requirements. The concept of a "balanced" collection in which all areas of subject knowledge are represented fairly and perhaps equally is certainly not realistic for libraries in times of limited resources and in fact never really was viable. No library is totally a library of record; therefore, implementation of the concept of a balanced collection is too costly to meet infrequent information requests received by all libraries. To do so has the potential for resulting in a waste of limited resources. What collection development librarians really need to know is the type of information their users require, and thus librarians cannot ignore use patterns.

Community studies that deal with information needs have tended to focus on the information requirements of library users alone. However, there is also a reason to determine the requirements of non-users in order to increase the relevance of the collection for this group. Nevertheless, these studies should be directed toward the identifiable constituencies of each library rather than including persons outside the scope or the geographical limits of the service area.

3. Identification of Other Community Information Resources. A community study should report the nature and extent of the holdings of nearby institutions. This is done with the expectation that these institutions will have resources which complement or supplement the library's own holdings. This should also apply to non-library information resources to which information seekers can be referred. In an information rich society, the information requirements of users frequently extend beyond libraries and conventional print formats. Therefore, whether the required information is in print form or otherwise, it is generally a sound policy for the library to avoid unnecessary duplication and to augment this with knowledge of local availability, to enable quick referral of users to the source of the required information.

Although a great deal has been written about the value of resource sharing, there are still many examples of inadequate knowledge or awareness of nearby library collections or other information resources that can supplement the holdings of each collection. Users are ill served by libraries that either waste their resources in unnecessary duplication or are unable to refer their users to other nearby information resources.

Policies

A collection development policy is a statement of the plan that a library develops to meet its collection objectives. It should identify collection priorities established by the library staff and based on the results of the community analysis. The policy statement is intended to provide stability and consistency in the collection development process as well as a resource to turn to when difficult choices must be made. It is difficult to understand how a library can develop its collection in a systematic and orderly fashion without a well reasoned collection development policy, which takes into account the full range of information needs of the community that the library serves. Therefore, the design of a collection development policy is an enterprise that should involve as many members of the library staff as possible, as well as representatives of the constituencies served.

There are standard features that a carefully planned collection development policy should include.[18] Since these are identified in several sources, it will not be necessary to discuss them all here. However, three have been selected for emphasis through further discussion. The first feature, the introduction or overview, should identify the mission of the library and the nature of the user community served by the library. Included should be a general indication of the information requirements of the user community. This should be augmented later in the policy statement by a more detailed description of user requirements in relationship to the subject areas that must be represented. Also included in the overview should be an indication of the way the library pictures its relationship to other institutions, and when such exist, a specification of the library's responsibilities in any cooperative acquisitions and collection development agreements.

A second feature, which should be a part of a collection development policy statement, is a clear and detailed subject and format analysis of the component parts of the collection. One author states that

> . . . the detailed subject analysis will require, at a minimum, an indication of the level of acquisition determined to be desirable for the continuing development of the library's collection in each subject or class, and an indication of the selector or unit with primary responsibility in the field.[19]

The purpose of this portion of the policy statement is to create a statement of collection priorities that can be used for day-to-day decision making when choices must be made.

The establishment of priorities implies the creation of a list of the levels of acquisition for various parts of the collection. Various authors have developed categories to indicate the levels of acquisition, but the four categories described by Evans appear to provide the clearest indication of the nature of collection development that would occur at each level.[20] The four levels of acquisition which he identifies are:

1. *General coverage.* This level of coverage that is intended to serve the general adult reader excludes the purchase of reference books and incorporates an ongoing program for the deselection of titles.

2. *Instructional or working collection.* This level of coverage includes current materials and excludes retrospective materials. It is limited to indexed periodicals and specifies limited collection of microform items.

3. *Comprehensive/research collection.* At this level, an attempt should be made to acquire all current materials on a subject, both for reference and circulation. Although Evans states that little or no weeding should occur, one could argue that periodically items could be reviewed for transfer to high-density remote storage.

4. *Exhaustive collection.* As the term implies, this level of collection requires an effort to collect everything related to the subject, with the objective of permanent retention. Efforts should be made to acquire funds for especially rare and expensive materials.

The third element of the collection development policy that is more general in nature deals with topics such as gifts and exchanges, weeding and discards, replacements and duplicates, complaints and censorship, and evaluation. These will not be discussed individually here, but two topics, weeding/discards and evaluation will be addressed as separate parts of this chapter.

A substantial amount of useful advice is available for libraries that plan to set about the process of planning and drafting a collection development policy.[21] Libraries should therefore utilize these resources to maximize the quality of the policy statement that they create.

The dynamic nature of collection development makes it imperative that the policy should be reviewed and updated periodically. Just as the community analysis process should be an ongoing effort, so too should the maintenance of an up-to-date collection development policy. It might even be desirable to record a development policy in a word processor to facilitate the updating process.[22]

Because this book is concerned with collection development of government publications collections, the authors have included sample policies from seven libraries (see Appendix A). In addition, Chapter 7 proposes a model collection development policy for federal documents depository collections. It is hoped that this book will aid libraries wanting to develop or revise a collection policy.

Selection

Of all of the elements of the collection development process, selection has probably received the most attention in the literature. As noted above, the early literature concerned with collection development dealt almost entirely with selection. The basic principles of selection for books and non-book materials are well established and available from a variety of sources. Several basic texts identify and describe these principles. Unfortunately, the principles of selection are often ignored in favor of expediency. For example, libraries that receive unexpected money for acquisitions near the end of the fiscal year may choose to use the funds to buy large sets in paper copy or microform. The reasons for this are typically, insufficient time to evaluate needed purchases, or insufficient time to place and receive numerous small orders prior to the end of the accounting period. This happened frequently during the days when federal funds were plentiful and time to spend them was short.

The best alternative to the ineffective use of funds that occurs if libraries acquire materials with limited time to select properly is to anticipate the problem and have orders ready to go. However, if it is not possible to order materials consistent with the collection development priorities, a serious question can be raised about the advisability of spending the funds at all. Spending funds for marginally needed materials violates both the basic principles of materials selection and the library's own collection development priorities. Additionally, the cost to the library of last minute purchases might in the long run be greater than if the money went unspent. The library's costs include processing and storing items which are not used.[23] Whether the items are in hardcopy or microform, there is still a cost involved, which will usually far exceed any benefit derived from the purchase of the items. Thus, it is the authors' contention that the principles of selection should be adhered to regardless of circumstances that might suggest deviations due to expediency.

The issue of consistent application of selection principles is especially pertinent to the area of collection development of U.S. government publications collections, the central theme of this book. In some, perhaps many, depository libraries, documents series have been selected without being subjected to the level of scrutiny mandated by proper selection procedures. This is due to limited information available from the Government Printing Office and to limited efforts by librarians to learn about the documents. The absence of a subject context for document selection is another factor. The notion of a subject orientation model for government document collection development will be dealt with more fully in in Chapter 4 of this book.

Another example of a decline in adherence to selection principles is increased reliance on standing order plans and their variant, approval plans. Standing order and approval plans reduce the amount of staff time required for materials evaluation. On the surface this would appear to be a positive feature of these services, and in many cases it is. However, approval plans result in a more cursory evaluation of the items sent for approval, and standing order plans generally result in no evaluation of individual titles. Although approval plan vendors incorporate a number of dimensions into the library acquisition profiles, there is no way they can assure the quality of all materials sent for examination. This means that the responsibility for the evaluation of items rests with those who examine them. There are two factors that work against adherence to careful evaluation standards in this process. One is the assumption many evaluators make that the profile is a fairly accurate reflection of the library's needs, therefore only superficial examination of titles need be conducted. The other is the cost to the library of returning any unwanted items. The result is a situation where a high rejection rate could indicate the library profile is not well designed, but if the rejection rate is low, it could reflect a lack of careful selection on the part of those who do the evaluation. Either way, titles could be acquired by default, and standards for the selection of materials might not be applied in a stringent fashion.[24]

Acquisition

The acquisition phase of collection development follows closely on the selection phase, and is interrelated in many respects. The activities or facets of acquisition include selection as well as verifying, ordering, receiving, and recording funds.[25] However, the acquisition and selection phases will be considered separately in this chapter.

Acquisition is usually regarded as the set of procedures required for the purchase of materials for the library. However, one author argues that the definition of acquisition should be expanded to include non-purchase means of acquiring library materials.[26] This includes not only gifts and exchanges, but also the automatic receipt of theses and dissertations in academic libraries or government publications in depository libraries. (In the case of depository programs, the publications cannot, in most cases, be considered as gifts because the governments responsible for distributing them retain title to the publications).

For successful implementation of a broadly based collection development process, acquisition of library materials must be coordinated in the various sub-units of the library. In a large, complex system, it is not uncommon for several units to have some measure of acquisition authority or responsibility. For example, microforms might be identified and acquired separately from monographs and serials. U.S. government publications might by acquired through a totally separate acquisition system. Without coordination, the potential for unwanted or unnecessary duplication of materials is great.

An example of this problem is evident with government publications that are distributed both by the Government Printing Office (as depository items) and by the National Technical Information Service (as sales items). In a library without a cataloged documents collection and without a verification program that extends to all parts of the collection, unwanted duplication could occur easily (and frequently does) with these two government publishers. Another example of unwanted duplication was observed in a specific library when it was learned that the British Parliamentary Papers (sessional papers) in paper copy from HMSO were being duplicated with a separate subscription to the parliamentary papers on Readex microprint. This unwanted duplication continued for several years, at great expense, before it was discovered.

Acquisition is largely a technical activity directed at bringing library materials physically into the library. Unless the acquisitions program is operated in a competent, businesslike manner and within the context of an overall collection development program, it can be counterproductive for successful collection development.

Weeding

Although weeding is the term most commonly used for the process of withdrawal of items from the collection, the authors of this book prefer to use the term deselection. Deselection carries the connotation of the careful application of the same principles as found in the selection process, only with a reverse intent: removal from the collection of those items no longer considered relevant to the user population.

The necessity for deselection in most library collections is brought about because the proliferation of newly published knowledge brings about inevitable obsolescence in existing knowledge. For most libraries, the permanent retention of published knowledge is costly far beyond any value that might be derived from its use. It is costly because of the financial resources that must be committed to indefinite storage and maintenance of materials that have little or no relevance to users. Studies have demonstrated that the relevance of a collection to its users is not randomly distributed, hence some portions of each collection are highly relevant to its users while other portions cease to be relevant and thus become obsolete.[27] If unbridled collection growth imposes the need for new or expanded facilities just to store the portion of the collection that is obsolete or non-relevant, then costs skyrocket.

Permanent maintenance of materials in any collection is costly in another way as well. The permanent retention of obsolete materials creates congestion in the means of access, particularly in the library catalog or classification scheme.[28] This congestion impedes user access to relevant materials. For example, in a library where the shelves are congested with obsolete publications interspersed with relevant material, the user who chooses to browse the shelves is presented with a frustrating experience. Similarly, a library catalog congested with obsolete items requires users to make a relevance judgment about numerous items based on the minimal information on the catalog entry or else go to the shelves to examine each item. If a high percentage of the items are not relevant, it is a costly and time-consuming experience for the user.

The costs associated with this problem can be reduced by means of a well planned process to determine which items are to be retained, which might be sent to a high density storage facility (if one exists), and which items are to be purged from the collection. Factors which work against this are: a) a philosophy that says it is the responsibility of the library to acquire and retain all items in certain areas. This philosophy is certainly questionable in times of limited resources and the expanding production of information. Faced with limited resources, any type of library should give careful thought to acquiring and retaining materials at the exhaustive level; b) a reluctance of librarians to discard publications because they might eventually be called for (Evans suggests the existence of two "natural laws" that inhibit librarians from engaging in an active deselection program: "(1) no matter how strange an item may seem, at least one person in the world will find it valuable; and (2) no matter how long a library keeps these strange items, ten minutes after one has been discarded, the one possible user in the world will walk in and ask for that item."[29]). The cost of providing infrequently requested materials when analyzed should serve as a motivation for librarians to abandon their allegiance to these "natural laws;" c) restriction on the ability of the library to discard certain types of materials. The best example of this, and one pertinent to the central theme of this book, is the policy of the GPO depository system limiting the discretionary power of depository libraries to engage in deselection programs. The rules and procedures imposed for discarding public documents do not allow libraries the level of freedom possessed with other parts of the collection. Also, with the procedures in effect, it means that the process of purging obsolete documents from depository collections is more costly than the disposal of other types of library materials. With many libraries understaffed, the result is less active deselection programs. The philosophy that leads to the existence of these rules for retention and discarding for depository libraries stems from the archival heritage of the GPO and represents the notion that public documents should be made available to the public. This concept, although laudatory, should be tempered by the understanding that availability can be impeded by the excessive retention of non-relevant or obsolete materials. It would seem to be an appropriate time for the depository system to examine the five year retention policy to determine if it is productive or counter-productive. Chapter 5 deals at greater length with the five year retention policy.

The deselection concept should be applied to all forms of materials, not only monographs. Obsolescence occurs with published material that appears in microform, technical reports, and other formats as well. Some materials almost seem to be immune from the deselection process. Microforms, because they require less space than paper copy equivalents, are often considered an appropriate substitute for items with limited relevance. However, the notion that the substitution of a format that requires less space in order to extend the retention of materials that have little or no relevance to the user population is questionable. For example, the decision to discard paper copies of obsolete items and substitute microfiche copies results from a failure to recognize at least one of the two problems mentioned earlier, the need to limit intellectual and bibliographic congestion of non-relevant items. Furthermore, microform copies if substituted in large numbers for paper copies eventually accumulate in sufficient quantities to present the same problem.[30]

The growing awareness of the need for active deselection has brought a greater sense of urgency to the principle and practice of resource sharing. DeGennaro, long an advocate of resource sharing, has indicated the reason for this increased interest:

> Powerful inflationary trends on the one hand, coupled with increasingly effective technological and resource-sharing capabilities on the other hand, are causing all academic research libraries to undergo a fundamental reassessment and reorientation of their traditional collection development goals and service strategies as they make the painful transition from the affluent sixties to the austere seventies and eighties.[31]

The deselection phase of collection development could be conducted in the same fashion that continuous revision occurs in a general encyclopedia. Various subject areas of the collection could be examined each year on a rotating basis with the result that over a ten year period of time the entire collection could be subjected to this process. Following the completion of a full cycle, the process would begin again. Although many librarians would argue that they lack the staff to do this, if carefully planned, staff resources could be allocated in most cases to carry out this process.

In order for the collection development process to proceed in a successful fashion, deselection must be an inherent and active part of the process. Failure to include this results in a congested system with a resultant impediment to intellectual and physical access.

Evaluation

The purpose of evaluation is to provide a feedback mechanism to determine if document delivery is proceeding smoothly (e.g., the operational process by which items appear on the shelves), and to determine if user information requirements are being met. This feedback mechanism can be used to determine if other elements in the collection development process are working effectively. It is also a mechanism to determine if the collection development process results in a collection with maximum utility for the user population and minimum expenditure of resources. It is through this activity that the accuracy of judgments made in community analysis, selection, and deselection can be assessed. Evaluation provides a means of assessing the quality of the written collection development policy, thus enabling the library to adjust the policy statement where necessary. Finally, evaluation provides a mechanism for reflecting on the effectiveness of the selection, acquisition, and deselection procedures. Procedures which impede successful selection development can be altered.

Collection evaluation is a complex process and there is no consensus on the single "best" way to achieve it. Various evaluation measures have been developed that are applicable to collection development. Robinson identifies the six categories of evaluation measures that have been employed to study the process of collection development:

1. Activity measures are the most popular and involve counting collection related activities for a period of time. For example, the number of items selected or added to the collection, the number circulated, the number of reference queries answered by government documents, etc.

2. Performance or effectiveness measures are gaining in popularity, but are more difficult to use. Performance measures attempt to measure the degree to which the collection meets particular user requests or needs. For example, the number of requested items held and available for users are measures of performance.

3. Impact measures are less frequently used. The impact of the documents collection might be measured by the extent to which potential users actually use the collection.

4. Cost measures are increasing in popularity. These may identify the total cost of providing the collection as a whole or may define the cost of providing an average document to the patron. Cost and benefit measures are frequently associated.

5. Outcome measures attempt to identify and count accomplishments or products which result from collection use. An example of this is research reports that were written using available documents.

6. Benefit or value measures would be the most helpful, but they are also the most difficult to apply. Benefit measures attempt to record the amount of societal good (based on broad assumptions of 'value') created by the use of the collection. Thus, they build upon and go one step further than outcome measures.[32]

Three basic requirements for collection evaluation are: 1) the collection be evaluated against an accepted standard; 2) this process be continuous; and 3) it result in meaningful changes in other elements of the collection development process. If these three requirements are not met, collection evaluation is not being conducted properly.

The first requirement, the use of an accepted standard against which the collection can be evaluated, raises the question: what type of standard? Robinson, responding to this question, notes that:

> Collection evaluation has historically focused on the degree to which the collection is 'adequate.' That leads to the obvious question of 'adequate for what' which in turn leads to a community analysis which provides reasonably clear specifications of what is needed. Adequacy is usually defined as the goodness or quality of the collection, as the ability to meet particular needs or wants, and as the degree to which a collection is complete.[33]

SUMMARY

This chapter, which has dealt with the general concept of collection development, has demonstrated that the concept as now understood is the result of an evolution of the theory from a more restricted notion in use at an earlier time. The chapter has also discussed the theoretical base and the elements that comprise an operational definition of collection development. The remaining chapters of the book fall within the conceptual framework established by this chapter. They explain and apply collection development principles to study the selection and use of government publications published through the depository library program operated by the Government Printing Office.

NOTES AND REFERENCES

1. Carl B. Roden, "Theories of Book Selection for Public Libraries," in Louis R. Wilson (ed.), *The Practice of Book Selection* (Chicago: University of Chicago, 1940), p. 6.
2. Ibid., p. 9.
3. David O. Lane, "The Selection of Academic Library Materials, A Literature Survey," *College and Research Libraries* 29 (September 1968): 364-372.
4. Roden, "Theories of Book Selection for Public Libraries," p. 10.
5. An informative review article which deals with collection building in academic libraries especially during the 1960s and 1970s is: Rose Mary Magrill and Mona East, "Collection Development in Large University Libraries," in Michael H. Harris (ed.), *Advances in Librarianship*, Vol. 8. (New York: Academic Press, 1978), pp. 2-54.
6. A good account of the history of approval plans in U.S. libraries is found in: H. William Axford, "Approval Plans: an Historical Overview and an Assessment of Future Values," in Peter Spyers-Duran and Thomas Mann, Jr. (eds.), *Shaping Library Collections for the 1980s* (Phoenix, Ariz.: Oryx Press, 1980), pp. 18-31.

7. Lane, "The Selection of Academic Library Materials, A Literature Survey," p. 372.

8. Robert Haro, "Book Selection in Academic Libraries," *College and Research Libraries* 28 (March 1967):104.

9. Hendrik Edelman and G. Marvin Tatum, Jr., "The Development of Collections in American University Libraries," in Richard D. Johnson (ed.), *Libraries for Teaching, Libraries for Research* (Chicago: American Library Association, 1977), p. 48.

10. Charles R. McClure, "An Integrated Approach to Government Publications Collection Development," *Government Publications Review* 8A (1981):5.

11. James C. Baughman, "Toward a Structural Approach to Collection Development," *College and Research Libraries* 38 (May 1977):242.

12. Ibid.

13. Several studies have demonstrated that a small percentage of titles in library collections account for a large percentage of use. An early study which provides evidence of this is: Richard W. Trueswell, "A Quantitative Measure of User Circulation Requirements and Its Possible Effect on Stack Thinning and Multiple Copy Determination," *American Documentation* 16 (January 1965):20-25. A study which provides more current evidence of this is: Allen Kent, et. al., *Use of Library Materials; The University of Pittsburgh Study* (New York: Marcel Dekker, Inc., 1979), pp. 9-55.

14. Robert D. Stueart and George B. Miller (eds.), *Collection Development in Libraries: A Treatise.* (Greenwich, Conn.: JAI Press, Inc., 1980).

15. G. Edward Evans, *Developing Library Collections* (Littleton, Colo.: Libraries Unlimited, 1979), p. 19.

16. A study which demonstrates the way use orientation affects the user's perception of relevance is: Carlos A. Cuadra and Robert V. Katter, "Opening the Black Box of 'Relevance'," *Journal of Documentation* 23(December 1967):291-303.

17. Evans, *Developing Library Collections*, pp. 97-118. See also: William A. Katz, *Collection Development: The Selection of Materials for Libraries* (New York: Holt, Rinehart and Winston, 1980), pp. 25-40.

18. A number of sources identify features of collection development policies. Among these are: Evans, *Developing Library Collections*, pp. 126-135; Katz, *Collection Development: The Selection of Materials for Libraries*, pp. 21-22; and Richard K. Gardner, *Library Collections: Their Origin, Selection, and Development* (New York: McGraw-Hill, 1981), pp. 225-228.

19. Sheila T. Dowd, "The Formulation of a Collection Development Policy Statement," in Robert D. Stueart and George B. Miller (eds.), *Collection Development in Libraries: A Treatise* (Greenwich, Conn.: JAI Press, Inc., 1980), p. 85.

20. Evans, *Developing Library Collections*, p. 129.

21. In addition to the standard texts cited in references 15, 17 and 18, there are other useful sources that provide guidance for drafting collection development policies. Among these are: David L. Perkins (ed.), *Guidelines for Collection Development* (Chicago: American Library Association, 1979); and Charles B. Osburn, "Some Practical Observations on the Writing, Implementation, and Revision of Collection Development Policy," *Library Resources and Technical Services* 23 (Winter 1979): 7-15. The ALA publication is the product of the Collection Development Committee of the Resources and Technical Services Division and as such it represents the work of task forces of that division assigned to develop practical guidelines.

22. Dowd, "The Formulation of a Collection Development Policy Statement," p. 85.

23. A major study that compared the cost of conventional storage of material as opposed to various compact storage systems indicated that in 1969, conventional storage cost $1.31 per volume, while very compact storage was as low as $0.49 per volume. These costs would of course be much higher today because of inflation. The study which

reports these costs is found in: Ralph Ellsworth, *The Economics of Book Storage in College and Research Libraries* (Washington: Association of Research Libraries, 1969), p. 18.

24. For further discussion on this topic see: Margaret Dobbyn, "Approval Plan Purchasing in Perspective," *College and Research Libraries* 33 (November 1972): 480-484. A range of opinions and experiences about approval and standing order plans can be found in the papers included in the following: Peter Spyers-Duran and Thomas Mann, Jr. (eds.), *Shaping Library Collections for the 1980s.* (Phoenix, Arix.: Oryx Press, 1980).

25. Ted Grieder, *Acquisition: Where, What, and How; a Guide to Orientation and Procedure for Students in Librarianship, Librarians, and Academic Faculty* (Westport, Conn.: Greenwood Press, 1978), p. 14.

26. Evans, *Developing Library Collections*, p. 29.

27. The topic of relevance has been addressed through the application of bibliometric studies as well as through other approaches. For a comprehensive overview of the results of these studies, see: Tefco Saracevic, "Relevance: A Review of and a Framework for the Thinking on the Notion in Information Science," *Journal of the American Society for Information Science* 26(November-December 1975): 321-343.

28. A review of catalog use studies can be found in: F.W. Lancaster, *The Measurement and Evaluation of Library Services* (Washington: Information Resources Press, 1977), pp. 19-72.

29. Evans, *Developing Library Collections*, p. 217. For additional information on the topic of weeding collections, see: Stanley J. Slote, *Weeding Library Collections* (Littleton, Colo.: Libraries Unlimited, 1975).

30. A conceptual model which enables persons responsible for collection development to identify reasons for acquiring government publications in microform can be found in: Peter Hernon, *Microforms and Government Information* (Westport, Conn.: Microform Review, 1981), p. 41.

31. Richard DeGennaro, "The Libraries in Transition," *Almanac* (February 10, 1976):305. Cited in: Allen Kent, "The Goals of Resource Sharing in Libraries," in Allen Kent and Thomas J. Galvin (eds.), *Library Resource Sharing* (New York: Marcell Dekker, 1977), p. 16.

32. William C. Robinson, "Evaluation of the Government Documents Collection: an Introduction and Overview," *Government Publications Review* 8A (1981), p. 112.

33. Ibid., p. 114

Chapter 2

Collection Development: Government Publications

A collection development policy sets the parameters of the documents collection, including the levels of government collected, a determination of how comprehensive or selective the collection should be, and criteria for selection and retention. It also demonstrates that collection development is an ongoing decision making process by which the staff members of a library guide all the collections to meet predetermined goals and objectives. Any subset of the whole collection, such as the documents holdings, must adhere to the overall library and institutional mission and goals. Documents, even those housed in separate collections or published in non-print formats, should not be treated as a specialized or unique resource isolated intellectually from other library holdings. Further, it should be recognized that they are not a free or inexpensive resource; this applies to even those received gratis on deposit upon the stipulation that they be made available for use by the public. They cost in terms of processing, storage, use, staffing, and the need for adequate finding aids (e.g., the purchase of commercially produced indexes).

Within the philosophical notion that libraries must control all parts of their rapidly expanding collections, this chapter presents an overview of collection development as applied to government publications. It also examines the relevant literature in the context of this philosophical notion and suggests that depository libraries, other than regionals, should be selective in the acquisition and retention of government publications, focusing on those most likely to be used. Infrequently requested items should be received through interlibrary loan.

THE NEED FOR COLLECTION DEVELOPMENT

Dramatic increases in costs with moderate increases in funding have forced many libraries to examine previously held assumptions about collection development. Assumptions subject to review here are those which relate to the size and growth of the government documents collection. As a result of the condition that has led to a reassessment of long held assumptions, many libraries have been faced with difficult decisions with regard to collection development practices. As funds for the expansion of collections become increasingly more limited, libraries must adopt carefully considered selection and deselection policies.

Most depository libraries and many non-depository libraries are now faced with congestion in the processing, servicing, and storage of government publications, particularly U.S. federal documents. At the same time this situation exists, staff reductions have occurred and space for the expansion of the collection is limited. To cope with these problems, some libraries have developed collection development policies that cover document holdings. It is the intent of this chapter to demonstrate the need for all libraries to include government publications in their collection development policies.

For libraries designated as depositories, the documents distributed by the Government Printing Office constitute the largest single means of acquiring U.S. documents. A look at the increase in GPO distribution of documents in the last few years demonstrates the magnitude of the problem. As shown in Table 2.1, the number of titles distributed by the GPO has increased dramatically each year. For example, in 1978, depositories received 14,473,656 copies of hardcopy documents and 1,544,755 copies of microfiche. For 1979, the number increased significantly: 19,580,302 hardcopy documents and 7,473,049 microfiche copies were distributed. For 1980, a total of 67,035 document titles were distributed in both hardcopy and microfiche. However, only 17.8 percent (11,933 titles) were distributed in both formats. Deducting the 11,933 titles from the total count reduces the individual title count to 55,102. To provide a basis of comparison, we can observe that the number of book titles published in the United States by non-government publishers was 45,182 for 1979 and for 1980 it is projected at 33,737.[1]

As is evident from these data, the United States government is a prolific publisher. Moreover, the depository system is receiving a higher percentage of titles published by the government than ever before. It is no

Table 2.1. Number of Titles Shipped by the GPO

Year	Hardcopy	Microfiche	Total
1978	30,102	4,054	34,156
1979	34,218	20,598	54,816
1980	43,377	23,658	67,035
1981 (anticipated)	41,144	39,823	80,967

wonder that an increasing number of depository libraries are acquiring less than the minimum percentage of item numbers recommended by the *Guidelines for the Depository Library System,* as adopted by the Depository Library Council in 1976 and amended in 1977.[2] Those depositories selecting the minimum 25 percent of item numbers in 1980 would have received approximately 14,000 titles. Regional depositories, on the other hand, are required to accept and retain all available titles. In addition to this large body of documents, many depository libraries acquire government publications printed and distributed outside the sphere of the Government Printing Office.

If libraries are to be effective and efficient providers of government information, they must give immediate attention to the problems that result from the vast amount of government publishing from which they must select and the limited funds for maintenance of services and staff. Librarians who argue this note that "if some adjustments are not made in the current regional system, it will collapse under its own weight." They believe that there must be federal funding to support service programs, improved access to the full range of government publishing, better bibliographic control, as well as "a lid on depository distribution by instituting a 'documents-on-demand' service."[3] Further, regional libraries, they note, are plagued with the following problems:

- Lack of space or storage facilities for:
  a. Hardcopy
  b. Microfiche
  c. Unusual formats

- Inability to provide required services:
  a. Interlibrary loan
  b. Visiting selectives
  c. Exchange lists
  d. Reference, training and consultation
  e. Promotional activities

- Inability to keep up with processing and maintaining material received:
  a. Labeling, cataloging, etc.
  b. Class corrections
  c. Preservation, replacement and retrospective acquisitions
  d. Purging superseded material

- Inadequacy of "Guidelines" and "Instructions" concerning regional status

- Inability to attend national meetings related to regional status
- Loss of information of possible historical interest due to increased purging of superseded material.[4]

Point four encompasses the need for meaningful goals and objectives, an improved inspection program, and detailed specification of evaluative criteria or performance measures.

Various solutions have been proposed for dealing with these and other problems facing the depository library program. For example, the Depository Library Council has recommended to the Superintendent of Documents that regional depositories need only to select and retain "material for their Standard Federal Region...when that material is offered in a series by geographic breakdown."[5] Other suggestions call for cooperative or shared regional responsiblities, greater flexibility in the disposition of dated material, the creation of an added structural level (e.g., super-regionals or a lending library of last resort), more rigorous deselection policies, increased distribution and retention of microfiche, the establishment of special regionals collecting by format (e.g., audiovisual material), and "on-demand" distribution of low-use titles and series. Some of these suggestions would require minor readjustments in the depository library program, while others are more far-reaching in their implications.

This chapter will not analyze the suggestions made above, but it should be noted that structural defects in the program cannot be adequately remedied by such suggestions. Instead of focusing on particular aspects of the system, greater attention should be given to the network as a whole and to the interrelationships among the various parts. Research is needed to provide insights into the present program, identifying its strengths and weaknesses. This research should have as its objective to guide the development of a national network, which is able to exploit fully technological advances and which can provide the American public with access to needed government information, regardless of the level of government producing it.[6]

COLLECTION DEVELOPMENT

Collection development is an activity that deserves the constant attention of all professional staff members. However:

> In many cases collection development for government publications is assumed to be a self-directed activity—one that operates almost by default. The acquisition of materials and their appearance on the shelves is assumed to be evidence of collection development—or is there more to this process?[7]

In fact, collection development for government publications should follow the same pattern applicable to other library materials, thus addressing such factors as determining how much and what material to acquire (by subject, content, format, and so on), the number of copies, how long to retain the material, and how to manage what is kept.[8] "A collection development policy is a plan that provides guidelines to the selectors as to the appropriateness of various types of materials for a particular collection."[9] The policy allows library staff members to guide the collection toward predetermined goals and objectives. However, as Yuri Nakata notes:

> The acquisitions budget and number of staff will determine whether the acquisitions program will be aggressive or of limited scope. Whatever design is envisioned as the final goal, the collection development process must be a well-planned and continuing activity.[10]

Some documents librarians may not view collection development in its full dimensions and may place a higher priority on processing and bibliographic control. Since assignment to specific tasks as well as other factors might dictate the commitment of a staff to collection development, research should examine the tasks performed by documents staff and determine the amount of time devoted to each. The purpose is to prioritize tasks, duties, and responsiblities so that the goals and objectives of the documents department and the overall library are realized.

Collection development is a planning process encompassing decision making regarding the selection and retention of material, as well as the initiation of an evaluation component. Through evaluation libraries can determine the extent to which their holdings provide for and meet the information requirements of their user groups, and gauge such factors as the types of resources needed and the most effective allocation of financial resources. Libraries can then set priorities among competing resource needs, better cope with limited spatial environments dictating the controlled growth of collections, and improve access to the major resources needed by client groups. The objectives of collection development can be summarized as:

> To provide for the information needs of the library's community; to increase the quality of information resources available to the library's community; to efficiently allocate available financial resources for the purchase of information resources; and to develop procedures by which the effectiveness of the collection, vis-a-vis the information needs of the community, are regularly evaluated.[11]

Partial depositories need to concentrate their acquisitions and retention on those government publications that are heavily used and to place less emphasis on those that are used infrequently or have been unused for a number of years. The more libraries try to acquire sources to meet single and infrequent requests, the more publications they must acquire. The more acquired, the higher the cost for processing, storage, and service. In addition, the excessive acquisition of materials creates a congestion on the shelves, which itself constitutes a reason for limited use of documents collections.[12]

Libraries that want to develop collections that emphasize the most frequently needed source material must be able to draw upon inter-institutional cooperation for lesser needed material. Thus, collection development techniques require attention in two areas: (1) collection development activities within the institution, and (2) the development of a system for the prompt and reliable delivery of requested source material among depository libraries. The lack of an effective document delivery system serves as a deterrent to libraries that want to limit documents collection building to a carefully selected body of materials. The lack of an effective delivery system also results in the further expansion of microform holdings as compensation for inadequate resource sharing. Although this might seem as a viable alternative to hardcopy acquisitions, extensive holdings in microform result in the same problems of congestion and expense as paper copy collections.

Figure 2.1, which depicts the role of collection development for libraries, shows that libraries, reflecting institutional goals and objectives, select from among available government publications those of current and potential interest to their client groups. Libraries must decide how widely to collect and how much to collect in each subject, discipline, topic, or area of study.[13] They do this by taking into account such factors as curriculum, subject literatures, institutional mission (supporting teaching and research interests), highest degree offered, format, publication quality, and cost.

The concept of collection development could extend to the referral process, that is, the situation in which many libraries serve as a clearinghouse for the referral of user requests to other agencies. Under these circumstances, the identification of appropriate "outside" sources of information is a logical extension of the collection building function of the library. Where this is the case, the word "published" should be dropped from the caption "universe of published government information." Government information appears in a variety of formats (including printed, machine-readable, audio-visual, microform, and so on) and libraries are but one mediator of government information for client groups. Consequently the middle category, depicted in Figure 2.1, could also be amended to reflect "mediating source provider," thereby placing depository libraries in the context of the full range of source providers (e.g., Federal

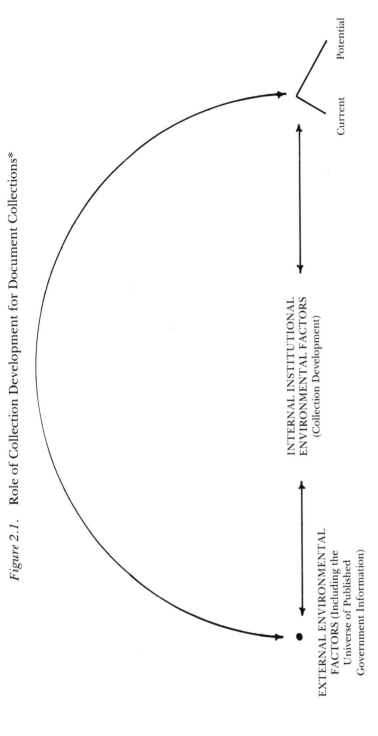

Figure 2.1. Role of Collection Development for Document Collections*

EXTERNAL ENVIRONMENTAL FACTORS (Including the Universe of Published Government Information)

INTERNAL INSTITUTIONAL ENVIRONMENTAL FACTORS (Collection Development)

Current

Potential

Source: *This figure is adapted from James Baughman, et. al. "A Survey of Attitudes toward Collection Development in College Libraries," in Robert D. Stueart and George B. Miller Jr. (eds.), *Collection Development in Libraries: A Treatise* (Greenwich, CT: JAI Press, 1980), p. 92.

27

Information Centers, GPO bookstores, NTIS bookstore, as well as government agencies and Congressional committees themselves).

As noted earlier, collection development consists of three phases: collection planning, implementation of the planning model, and evaluation. The planning phase extends to the decision making involved in determining what is appropriate for selection and retention. It must reflect institutional and library goals, objectives, and priorities. The next phase, implementation of the planning model, encompasses the process of making documents accessible for use. Evaluation is a necessary component for refining the planning model and the process by which it is implemented.[14]

THE LITERATURE

Overview

The following is a review of the literature of government publications concerned with collection development as examined within the context of the viewpoint expressed earlier in this chapter. In some instances specific authors are noted, but in other cases, a point is made that represents a synthesis of the writings of several authors.

Some authors encourage libraries facing space shortages and a decreasing number of staff assigned to documents work to be more selective in the acquisition and retention of paper copy. In addition, they favor expanded microfiche selection in order to maintain the past level of collecting or to increase the size of the immediate collection. The need for a higher level of collecting is rationalized on the premise that these resources have potential public interest or educational value and that at some point in time a client might want a particular publication. Such authors fail to recommend the examination of all document holdings in the context of functional collections and the retention of only the more heavily needed source materials.[15]

The central weakness to much of the reported literature on government publications collection development is that it does not draw upon solid research findings relating to government publications. This is, however, less a commentary on these writings than on the state of knowledge and thinking concerning collection development for public documents at this time. For example, the *Guidelines for the Depository Library System* recommend that "each depository library should maintain a basic collection available for immediate use consisting of all titles in Appendix A."[16] The rationale for labeling these twenty-three titles as central to all types of depository libraries (e.g., state, federal, law school, and academic) is not provided in that source or elsewhere. The existence of such a list, with its implied mandate to depository libraries, gives rise to the question: should titles such as *Historical Statistics of the United States, Subject Bibliographies* (S.B. Series), and *Congressional District Data Book* be common to all depository collections? Further, is there indeed a core of titles which *all* depositories need and what is the rationale for the existence of a list of core titles required for selection?

Many writings have touched upon aspects of collection development, ususaly those which relate to selection and acquisition. Frequently, suggestions are offered on what to select for a particular type of library (e.g., school, or small to medium-sized public or college) and how to acquire it.[17] A number of writers have advised librarians to build collections taking into account such factors as curriculum and user needs. As Anne M. Boyd and Rae Elizabeth Rips note, proper selection is important for any type of resource acquired by libraries, but it is perhaps most important for government publications. Their reason for believing this is that the federal government produces a "multiplicity of material" and

> ...that, of the thousands of individual publications appearing each year, only a limited proportion can possibly be made currently available to users in libraries, even if all this material were of equal value, which it is not. The principles of book selection which apply to other classes of library material apply also to federal government publications.[18]

To this Ellen P. Jackson adds:

> The major research library will doubtless select all but a few of the series offered, but careless and indiscriminate over-selection is bad, both for the library in waste of time for handling and of space for storage, and for the public interest in waste of funds. Too limited selection, on the other hand, may jeopardize the value of the collection, in the unforeseen future, if not at present. An intelligent selection requires a broad view of the possible needs and interests of all segments of the library's patronage and a general knowledge of the nature of the publications of all federal government agencies.[19]

The problem of making documents available when needed by library users may be different by an order of magnitude from providing other library materials, given the high rate of obsolescence for many documents and the ephemeral nature of a substantial proportion of the material.

Specific Writings

Aside from the general writings, there is a recent developing body of literature which addresses collection development in the context of Figure 2.1. One writer encourages libraries to maintain functional collections, ones which focus on selection and retention of the more frequently needed source material and which rely on inter-institutional cooperation to fulfill other requests. He also notes that research, although still exploratory in nature, suggests that there are distinct patterns among the documents used and that these patterns are discernible among different groups of documents users.[20]

The problems that surface with the addition of microformatted government publications to the collection have also been considered in the recent literature. Charles R. McClure "provides a framework for identifying the administrative parameters that affect the handling of microformatted government publications in a library."[21] He observes that administrative integration of microformatted government publications is achieved

> ...when the patron has the same awareness of the information sources available in microformatted government publications as of other material in the library, when he has the same probability of bibliographic access to this material as to other types of material, when he has the same probability of physical availability of this material as of other types of material, and when he deals with professional librarians who are as competent with microformatted government publications as other librarians are with their areas of responsiblity.[22]

McClure has further expanded on the handling, organization, space requirements, and facilities for microformatted documents in his column for *Government Publications Review*.[23] His insights, however, apply to hardcopy as well as microform collections. For example, in another article, McClure "suggests that the overall effectiveness and integration of government publications will be determined largely by the degree to which government publications are included in the overall philosophy of library collection development." Further, administrative integration is dependent upon needs assessments and adherence to collection development.[24]

Bernard M. Fry also endorses the administrative integration of government publications: their incorporation "into the mainstream of library services should be considered a priority goal for both government and libraries in providing public access to government produced information." While offering suggestions on how to accomplish integration, he notes that documents collections should be "designed to fit the needs of both current and potential users" and that "there will be need for greater emphasis on weeding and selective acquisition of government publications in order to avoid congestion in processing and servicing and in storage space."[25]

Although focusing on the selection process, Fred W. Roper provides an overview of deselection and evaluation. He reaffirms that selection policies for government publications should be consistent with the overall library selection policy. Further, selection policies should be based on community analyses and take into account the information requirements of client groups.[26]

Surprisingly few collection development statements for government publications have appeared in the literature.* Recognizing this fact, Bruce Morton developed a statement of policy for Carleton College "as a modular component of an overall policy statement" and "as a guide to the process of collection development." As he notes, "in order to make judicious decisions which will permit the depository collection to grow in a manner responsive to its own needs, as well as to various curricular and community needs, a framework of policy must exist."[27] In a separate statement, Yuri Nakata expands on this theme. She states:

> If special consideration is to be given to the collection of government publications, a separate acquisitions policy statement should be developed to answer such questions as: who are to be served (the library's public)? What will be selected? Who will do the selecting? How will the materials be obtained (deposit, purchase, gift, exchange)? Where will the materials be housed?

In addition, she addresses the issue of library cooperation in collection development by noting that "access to government publications in [other] libraries will affect the depth of collection development."[28]

The documents department at the University of California, Berkeley, carried out a year long self-study, which led to reorganization of the department, staff responsiblities, and service functions. The collection policy, which comprised one component of the study, has relevance to this chapter. Since "too many ephemeral publications are received that do not belong in a large academic and research library," it was suggested that the library could drop "certain depository categories without losing potentially valuable publications" and place greater reliance "on the regional depository library to maintain items of little or no use."[29]

Use studies, which can be used to identify collection requirements, can be categorized into three types: (1) library surveys (typically these identify what documents libraries select and what they perceive as used); (2) user surveys (most of these to date have examined the use of federal documents by faculty members at academic institutions); and (3) citation analyses. In a review essay published in 1978, Terry L. Weech analyzed the three types and discussed their application to the documents field.[30] The following discussion provides additional examples of each means for data collection.

*Appendix A reprints collection development policies from seven libraries.

Library Surveys

During the 1930s two studies were undertaken to determine which federal publicaitons were most useful in a college curriculum. Use, the first study asserted, was enhanced by the careful acquisition, weeding, and organization of government publications. In the study, Paul Fossum, professor of economics at Carleton College identified which government publications were used by thirteen departments at that institution. He did not examine individual course use but advocated a rational selection policy.[31] Kathryn Miller, a student at the Graduate Library School at the University of Chicago, surveyed college instructors and librarians in order to determine the relative value of U.S. serial documents to liberal arts colleges. Her objective was to get these institutions to place selection policies on a more scientific basis. Libraries, it was hoped, would acquire only those publications that would be utilized and would not approximate use from observation and supposition. Her study did not determine classroom use of government publications but reaffirmed the need for a closer working relationship between faculty members and librarians concerning the acquisition and use of these publications.[32]

Shirley Edsall, who surveyed fifty-one community college depository libraries, focused on selection and receptivity to expanded microform collections, but did not deal with other aspects of collection development. Nonetheless, her survey revealed that these libraries select the more frequently needed source material and that they do not require extensive documents collections.[33]

Kathleen Larson discussed subject areas in which law school depository libraries might want to select government publications. In addition, she looked at the types of documents potentially useful to these libraries.[34] In another article concerned with documents in law libraries, Kay Schlueter tried to identify the core documents selected by law school libraries. The results "revealed few consensus choices" and that the concept of a "basic" collection was open to interpretation. Appendix B of her article listed titles and types of government publications received by at least two-thirds of the responding libraries.[35] Such information might prove useful for law schools as well as other libraries that are interested in defining core collections. The list of items, however, would have been more useful and valid if viewed within the context of specialities within the legal field and the curricular emphases of the law schools surveyed. Law schools do not all have the same thrust and program strengths.

User Studies

User surveys have been limited to one segment of academic library users, faculty members. Students and other non-faculty groups need to be surveyed and user studies should extend beyond the academic community. By documenting use patterns and information seeking strategies, libraries can conduct the community analysis necessary for developing collections reflecting the information requirements of client groups. To illustrate the value of user studies, it should be mentioned that faculty members in the disciplines of economics, history, political science, and sociology rely primarily on only a few types of government publications. Sources which contain statistical data are at the forefront of the list. Other types considered important by these users include government periodicals, Congressional hearings, annual reports of departments and agencies, census reports, reports of investigation and research, Congressional reports and committee prints, decisions and opinions, and ephemera (e.g., agency newsletters and press releases describing current developments, and agency distributed bibiliographies).[36] On the basis of these findings, it would seem that documents librarians undertaking a needs assessment could investigate documents use by persons in various disciplines and construct lists of the most frequently used titles. A principle of diminishing return with respect to collection utilization has implications for the number of titles acquired and for the length of time that publications are retained.

Citation Analyses

Citation studies provide one way for determining use patterns and identifying those sources that authors cite in their scholarly works. One weakness to these studies is that they do not reflect the range of sources that scholars consult in the process of preparing their books, articles, and reports. Despite this and other limitations, the data collected supplement those gathered by other means.

A study of the government publications contained in the 1979 *Social Sciences Citation Index* underscores the importance of serial titles to social scientists and suggests some of the most frequently cited titles. This type of information is useful for guiding decision making regarding collection maintenance, selection, and retention. Identification of the rate of obsolescence provides an objective indicator of the number of years that a particular title ought to remain in the active file.[37]

Before concluding the discussion of the literature relating to collection development for government publications, five other works merit mention. First, Terry L. Weech relates weeding to his experiences with Illinois libraries and regards the provision of weeding of depository collections as "one of the most important sections of the Depository Library Act of 1962."[38] William C. Robinson provides an excellent overview of the role of evaluation, the need for continuous evaluation, and various techniques of evaluating library collections. This article is especially useful because, as he notes, "substantial literature on government document collection evaluation does not exist."[39] His article appears in the special issue of *Government Publications Review* devoted exclusively to collection development for government publications. This issue is the first extended treatment of collection development across levels of government.[40]

The final two works are representative of the writings dealing with report literature. According to Wilda Newman and Michlean Amir, the documents collection of the John Hopkins University, Applied Physics Laboratory, became so large that it consumed too much space, staff and computer time, and money. To remedy the situation, the laboratory adopted such measures as "defining the purpose of the report collection," "screening items received on automatic distribution," "establishing guidelines for a routine weeding policy," and "considering retention of microfiche versus paper copy."[41] It was decided that reports would not be collected and retained for archival purposes, but rather

> . . .would be screened for retention, in a viable library collection, the size of which would be controlled by cost and space, and the content of which would be defined in terms of user needs. Only material relevant to the laboratory's interests, and not readily obtainable elsewhere would justifiably be maintained.[42]

Gary Purcell, in an examination of the National Technical Information Service, identifies principles basic to maintaining a collection of NTIS reports, whether they are in hardcopy or microfiche. He believes that a collection should follow stringent selection and retention policies and minimize storage congestion. Further, to best serve their clientele, libraries should acquire reports soon after their publication, discard them once the information content becomes outdated, and rely upon inter-institutional cooperation for the delivery of infrequently required publications.[43]

CONCLUSION

The accumulation of large numbers of publications that are never or infrequently used has implications far beyond individual libraries, in that printing, distribution, and library handling costs all are affected.[44] Depository, as well as non-depository, libraries need to carry out active weeding programs, to acquire government publications selectively, and to review and revise selection criteria on a regular basis. Elimination of ephemeral, trivial, superseded, and duplicative publications from documents collections will better serve user needs. Libraries should therefore identify and acquire high-interest publications and rely on resource sharing for material seldom used. As Bernard Fry points out:

Library administrators need to consider government publications collections as an information resource on an equal basis with books and serials, to the extent that they are integrated in information services, whether shelved as separate collections as in many major research libraries. The relationship between the documents collection and other library collections should be that of a single resource in meeting user needs. To restate: the key to a good government documents collection is integration into the mainstream of library information services.[45]

As an aid to administrative integration, this chapter has provided an overview of collection development for government publications and summarized the literature on the topic. This literature unfortunately reflects neither the range of issues nor the research findings found in the writings for other library genre. To be fair, however, the concept of collection development, devising and implementing a planning model as well as initiating an evaluation component, is relatively new to the documents field. The literature will undoubtedly increase and additional research will be conducted. The remaining chapters will address these and other issues as one step toward improving access to government publications and toward identifying those government publications most likely to be in demand.

The chapters reinforce the thesis that since use centers on a comparatively few document types and titles, libraries can develop collections focusing on the more frequently needed source material. The more depository libraries try to acquire sources to meet single requests, the more documents they must acquire. The more acquired, the higher the cost of processing, storage, and service. Libraries therefore need to determine how many demands they want to meet internally and to rely on resource sharing for lesser-used titles.

NOTES AND REFERENCES

1. For a discussion of the book title output see: Chandler B. Grannis, "Book Title Output and Average Prices, 1980 Preliminary Figures," in *The Bowker Annual, 1981* (New York: Bowker, 1981), pp. 329-335.
2. See George W. Whitbeck, Peter Hernon, and John Richardson Jr., "The Federal Depository Library System: A Descriptive Analysis," *Government Publications Review* 5 (1978): 253-267; and John V. Richardson, Jr., Dennis C. W. Frisch, and Catherine M. Hall, "Bibliographic Organization of U.S. Federal Depository Collections," *Government Publications Review* 7A (1980): 463-480.
3. Sandra McAninch, "Memorandum: Position Paper on Proposed Solutions to the Problems of Regional Depositories for U.S. Government Publications," Unpublished report prepared for the Depository Library Council and dated March 30, 1981, p. 5.
4. Ibid., p. 1.
5. "Resolutions Approved by the Depository Library Council to the Public Printer," *Documents to the People* 9 (July 1981): 160.

6. For an analysis of the depository library program and recommendations for change see: Peter Hernon, *Microforms and Government Information* (Westport, CT: Microform Review, Inc., 1981), and Charles R. McClure, "Structural Analysis of the Depository System: A Preliminary Assessment," in Peter Hernon (ed.), *Collection Development and Public Access of Government Publications. Proceedings of the First Annual Library and Government Documents Conference* (Westport, CT: Meckler Books, 1982).

7. Charles R. McClure, "An Integrated Approach to Government Publication Collection Development," *Government Publications Review* 8A (1981): 5.

8. Michael K. Buckland, *Book Availability and the Library User* (Elmsford, N.Y.: Pergamon Press, 1975), p. 3.

9. McClure, "An Integrated Approach to Government Publication Collection Development," p. 5.

10. Yuri Nakata, *From Press to People* (Chicago: ALA, 1979), p. 39.

11. McClure, "An Integrated Approach to Government Publication Collection Development," pp. 5-6.

12. Peter Hernon, *Use of Government Publications by Social Scientists* (Norwood, N.J.: Ablex Publishing Corp., 1979).

13. James Baughman, et al., "A Survey of Attitudes toward Collection Development in College Libraries," in Robert D. Stueart and George B. Miller Jr. (eds.), *Collection Development in Libraries: A Treatise* (Greenwich, CT: JAI Press, 1980), p. 94.

14. Ibid., pp. 93-94.

15. For a discussion of this point see: Hernon, *Microforms and Government Information*.

16. *Guidelines for the Depository Library System*, as adopted by the Depository Library Council to the Public Printer (October 18, 1977), p. 3.

17. For example, there are: W. Philip Leidy, *A Popular Guide to Government Publications* (New York: Columbia University Press, 1976); Walter L. Newsome, *New Guide to Popular Government Publications* (Littleton, CO: Libraries Unlimited, 1978); Nancy Patton Van Zant, *Selected U.S. Government Series* (Chicago: ALA, 1978); and Alice J. Wittig, *U.S. Government Publications for the School Media Center* (Littleton, CO: Libraries Unlimited, 1979).

18. Anne Morris Boyd and Rae Elizabeth Rips, *United States Government Publications* (New York: H. W. Wilson, 1949), p. 555.

19. Ellen P. Jackson, *The Administration of the Government Documents Collection*, ACRL Monographs No. 5 (Chicago: Publications Committee of the Association of College and Reference Libraries, 1953), p. 2. See also Rae Elizabeth Rips, "The Reference Use of Government Publications," *Drexel Library Quarterly* 1 (October 1965): 17.

20. Peter Hernon, "Developing the Government Publication Collection," in *Collection Development in Libraries*; Peter Hernon, "Functional Documents Collections," *Microform Review* 9 (Fall 1980): 209-219; and Hernon, *Microforms and Government Information*.

21. Charles R. McClure, "Administrative Integration of Microformatted Government Publications: A Framework for Analysis," *Microform Review* 6 (September 1977): 259. Also see: Charles R. McClure, "Administrative Basics for Microformatted Government Librarians," in *Microforms and Government Information*.

22. McClure, "Administrative Integration of Microformated Government Publications: A Framework for Analysis," p. 269-270.

23. For example, see: Charles R. McClure, "Microformatted Government Publications," *Government Publications Review* 5 (1978): 511-515; and McClure, "Microformatted Government Publications: Space and Facilities," *Government Publications Review* 6 (1979): 405-412. Also see: Vicki W. and John B. Phillips, "Microformatted Government Publications," *Government Publications Review* 8A (1981): 127-133.

24. Charles R. McClure, "An Integrated Approach to Government Publication Collection Development," *Government Publications Review* 8A (1981): 5-15.

25. Bernard M. Fry, "Government Publications and the Library: Implications for Change," *Government Publications Review 4* (1977): 111-115. Also see: Bernard M. Fry, *Government Publications: Their Role in the National Program for Library and Information Services*, Prepared for the National Commission on Libraries and Information Science (Washington: GPO, 1978).

26. Fred W. Roper, "Selecting Federal Publications," *Special Libraries* 65 (August 1974): 326-331.

27. Bruce Morton, "Toward a Comprehensive Collection Development Policy for Partial U.S. Depository Libraries," *Government Publications Review* 7A (1980): 41. The policy statement of the Arizona State University Library Documents Service is contained in Peter Hernon and George W. Whitbeck, "Government Publications and Commercial Microform Publishers: A Survey of Federal Depository Libraries," *Microform Review* 6 (September 1977): 280-281. Government publications are included as part of general collection development statements in Elizabeth Futas, *Library Acquisition Policies and Procedures* (Phoenix, AZ: Oryx Press, 1977).

28. Nakata, *From Press to People*, p. 38.

29. University of California, Berkeley, General Library. *Report of the Documents Department Study Group.* Prepared by Suzanne Gold, et. al. (November 1976), p. 29. Also see Catherine C. Gordon, "Administrative Reorganization: An Attempt to Control Government Documents in the Library," *Government Publications Review* 6 (1979): 241-248.

30. Terry L. Weech, "The Use of Government Publications: A Selected Review of the Literature," *Government Publications Review* 5 (1978): 177-184.

31. Paul Fossum, "Government Documents in Liberal Arts Colleges," *Bulletin of the American Library Association* 25 (1931): 581-585.

32. Kathryn Naomi Miller, *The Selection of United States Serial Documents for Liberal Arts Colleges* (New York: H.W. Wilson, 1937).

33. Shirley Edsall, "A Study of the Administration, Utilization and Collection Development Policies of Government Document Collections in Community College Libraries Which Have Been Designated as Depositories" (ED 146 954).

34. Kathleen T. Larson, "Establishing a New GPO Depository Documents Department in an Academic Law Library," *Law Library Journal* 72 (Summer 1979): 484-496.

35. Kay Schlueter, "Selection of Government Documents in Law School Libraries," *Law Library Journal* 71 (August 1978): 477-480.

36. Hernon, *Use of Government Publications by Social Scientists*. Also see Gary Purcell, "The Use of Tennessee State Government Publications," *Tennessee Librarian* 32 (Spring 1980): 25.

37. Peter Hernon and Clayton A. Shepherd, "Government Documents in Social Science Literature: A Preliminary Report of Citations from the Social Sciences Citation Index," in *Collection Development and Public Access of Government Information*. Also see Robert Goehlert, "A Citation Analysis of International Organization: The Use of Government Documents," *Government Publications Review* 6 (1979): 185-193.

38. Terry Weech, "Weeding of U.S. Government Publications in Illinois Depository Libraries," *Illinois Libraries* 53 (June 1971): 394-399.

39. William C. Robinson, "Evaluation of the Government Documents Collection: An Introduction and Overview," *Government Publications Review* 8A (1981): 111-125.

40. "Collection Development for Government Publications," *Government Publications Review* 8A (1981): Numbers 1 and 2.

41. Wilda B. Newman and Michlean J. Amir, "Report Literature: Selecting Versus Collecting," *Special Libraries* 69 (November 1978): 415.

42. Ibid., p. 416.

43. Gary R. Purcell, "NTIS Micropublishing Program," in *Microforms and Government Information*. Although outside the scope of this book, it should be noted that there are

three excellent sources covering collection development for United Nations material. These are: Peter I. Hajnal, "Collection Development: United Nations," *Government Publications Review* 8A (1981): 89-109; Luciana Marulli-Koenig, "Collection Development for United Nations Documents and Publications," in *Collection Development and Public Access of Government Information*; and Luciana Marulli, *Documentation of the United Nations System* (Metuchen, N.J.: Scarecrow, 1979).

44. Fry, "Government Publications and the Library: Implications for Change," p. 115.
45. Ibid.

Chapter 3

Selection Patterns For Depository Collection Development

The first two chapters established a framework for the consideration of collection development. Chapter 1 addressed collection development as it applied to all components of the library collection. Chapter 2 narrowed the focus and examined the development of collections of government publications, with specific emphasis on U.S. depository collections.

Chapter 2 noted that a lack of research makes it difficult to recommend improvements in the process of developing depository library collections. In both this chapter and Chapter 5, the authors report the results of research that examines aspects of depository library collection development. The research reported here deals with patterns of document distribution to selective depository libraries and library characteristics related to depository collection development. Only selective depositories are examined in this chapter because regional depositories receive all items distributed by the GPO and consequently do not participate in the same type of collection development process as do selective depositories. Thus, the forty-nine regional depositories are excluded from all analysis presented in this chapter.

Identification of patterns of document distribution to selective depositories enables the authors to make inferences about the process of collection development as currently practiced by depository libraries. These inferences serve as a guide to subsequent recommendations and lead into the discussion of depository collection development viewed within a subject context, discussed in the next chapter.

ITEM NUMBER SELECTION

Patterns of document distribution to depositories have been identified through the analysis of files made available to the authors by the U.S.

Government Printing Office (GPO). These files are augmented by a file of additional information collected by the authors. The files from the GPO were made available through the permission of Mr. Carl LaBarre, former Superintendent of Documents, with the assistance of several members of his staff. However, conclusions derived from the analysis of this information are the responsibility of the authors and do not necessarily reflect the judgment or opinions of the staff of the GPO.

The information which forms the basis of this chapter comes from the following four files, three of which were obtained from the GPO.

Depository Library Directory. A file that identifies all depository libraries by name, address, depository library number, and status (e.g. whether a regional or selective depository). This file was current as of August 7, 1980 and includes 1,340 depositories of which 1,291 are selective depositories and forty-nine are regionals.

Item Selection File. A file that includes all item numbers received by selective depositories in January 1981. The records for item numbers received by regional depositories are not included in this file. At the time the magnetic tape was produced, there were 1,295 selective depositories and 5,077 items were available for selection. When the authors acquired the Item Selection File, it was arranged by item number, followed by a list of all selective depositories that received that item number. To facilitate the utilization of the data, the file was recoded and arranged by depository library number, with all item numbers received by each depository listed under the depository library number.

Biennial Survey, 1979. A file that records the responses of depository libraries to a survey that the GPO Library and Statutory Distribution Service conducted in October 1979. Some 1,286 depository libraries responded to it (including all regionals but not all selective depositories). Although questions included in the survey were intended to provide the GPO with information that would improve the depository distribution system, there are several questions that provide some insight into the collection development procedures of depository libraries. The most useful of these have been selected for examination and analysis in this chapter.

Supplementary Information File. A file that contains data collected by the authors about depository libraries. There are 1,340 depositories represented in this file of which 1,291 are selective depositories and forty-nine are regionals. Included in this file are data that indicate the type of library, the size of the collection, and for academic libraries the size of the student body, the highest degree or certificate offered, and the form of control for the institution in which the library is located (for example, whether it is a state supported or private, non-profit institution). This file was created to augment information in the other files. However, not all of the information in this file was subjected to analysis due to limitations in the financial resources available to the authors.

The number of depositories included in each of the four files differs slightly from one file to another. The variations can be explained by the fact that the files were created at different times and that one of the files (the Item Selection File) does not include regional depositories. Consequently, when an analysis is made that requires a combination of any two of these files, the number of observations will be determined by the file with the smallest number of depositories. The result of this is a variation in the number of observations reported in the tables.

Before analyzing item number distribution to depositories, an explanation of item numbers and their application to this study is in order. All government publications distributed through the GPO depository system are designated by an item number. Item numbers are the categories used for the systematic and convenient dissemination of documents. At the time the Item Selection File was created, more than 5,000 item number categories were in use. In some instances, an item number is used to designate a single publication such as the *Congressional Record* or the *Statistical Abstract*. In other cases, miscellaneous publications that deal with different topics are included in a single item number category. However, all publications distributed by the GPO to depositories, whether in paper copy or microform, are designated, and hence distributed by an item number.

The list of item number selections serves as a record of the current depository collection development choices of this group of libraries. The list represents only current choices, however; it does not reflect retrospective holdings. The item number choices made by individual libraries reflect the depository collection development practices of those libraries. Each item number selected by a depository library indicates an active decision on the part of the library to receive the documents distributed through that item number. Whether this decision is made with full knowledge of the content of the item number or its possible use by the clientele served by the library cannot be determined by examining the aggregate list of item numbers received by all libraries. However, for the purpose of the analysis of the Item Selection File, it is assumed that depositories have, at least, made a conscious decision to receive an item number and do not do so by default.

The summing or aggregation of item number choices by depository libraries is a means of portraying the item number preferences of depositories, thus indicating priorities in the choice of specific government publications or categories of government publications. This aggregation of choices provides an indication of the patterns that exist in document selection by depository libraries. An examination of aggregate preferences for item numbers, when related to the characteristics of depository libraries, provides insights into the patterns of document selection. These patterns, in turn, can be used to infer collection development practices. For example, item number choices can be related to library characteristics such as type of library, size of collection, or, in the case of academic libraries, the highest degree offered by the institution. These patterns show how or if preferences for item numbers differ in a systematic fashion among libraries with different characteristics. It can then be inferred that the process of making item number choices does or does not differ in a systematic fashion among depository libraries. Knowledge of this will increase understanding of depository collection development.

There are clear limitations to the inferences that can be made from these data. These findings are especially limited in their potential to shed light on the depository collection development practices of individual libraries except where a library might wish to compare its selections with the existing patterns. However, the value that these data have is to demonstrate that patterns do exist in item number selection, and to suggest areas of further study as well as the need for more sophisticated resources to facilitate the selection of publications distributed by the depository system. A method for developing a subject approach to item selection is presented in Chapter 4, and an example of its application is demonstrated in Chapter 7.

ANALYSIS OF DEPOSITORY ITEM NUMBER SELECTION

The analysis of depository item number selection will focus on one major concept. This is the frequency with which specific item numbers are selected by depositories. The frequency of selection of item numbers is used here as a measure of the consensus that exists among depositories as to the value of government publications represented by an item number. This concept will be referred to by the authors as CONSENSUS. The ranking by frequency of selection of item numbers will be used as the means of depicting CONSENSUS. The frequency of selection is thus central to this analysis of the Item Selection File.

It is appropriate at this point to note that in depicting CONSENSUS, the authors do not mean to suggest that the most frequently selected items are the most significant government publications. The inference that can be made is that the most frequently selected items are perceived by the greatest number of depositories as having value to their constituents. The usefulness of this concept, then, is in its reflection of the perceived value to depository libraries of the item number choices available through the depository system.

In order to state the concept of CONSENSUS in operational terms, the authors formulated the following research questions. These are:

- Which item numbers are selected most frequently by all selective depositories?
- Which item numbers are selected least frequently by all selective depositories?
- Which item numbers are selected most frequently by selective depositories in different types of libraries?
- Are differences in item number choices associated with differences in the percentage of depository items received by depositories?

Because significant differences exist among depositories, even within type of library categories, the authors wanted to see if there was an increase or a decrease in CONSENSUS when libraries of the same type were placed in even more homogeneous categories. Other chapters in this book are concerned with the use and treatment of depository collections in academic libraries. Therefore, academic libraries were selected for examination of CONSENSUS in more homogenous library categories. A research question was formulated to determine if CONSENSUS was associated with systematic differences in academic libraries. This question was:

- Are differences in item number choices associated with differences in the highest degree offered by academic institutions?

The five research questions stated above are basic to determining the types of patterns that exist in the distribution of item numbers through the depository system. Each of these questions deals with the concept of CONSENSUS, either as applied to all selective depositories or to academic depositories. These questions were made operational by means of ranking the item numbers selected by depositories. The rankings of item numbers selected by depositories to determine CONSENSUS are reported in five tables that are titled as follows:

- *Table 3.1.* Ranking of the 200 item numbers most frequently chosen by selective depositories.
- *Table 3.2.* Inverse ranking of the 200 item numbers least frequently chosen by selective depositories.
- *Table 3.5.* Number and percent of selective depositories that choose the 200th most frequently selected item number, by type of library.

- *Table 3.6.* Ranking of the 200 item numbers most frequently chosen by percent of available item numbers selected by the depository.
- *Table 3.7.* Ranking of the 200 item numbers most frequently chosen for academic libraries by highest degree offered by the academic institution.

In each of the above rankings, the 200th item number has served as the cutoff point. This number was chosen because on the basis of preliminary evidence, this figure appeared to provide an adequate range for demonstrating systematic differences that might exist among depositories in their selection of item numbers.[1] The range provided by using the 200th most frequently selected item number as a cutoff point is demonstrated in Table 3.1. In order to portray item number selection patterns with more precision, four benchmark ranking points were established to indicate the degree to which CONSENSUS exists at each of four incremental levels. The benchmarks indicate the number of libraries that have selected the 1st, 50th, 100th, and 200th most frequently selected item numbers. By use of these benchmark rankings, a better sense of the rate of CONSENSUS can be determined.

The rankings are displayed in the several tables usually by means of three columns. The first column indicates the variable against which the ranking is made (e.g., type of library). The other two columns indicate the frequency of libraries that receive the "nth" ranked item number and the percentage of libraries that receive that item number. The rank of an item number is a measure of CONSENSUS among libraries as to the potential value to their users of the documents distributed through that item number. The percentage of libraries that receive the nth item number is a reflection of the CONSENSUS that exists. Thus, it is important to observe the column that shows the percentage of libraries that receive item numbers at each or any of the four benchmark points. This column reflects the decline in CONSENSUS at each of the four benchmark rankings. The more rapidly the percentage decreases, the more quickly CONSENSUS fades. Following are the tables and explanations of the rankings.

Ranking of the 200 Item Numbers Most Frequently Chosen by Selective Depositories

Table 3.1 displays the results of a ranking of the frequency of item numbers selected by all selective depositories. At the time this file was created, item numbers distributed to regional depositories were not recorded in the Item Selection File. The total number of selective depositories represented in this file is 1,295.

Table 3.1. Ranking of the 200 Item Numbers Most Frequently Chosen by Selective Depositories

	N = 1295	
Item Number Rank	*Number Libraries Selecting*	*Percent Libraries Selecting*
1	1281	98.9
50	1026	79.2
100	907	70.0
200	787	60.8

An examination of Table 3.1 shows that the decrease in CONSENSUS for even the 200 most frequently selected depository item numbers is rather precipitous. The 200th most frequently selected item number represents less than 4 percent of the 5,077 items available for selection at the time this file was produced. Total CONSENSUS does not exist for any item. The most frequently received item number is received by 98.9 percent of the selective depositories. By the time the ranking drops to the 50th ranked item number, only 80 percent of the selective depositories choose to receive the item. By the time the ranking has dropped to 200, fewer than two-thirds of the libraries select the item. Although the data do not show the percentage of libraries that receive fewer than the first 200 items, it is reasonable to assume that the rate of CONSENSUS continues to decline proportionally.

Of interest to persons responsible for the distribution and the selection of item numbers are the series titles of the most frequently selected item numbers. Table 3.2 lists the series titles for the fifty most frequently selected item numbers. (Appendix B lists the series titles of the 200 most frequently selected item numbers.) Perusal of this table shows that many of the titles are commonly used reference publications or well-known serial publications. Included on this list are most of the titles that the depository system indicates should be received by all depositories. It is suggested in Appendix A of the publication *Guidelines for the Depository Library System*, issued by the GPO, that twenty-three document series be acquired by all depositories.[2] However, it is evident from the data reported here that not all depositories follow this suggestion because none of the titles identified in the *Guidelines* is received by all selective depositories.

The list of the fifty most frequently selected item numbers raises a number of questions. For example, why are the publications that the GPO recommends not received by all depositories? Also, why are there depositories that do not receive publications such as the *Congressional Directory* or the *Zip Code Directory*? These are publications one might expect every depository to receive. A closer examination of the recommendations to

Table 3.2. The Fifty Item Numbers Chosen Most Frequently by Selective Depositories

N = 1295

Rank	Series Title	Number Libraries Selecting	Percent Libraries Selecting
1	Monthly Catalog	1281	98.9
2	Statistical Abstract	1274	98.4
3	U.S. Government Manual	1269	98.0
4	Congressional Directory	1255	96.9
5	Statistical Abstract Supplement	1241	95.8
6	Zip Code Directory	1207	93.2
7	Monthly Labor Review	1205	93.1
8	Department of State Bulletin	1192	92.0
9	U.S. Code and Supplement	1183	91.4
10	Federal Register	1166	90.0
11	L.C. Subject Headings and Supplement	1165	90.0
12	Educational Directory	1163	90.0
13	Catalog of Federal Domestic Assistance	1154	89.1
14	Public Papers of the President	1147	88.6
15	Statutes at Large	1147	88.6
16	Uniform Crime Reports	1136	87.7
17	Congressional Record	1129	87.2
18	Weekly Compilation of Presidential Papers	1119	86.4
19	Agriculture Department Yearbook	1115	86.1
20	Monthly Checklist of State Publications	1113	85.9
21	Survey of Current Business Statistics	1112	85.9
22	Your Federal Income Tax	1103	85.2
23	Congressional District Atlas	1102	85.1
24	Budget of the United States	1099	84.9
25	Publications Reference File	1098	84.8
26	Economic Report of the President	1098	84.8
27	United States Reports	1094	84.5
28	Digest of Public General Bills	1093	84.4
29	Treaties in Force	1092	84.3
30	Occupational Outlook Handbook	1088	84.0
31	Budget in Brief	1087	83.9
32	Price List (#36 only one still published)	1081	83.5
33	American Education	1078	83.2
34	Occupational Outlook Quarterly	1078	83.2
35	Code of Federal Regulations	1076	83.1
36	Pocket Data Book	1065	82.2
37	Background Notes on Various Countries	1055	81.5
38	Handbook of Labor Statistics	1052	81.2
39	Social Security Bulletin	1050	81.1
40	Selected U.S. Government Publications	1050	81.1
41	Vital Statistics	1047	80.8
42	U.S. Government Purchasing and Specification Directory	1040	80.3

Table 3.2. (Continued)

		N = 1295	
Rank	Series Title	Number Libraries Selecting	Percent Libraries Selecting
43	Reports and Publications—National Commission on Libraries and Information Science	1039	80.2
44	FDA Consumer	1038	80.2
45	Subject Bibliographies	1038	80.2
46	L.C. Classification Schedules	1037	80.1
47	U.S. Treaties and Other International Aggreements	1036	80.0
48	Consumer Price Index	1033	79.8
49	Bureau of Census, Catalog of Publications	1031	79.6
50	Aging	1026	79.2

depository libraries by the GPO might be in order to determine if indeed it is necessary or appropriate to the needs of all depositories to acquire the twenty-three document series identified in the *Guidelines for Depository Libraries*. Also, it might be useful to investigate why certain depositories do not request very basic items. It would also be of interest to know the characteristics of those depositories that do not select items considered to be basic.

Inverse Ranking of the 200 Item Numbers Least Frequently Chosen by Selective Depositories

The 200 items least frequently chosen by selective depositories were also ranked. This was done to determine which types of documents are seldom selected, and to learn how frequently or infrequently they are selected. An examination of the data reported in Table 3.3 shows that the rate of change between the 1st and the 200th least frequently selected items is substantially less than a comparable range among the most frequently selected item numbers. There were four items that were selected by only one library each, and then the number jumps sharply to thirty-two. At the 50th ranked item from the bottom, only 3.6 percent of the selective depositories made the selection. By the 200th ranked item, only 6.9 percent of the depositories made the selection. This is a difference of only 6.9 percent from the very least frequently selected to the 200th least frequently selected item. This is a sharp contrast to the other end of the scale where more than 38 percent separated the 1st ranked and 200th ranked item numbers.

Table 3.3.   Inverse Ranking of the 200 Item Numbers Least Frequently
Chosen by Selective Depositories

N = 1295

Item Number Rank From Bottom	Number Libraries Selecting	Percent Libraries Selecting
1	1	.1
50	47	3.6
100	79	6.1
200	90	6.9

The authors examined the series titles at the low end of the spectrum and found that their nature is quite different from those at the other end. For example, nearly one-fourth of the least frequently selected items are state flood control reports. Also, military publications account for a large percentage of the least frequently selected 200. Thus, the publications at the low end of the spectrum are clearly quite specialized with little general appeal to the broad range of depository libraries.

The conclusion that one can draw from the results of these rankings is that a substantial number of titles are selected by very few libraries, while very few items of the more than 5,000 available are selected by more than two-thirds of the depositories. Thus, when examining the concept of CONSENSUS, as evidenced by the choices made by selective depositories, one must conclude that CONSENSUS is not very strong except at the very top end of the scale. On the other hand, one can argue that there is another type of consensus at work in item number selection, and that is a consensus that a high percentage of item numbers have limited value to most libraries. This finding suggests to the authors that the range of choices available to most depository libraries extends well beyond their needs and perhaps beyond their ability to make informed choices. This is not to imply that the choices should not be available to them, but rather that the resources designed to enable depositories to make informed choices should be strengthened.

Number and Percent of Selective Depositories That Chose the 200th Most Frequently Selected Item Number, by Type of Library

The authors established six types of library categories, coded all depositories, and assigned each depository to one of the type of library categories. This information was incorporated into File 4, the Supplementary Information File. The frequency of selective depositories in this file, listed by type of library, is reported in Table 3.4. Data from this file were

Table 3.4. Frequency and Percent of Selective Depository Libraries by Type of Library

N = 1291*

Type	Frequency	Percent
Academic Libraries	732	56.7
Public Libraries	269	20.8
Law Libraries	181	14.0
U.S. Government Libraries	52	4.0
State Libraries	36	2.8
Special Libraries (e.g., Boston Atheneaum and American Antiquarian Society.)	21	1.6

Note: The number of depositories in this table is fewer than the number in Tables 3.1, 3.2 and 3.3 because four depositories were added after the directory was compiled from which data on this table was derived.

then combined with data from the Item Selection File in order to obtain a ranking of the most frequently selected item number categories by type of library. Table 3.5, which reports the combination of data from the two files, is discussed more fully below. Because the Item Selection File does not include records for regional depositories, Tables 3.4 and 3.5 only report data from selective depositories.

An examination of Table 3.4 shows that more than half of the selective depositories are found in academic libraries. Although not reported in the table, it is noteworthy that twenty-seven of the forty-nine regional depositories are also academic libraries. Table 3.5 reports the frequency

Table 3.5. Number and Percent of Selective Depositories That Chose the 200th Most Frequently Selected Item Number, by Type of Library

Type of Library	Number of Libraries Selecting 200th Item	Percent
State Libraries N = 36	26	72.2
Academic Libraries N = 732	518	70.8
Public Libraries N = 269	175	65.1
ALL LIBRARIES N = 1291	787	61.0
Law Libraries N = 181	98	54.1
U.S. Government Libraries N = 52	23	44.2
Special Libraries N = 21	8	38.1

of item number selection by type of library only at the 200th benchmark ranking to allow for easier comparison among the types of libraries. For comparison purposes, the 200th ranked item number for ALL selective depositories is also reported. The series title of the 200th ranked item for each type of library is almost certainly different from that of each other type of library because the ranking applies only to libraries coded in that type of library. The type of library categories are listed in order beginning with the type for which CONSENSUS was greatest at the 200th ranking down to the type of library that had the least CONSENSUS.

The results of this ranking demonstrate that there are substantial differences in item number CONSENSUS that exist among depositories in different types of libraries. State libraries display the strongest CONSENSUS at the 200th ranked item number, while special libraries display the weakest CONSENSUS. Public, academic, and state libraries are well above the average for all libraries. However, it is interesting to note the lack of CONSENSUS that exists within each of the six types of libraries even at the 200th ranked item number level. This especially true among those libraries of a specialized nature. This is probably to be expected among special libraries and U.S. government libraries because of the different clientele and perceived user requirements that they try to meet.

The lack of CONSENSUS among law libraries is more difficult to explain. Perhaps differences in the institutional context of law libraries account for part of it. For example, some law libraries are associated with universities and thus might be in close geographic proximity with another depository. Others, more isolated perhaps, perceive a need to acquire a wider range of materials. Possibly law libraries outside of an academic environment are more restrictive in their selection. Some serve a student population, while others serve a more diverse legal clientele. In any case, whatever the explanation, it is interesting that only 54.7 percent of the law libraries that are selective depositories obtain the 200th most frequently ranked item number. The fact that barely half of the law libraries have CONSENSUS on the 200th item number appears to reflect limited interest on the part of many law libraries to take advantage of the full range of item numbers available to them. They apparently are only interested in a limited number of items. This suggests that for many law libraries, the selections fall within a rather narrow range. The findings of this analysis appear to coincide with the study by Kay Schlueter, who examined the document selection process in academic law libraries. She summed up by saying:

> In conclusion, only a few documents titles can be considered completely essential to all law school libraries. More important considerations seem to be law school curriculum and research needs of patrons.[3]

Further study of the patterns of distribution of depository items to law libraries seems warranted, especially in light of the legislation that enables all accredited law schools to become selective depositories, if they so choose.

Ranking of the 200 Item Numbers Most Frequently Chosen by Percent of Available Item Numbers Selected

A question included in the *Biennial Survey* shows the relative percentage of item numbers received by selective depositories. Question 15 on the survey asks depositories to indicate the percentage of item numbers that they selected. Possible responses range from "ALL" to "less than 10%." Responses to this question from the Biennial Survey File were combined with data from the Item Selection File in order to determine if CONSENSUS was systematically associated with the percent of item numbers received by depositories. The results are reported in Table 3.6. The number of depositories analyzed in this question (1,237) deletes the regional depositories as well as those which failed to respond to the questionnaire or to question 15.

A brief explanation of the way data in this table were derived is necessary in order to understand their meaning. The Item Selection File did not report item selections for regional depositories, but the Biennial Survey File did include responses from regional depositories. These responses were included under the category heading "ALL" which implies that depositories responding to this category received all item numbers. Therefore, to make the two files compatible, the forty-nine regional

Table 3.6. Ranking of the 200 Item Numbers Most Frequently Chosen by Percent of Available Item Numbers Selected

N = 1237*

Libraries by Percentage of Item Numbers Selected	Libraries Selecting That Percentage Category	
	Number	*Percent*
ALL	19	100.0
75%	115	100.0
50-75%	172	91.5
25-50%	248	74.3
10-25%	163	46.6
Under 10%	53	25.4

Note: *The number of depositories included in this table is based on the responses to the Biennial Survey with the regional libraries deleted.

depositories were deducted from the total number of libraries (sixty-eight), which responded by indicating they received all item numbers. When this was done, only nineteen selective depositories remained in the "ALL" category. Further explanation is also required. The questionnaire used in the *Biennial Survey, 1979* was worded so that depositories that selected 75 percent or more of the available item numbers were required to choose between two categories, "ALL" and "75%." The number of selective depositories that responded by indicating "ALL" is nineteen. However, the actual number of selective depositories that select all item numbers is far fewer.[4] Thus, some or perhaps most of the libraries that marked "ALL" in response to this question fall somewhere between 75 percent and 100 percent.

The data in Table 3.6 report the level of CONSENSUS for the 200th ranked item number by each of the six responses to categories on question 15 of the *Biennial Survey*. The data show that 100 percent CONSENSUS exists at the 200th ranked item number among depositories that receive 75 percent or more of the available item numbers. This finding is not unexpected because depositories that select all or nearly all of the item numbers select nearly the same items. A high percentage of depositories (91.5 percent) that receive 50-75 percent of available item numbers also show CONSENSUS at the 200th ranked item number. However, CONSENSUS erodes rapidly among libraries that select less than 50 percent of the items. Under 25 percent, fewer than half of the depositories show CONSENSUS and under 10 percent only one-fourth do so.

The findings reported in this table reveal the systematic difference in CONSENSUS when compared to the percentage of item numbers selected. Among depositories that select a limited number of items, there is a wide variation in the choices made. The number of libraries which receive 25 percent or fewer item numbers is 562, or roughly 40 percent of all selective depositories. Because this group represents a rather sizeable part of the entire depository system, it would be of value to learn more about the characteristics of depositories that comprise this category. These findings suggest a need for further study of these depositories.

Ranking, for Academic Depositories, of the 200 Item Numbers Most Frequently Chosen, by Highest Degree Offered by the Academic Institution

As previously noted, a more detailed breakdown of type of library characteristics was undertaken for academic libraries. Because the general type of library ranking of item numbers did not take into account significant differences known to exist among libraries of the same type, the authors decided to create more homogenous groupings of one type of library. Elsewhere in this book (Chapter 5), the authors have examined the use of depository publications by economists who work in an academic setting and who use their institutional libraries. The authors have also examined the treatment of depository items by academic libraries that serve the economists studied (Chapter 4). Therefore, academic libraries were chosen as the type of library that would be used to determine if systematic differences existed in item number selection among libraries that are more nearly alike.

Several means of differentiating among academic libraries were identified. These included: 1) highest level of degree offered; 2) type of institutional support or control for the academic institution in which the library is located; 3) size of student body; and 4) size of general collection. The first of these appeared to provide the best distinction among types of institutions. Therefore, the 200th most frequently received item numbers were identified by the highest level of degree offered. The results are reported in Table 3.7.

The characteristics of the host academic institutions cannot be explained fully by the coding of schools by highest degree offered. Variability

Table 3.7. Ranking, for Academic Depositories, of the 200 Item Numbers Most Frequently Chosen by Highest Degree Offered by the Academic Institution*

N = 732

Highest Level of Degree Offered	Number Libraries Selecting	Percent Libraries Selecting
Two or more years, but less than four years N = 58	27	46.6
Four or five year baccalaureate N = 163	87	53.4
Master's degree N = 206	148	71.8
Beyond master's but less than doctorate N = 80	66	82.5
Doctorate N = 211	164	77.7
Not reported N = 14		

Note: *The source for information about the highest degree offered by each academic institution was taken from: *Education Directory, Colleges and Universities 1979-80,* by Richard J. Petersen and Geneva C. Davis. Washington: National Center for Education Statistics, 1980.

exists even among schools that offer the same level of degree or certificate. However, less variability exists among schools that offer the same level of academic attainment than exists among all academic institutions considered together. Table 3.7 shows that the greatest levels of CONSENSUS exist among academic libraries in institutions that have degree offerings at the master's level or above. The lowest levels of CONSENSUS are found among those institutions which offer a baccalaureate degree or less as the highest level of academic attainment. The size of the institution is probably a related factor, at least at the top end of the scale. However, size alone cannot account for the difference in CONSENSUS because many schools that offer graduate programs are smaller than some that offer the baccalaureate degree or less. Another likely explanation for the variability is that institutions that do not offer advanced degrees probably have a greater range of variability, from one to another, in their programs than do institutions that offer higher level degrees.

A definitive explanation cannot be given because the data are limited, but it is evident that there is a systematic difference in the level of CONSENSUS among academic libraries in different types of schools. However, these differences are not as great as the differences found to exist among various types of libraries. This seems to support the notion that CONSENSUS increases with an increase in similarity among depositories.

The preceding several sections of this chapter have reported on factors that were examined in terms of their association with the concept of CONSENSUS. CONSENSUS, as it is defined in this context, is a measure of the frequency with which depositories select item number categories distributed by the GPO. CONSENSUS is measured by ranking item numbers and then determining the percentage of depositories that receive item numbers at various benchmark levels. The meaning of the findings of this study of item number distribution has been discussed in each section presented thus far. Conclusions that can be drawn from these findings will be presented at the end of the chapter, in combination with the results of the cross tabulations derived from the *Biennial Survey*, which are reported in the next section of this chapter.

BIENNIAL SURVEY AND FACTORS
RELATED TO COLLECTION DEVELOPMENT

The 1979 *Biennial Survey* included fifty-one questions. Several of these provide additional insight into patterns of depository library collection development practice and consequently have been analyzed for that purpose. Each of the questions that was used for this analysis was treated as a variable and was given a variable name, which described the aspect of collection development with which it dealt. These names and the results of the cross tabulations are reported and analyzed below. It should be emphasized that one variable in particular is useful for differentiating among depositories. This is question 15 on the *Biennial Survey*, which asked depositories to indicate the percentage of available item numbers that they received. This question was discussed above in the analysis of CONSENSUS. For the purpose of the analysis of questions taken from the *Biennial Survey*, this variable was given the name PERCENT and was compared with all other variables considered to have collection development implications. The results of these comparisons are reported under the names of the other variables.

As noted above, question 15 was worded in an ambiguous fashion and the consequence of this was that libraries that selected 75 percent or more depository items had to select between two categories, "ALL" and 75%," neither of which accurately represented their situation. Thus, for libraries that select over 75 percent, it is not possible to determine if they selected the higher or lower figure, and the results might not be an accurate reflection of the percentage of their item number selections. It is known that few depositories (other than regionals) receive all items distributed by the system, so the number of depositories that indicated they received "ALL" items does include some depositories that fall between 75 percent and 100 percent. For the purpose of this analysis, regional depositories were subtracted from the number that indicated they received "ALL", so the percentages reflect responses from selective depositories only.

Sufficiency

The question that became the variable named SUFFICIENCY (question 28) asked "Does the depository selection provide sufficient coverage of government publications to handle the documents needs of your library users?" The overall response to this question indicates that 1,120 depositories (87.1 percent) are satisfied while 146 (11.4 percent) are not; 7 (1.6 percent) did not respond to this question. Comparison of this variable with the percentage of item numbers received (PERCENT) reveals that depositories do respond to this question differently, depending on the percentage of item numbers that they receive. Table 3.8, which reports the results of this comparison, shows that nearly one-third of the libraries that claim to receive all item numbers believe the choice is not sufficient. The level of satisfaction improves slightly for those that receive 75 percent of the items and by the time one gets to the depositories that receive 50 percent or fewer of the depository choices, the level of satisfac-

Table 3.8. Sufficiency of Item Number Coverage by Percent of Item
Numbers Selected for Depository Collections

N = 1237*

Libraries by Percent Item Numbers Selected	Percent Yes	Percent No
ALL	61.0	39.0
75%	70.2	29.8
50-75%	87.2	12.8
25-50%	92.3	7.7
10-25%	94.2	5.8
Under 10%	92.3	7.7

Note: *The number of depositories included in this table is based on the responses to the Biennial Survey regional libraries deleted. This is true for Tables 3.8-3.16.

tion with the choices available is greater than 90 percent, which can be considered very high.

The results of this table can probably be explained by the range and difficulty of document retrieval requests directed to libraries of different types. Libraries that select a high percentage of item numbers are typically in large, general purpose academic institutions, with doctoral programs, and thus perceive a need to supply very specialized public documents. On the other hand, depositories that serve a less specialized, and perhaps less demanding, clientele can be satisfied with the choices that are available.

Another factor that might explain this difference is that the libraries that make choices for a smaller percentage of item numbers are reluctant to increase their depository choices because they do not want to increase substantially the number of documents received. Although a large number of items are available in microfiche, for small libraries the acquisition of items in microfiche still requires additional record keeping and staff time as well as the purchase of viewing and reproduction equipment. Consequently, a larger range of choices has limited value to them and, in fact, might be counterproductive because of the additional time required to make item number choices. This is an area where additional research would be valuable. In any case, whatever the explanation, there is evidence that about one-third of the depositories that receive a substantial number of items would prefer to have the range of choices increased, while most depositories are satisfied with the numbers as they now stand.

Resource Sharing

Resource sharing has been advocated elsewhere in this book as a means of giving responsible attention to the issue of collection development.

One element in collection planning is cooperative work with other libraries to share information resources. This implies sharing information
about the nature and size of the collection. Question 10 on the *Biennial
Survey* asked depositories if they had a program for informing other
libraries in their geographical area of the services and publications available from the depository. The response on the survey indicated that 485
(37.7 percent) of the depositories had such a program but 791 (61.5
percent) did not (with .8 percent not responding).

The authors were interested in determining if there was any association betwen responses to this question and the variable named PER-
CENT. When the data from PERCENT and RESOURCE SHARING
were compared, reported in Table 3.9, it was found that the existence of
a resource sharing program was not common among depositories of any
size. The data show that fewer than half of the libraries in any of the
categories indicate that they have such a program. Regional libraries,
which have a legal responsiblity to do this, are excluded from this analysis, so the results reflect only responses from selective depositories. Among
very small depositories, (e.g., those which receive under 10 percent of
the item numbers), less than a quarter have a program for informing
other libraries about their depository collection. The results of this comparison suggest that the actual practice of resource sharing, as it pertains
to depository collections, is very limited. It would seem to be crucial to
successful resource sharing that libraries which hold depository collections make their holdings known, not only to libraries with depository
collections, but to other libraries as well. Without this, resource sharing
would seem to have limited potential. If an automated item selection file
were available to depositories so that lists of item numbers received by
other depositories within a defined geographical area could be made
known, this might encourage greater resource sharing, at least among
depositories.

Table 3.9. Resource Sharing: Program for Informing
Adjacent Libraries of Documents Service by Percent of Item Numbers
Selected for Depository Collections

N = 1237

Libraries by Percent Item Numbers Selected	Percent Yes	Percent No
ALL	44.4	55.6
75%	40.5	59.5
50-75%	43.9	56.1
25-50%	39.5	60.5
10-25%	39.8	60.2
Under 10%	21.9	78.1

Collection Review and Discarding

Two questions on the *Biennial Survey* dealt with collection review and discarding practices of depository libraries. These questions were cross tabulated separately with the PERCENT variable. However, they will be analyzed together because they are related to similar aspects of the collection development process. The first question, number 16, was phrased "Has your library reviewed its depository selections in the past two years, deleting and adding according to your community requirements?" This variable, which was named COLLECTION REVIEW, is useful in that it provides an indication of the extent to which depositories try to relate item number choices to their user community. The vast majority of depositories responded to this question by indicating that they had reviewed their selections within the previous two years. The response indicated 1,165 depositories (90.6 percent) had and 87 (6.8 percent) had not; 34 (2.6 percent) did not respond. It would be of value to know how the collection review was conducted in these depositories, whether on the basis of user studies, experience, intuition, or some other means. The comparison with the PERCENT variable shows that the review process is fairly evenly distributed among all categories used in question 15 of the *Biennial Survey*.

A second question, number 23, dealt with the discarding practices of depositories. This question, which was given the name DISCARDING, asked "Have you discarded publications retained for five years or more during the past twelve months?" The response indicated that 603 (46.9 percent) had discarded documents while 652 (50.7 percent) had not; 31 (2.4 percent) did not respond. The response to this question was very nearly evenly divided among those depositories in the middle categories of the PERCENT variable, while depositories which receive a high percentage (ALL) or a low percentage (under 10%) responded in a notice-

Table 3.10. Review of Collection in the Previous Two Years by Percent of Item Numbers Selected for Depository Collections

N = 1237

Libraries by Percent Item Numbers Selected	Percent Yes	Percent No
ALL	89.4	10.6
75%	95.7	4.3
50-75%	97.3	2.7
25-50%	95.6	4.4
10-25%	95.1	4.9
Under 10%	91.8	8.2

Table 3.11. Discarding of Materials in the Previous Twelve Months by Percent of Item Numbers Selected for Depository Collections

N = 1237

Libraries by Percent Item Numbers Selected	Percent Yes	Percent No
ALL	21.1	78.9
75%	54.8	45.2
50-75%	60.4	39.6
25-50%	52.1	47.9
10-25%	53.8	46.2
Under 10%	27.5	72.5

ably different fashion. In these two categories, roughly three-fourths of the depositories indicate that they undertook no discarding. However, in the other four categories, in most cases, barely more than half of the depositories indicated that they had discarded depository items within the past twelve months. The results of this comparison show that many depositories are not actively involved in the deselection process. It would thus appear that for many depositories, the primary procedure for adjusting or adapting the depository collection is adding or deleting item number choices (as suggested in Table 3.10) rather than the physical removal of documents from the collection (as suggested in Table 3.11).

An explanation of the findings reported in this table leads to one of the following conclusions: 1) the libraries have done an excellent job of selecting the item numbers that they receive and expect to maintain permanent retention, even of documents that are superseded; 2) the libraries lack the staff and time to conduct this activity; 3) government documents are given low priority as an information resource in the library; or 4) the libraries are in states which have no regional library, thus complicating the procedures for discarding. Additional understanding of this matter might be gained by inserting a question in the next *Biennial Survey* asking depositories to estimate, in some fashion, the quantity of documents that they had discarded, and to indicate the number of new item numbers received or item numbers discarded. They might also be asked to indicate the reason they had not discarded during the previous twelve month period of time.

The authors wanted to determine if the REVIEW and DISCARD variables were evenly distributed among depository libraries when these variables were compared to the RESOURCE SHARING variable. It could be assumed that depositories that inform adjacent libraries of their holdings might be more diligent in reviewing item number selections based on user needs, or in discarding documents no longer found to be of

Table 3.12. Resource Sharing/Review: Program for Informing
Adjacent Libraries of Documents Service by Review of Collection in
the Previous Two Years

	N = 1237	
Resource Sharing	*Review*	
	Yes	No
Yes	98.0	2.0
No	98.3	1.7

value. Tables 3.12 and 3.13 report the results of these comparisons. In the case of the combination of the REVIEW and RESOURCE SHARING variables, (Table 3.12), there is little difference in the way the two groups of libraries respond. Almost all of the depositories in both categories reviewed their holdings within the previous two years.

In the case of the other variables, RESOURCE SHARING and DISCARD, (Table 3.13) the percentage of libraries in each category was nearly the same, but there were some differences. The results conform to the expectations of the authors that there would be slightly more emphasis on discarding of materials by those depositories that informed other libraries of their depository programs and services than by those that did not. The percentage difference, however, is not very great, and thus one is led to the conclusion that deselection of materials is not strongly associated with resource sharing, if this is measured by the level of activity that a depository displays in informing other libraries of its collection and services.

Collection Organization and Use of the Superintendent of Documents Classification System

Two questions on the *Biennial Survey* were concerned with the system for organizing the documents' collections (e.g., whether the depository

Table 3.13. Resource Sharing/Discard: Program for Informing
Adjacent Libraries of Documents Service by Libraries Discarding
Publications Within the Previous Twelve Months

	N = 1237	
Resource Sharing	*Discard*	
	Yes	No
Yes	55.4	44.6
No	46.1	53.9

was housed in a separate department or otherwise), and whether the depository used the Superintendent of Documents Classification System. These questions, number 18 and number 37, have a collection development implication for at least two reasons. First, it might be assumed that libraries where documents are housed in a separate department typically have persons assigned to the collection as a documents librarian or a documents assistant, with greater attention given to documents service than those libraries where there is no separate department. Second, a depository library in which there is a separate department is likely to have greater interest in the "item number" as a means of collection development because of the close correlation of item numbers with the SuDocs classification number. The SuDocs number is a primary means of determing the provenance or publishing agency, and thus by inference, the possible subject matter of a document series.

For the purpose of analysis, the variable which indicated whether depository items were located in a separate department was named COLLECTION ORGANIZATION, and the variable which indicated whether a library used the Superintendent of Documents Classification System was named SUDOCS.

The *Biennial Survey* reported that for the variable named COLLECTION ORGANIZATION, 841 depositories (65.4 percent) maintained the documents collection in a separate department, while 415 (32.3 percent) did not; 30 (2.3 percent) failed to respond. For the variable named SUDOCS, 1,149 (89.3 percent) used the SuDocs classification system for the major portion of the documents, with 121 (9.4 percent) using some other system; 16 (1.2 percent) did not respond.

The responses to these two queries on the survey raised questions about the relationship between the two variables, and their distribution among depositories that received varying percentages of item numbers. The relationship between the two variables was examined by comparing COLLECTION ORGANIZATION and SUDOCS; the results are reported in Table 3.14. There is an expected strong relationship between those depositories that have a separate collection and those that use the SuDocs system. Ninety-seven (97) percent of the libraries that have a separate documents department use the SuDocs system. However, a surprising finding emerged: 307 (76.6 percent) of the libraries that do not maintain a separate department for the depository collection also use the SuDocs classification system.

It is useful to compare this find with the descriptive study of depositories by Whitbeck, Hernon, and Richardson. In their study, the choice of four methods of arrangement for the depository collection was presented to respondents.[5] These four methods of arrangement were: 1) entirely separate collection; 2) totally integrated collection; 3) partially integrated

Table 3.14. Collection Organization/SuDocs: Documents Collection
Organized in Separate Department by SuDocs System Used for
Classifying Documents

N = 1237

Separate Department	SuDocs System Used	
	Yes	*No*
Yes	97.0	3.0
No	76.6	23.4

collection; and 4) mixed. Their findings showed that only 82 of 1,048 depositories had totally integrated collections, but the libraries that used separate collections were divided between those that were entirely separate (322) and those that were partially integrated (623).[6] The fact that respondents were given four choices in this study enabled the researchers to make more precise distinctions among possible alternatives to collection organization than was possible from the data obtained from the *Biennial Survey*. It would be useful if the *Biennial Survey* could enlarge the number of choices provided to depositories that they could use to describe their method of collection organization.

These same two variables (COLLECTION ORGANIZATION and SUDOCS) were computed with the PERCENT variable to see if there was any pattern in their distribution among libraries that received different frequencies of item number selections. Tables 3.15 and 3.16 report the results of these comparisons. In the case of the variable COLLECTION ORGANIZATION, the results in Table 3.15 show a steady decrease in the percentage of libraries that maintain a separate docu-

Table 3.15. Documents Collection Organized in Separate Department
by Percent of Item Numbers Selected for Depository Collections

N = 1237

Libraries by	Documents Collection in Separate Department	
Percent Item Numbers Selected	*Yes*	*No*
ALL	78.9	21.1
75%	80.7	19.3
50-75%	77.7	22.3
25-50%	77.3	22.7
10-25%	57.9	42.1
Under 10%	42.4	57.6

Table 3.16.   Use of SuDocs System for Classifying Documents
Collections by Percent of Item Numbers Selected for
Depository Collections

N = 1237

Libraries by Percent Item Numbers Selected	SuDocs System USED for Major Proportion of Documents Collection	SuDocs System NOT USED for Major Proportion of Documents Collection
ALL	100.0	0.0
75%	93.9	6.1
50-75%	94.7	5.3
25-50%	95.9	4.1
10-25%	88.0	12.0
Under 10%	77.9	22.1

ments department as the percentage of item numbers decreases. The most noticeable drop occurs with libraries that receive 25 percent or fewer of the depository items. This indicates that many libraries receiving a limited number of item number choices understandably do not deem it necessary to maintain a separate documents collection.

The other comparison involved the variables SUDOCS and PERCENT. The results of this cross tabulation, reported in Table 3.16, show a steady increase in the use of the SuDocs system as the percentage of item numbers selected increases. It is interesting to note the high percentage of depositories that select 25 percent or more of the item numbers which use the SuDocs system. However, the percentage is reasonably high for all categories. This suggests that depositories in all size ranges continue to find the SuDocs system to be of value. Further exploration of the relationship between the SuDocs system and depository collection development might result in some valuable insights about the way depository items are selected.

The meaning of these findings for collection development in depository libraries is unclear. Perhaps the SuDocs classification scheme is used as a major tool in making collection development decisions. The "List of Classes," which is distributed to all depository libraries, arranged by SuDocs classification number, may well be the major selection tool used by many depository libraries, particularly smaller depositories. Naturally, if this were the case, choices would be modified by the experience of the library staff. However, it is possible that some choices, made largely through the list or through the surveys distributed when new items are to be distributed, would be based largely on the classification scheme because the classification scheme is arranged by issuing agency, using the concept of provenance. If this were so, it could mean that the decisions are based largely on the basis of librarians' perceptions of the relationship of the publishing agency to the information needs of users. This, in turn, would require better subject access resources than are available at present for optimal subject selection. This further underscores the necessity of the type of research reported in Chapter 4.

CONCLUSIONS

In this chapter, data derived from the four files have been used to identify patterns of distribution of item number categories to depository libraries and to examine some characteristics of collection development procedures used by depository libraries. The data used for the analyses reported in this chapter were derived largely from files made available by the Superintendent of Documents, augmented by a file compiled by the authors. The patterns of item number distribution that were examined represent only a few of the many possible variations that might have been examined. Those selected were chosen because they were considered to have the most potential for revealing information, which in turn could be used to infer depository collection development patterns. The same is true for the questions selected for analysis from *Biennial Survey*.

What can be learned from this examination of patterns of distribution of depository item numbers and from the "collection development" variables found in the *Biennial Survey*? First, the study of item number patterns will be considered. The item number patterns were examined by means of a measure of the frequency of distribution of item numbers to depositories. This measure was named CONSENSUS for the purposes of this study. CONSENSUS is a measure of both the concentration and the dispersion of item numbers to depository libraries. Where a high degree of CONSENSUS exists, there is a concentration of libraries that place value on the item number for their users. Where little consensus exists, the distribution of an item number is widely dispersed among the total population of depositories.

The study of patterns of item number distribution showed a rather high degree of dispersion, with limited distribution of most item numbers. This results in a rather high degree of variability in the selection of item numbers by selective depositories. Whether this can be explained by adherence to good collection development practices or to other factors cannot be determined through the data available through this study. However, the authors rather suspect that other factors are at work because the mechanisms that would lead to good collection development practices and the resources, which libraries can draw on for informed choices among item numbers, simply are not available at the present time, especially for libraries with limited resources.

When CONSENSUS is used as a measure of concentration and dispersion, the study shows that it is associated in a meaningful way with type of library. There is greater CONSENSUS among some types of libraries than others. There is also greater CONSENSUS among libraries of the same type, when grouped in more homogenous subtypes. This was demonstrated by ranking item numbers received by academic depositories, grouped by highest degree offered. The meaning of this is that libraries of a similar nature tend to perceive their public document requirements in a similar fashion. This knowledge is useful in that it can provide the basis for the development of "core" lists of item numbers for libraries that serve the same types of user groups.

As noted above, one can consider the concept of CONSENSUS with a reverse twist as well. It is quite possible that where low frequencies are found to exist among depositories in their choices of item numbers, this indeed does represent CONSENSUS, a consensus as to the lack of value of some of the item numbers distributed by the depository system. The limited frequency of selection for such a large number of items might well signify that many depositories find there are simply too many item number categories in the system to cope with. This is a facet of depository distribution that should be given further thought, both by depositories as they make their choices and by the Government Printing Office. It might well have implications for the restructuring of the depository distribution system.

What size library typically can cope with the full range of item number choices? Although there is no magic number for total holdings at which a depository library should expect to receive all or most of the item numbers, it would certainly seem that libraries with fewer than 1,000,000 volumes would find it difficult to justify building an "exhaustive" collection implied by the selection of a large percentage of depository item numbers. Data compiled by the authors revealed that 137 depositories are in libraries that have collections over 1,000,000 books (excluding public documents). These libraries would presumably be over the "threshold" in terms of the resources available to build an exhaustive collection, hence would benefit from the wide range of item number choices available. However, the item number selection records show that the tendency among selective depositories is to opt for more limited sized collections rather than comprehensive collections. It is interesting to note that although the *Guidelines* suggest a depository should select a minimum of 25 percent of the item numbers, a substantial number receive less than this now, and the number of depositories that select fewer than 25 percent is likely to grow as the number of item number choices increases.

The results of this study suggest that the GPO and the Depository Library Council should study the relationship of the number of item numbers distributed and the expected and actual percentages of item numbers selected by depositories.

The use of data derived from the *Biennial Survey* resulted in some additional insights about patterns of depository collection development. The question which served as the most useful variable for examining the results of this survey was the percentage of item numbers received by depositories (PERCENT). This question enabled the authors to determine if variables derived from other questions were associated in a systematic way with the range of depository items received. It was observed that there were differences that could be explained by this variable, including the perception of the sufficiency of the item number distribution choices. There were other variables that seemed to be fairly evenly distributed by the PERCENT variable, and thus represent phenomena not associated with the percentage of item numbers selected.

The results of the study lead the authors to propose that whenever possible, questions on the *Biennial Survey* request that depositories supply actual numbers rather than respond to categories. For example, with the automated selection file, each depository could indicate the actual number of items received rather than estimate the percentage and respond in the appropriate category. The use of actual numbers would increase the strength of the inferences that could be made from the data. Also, additional questions directed at collection development practices in depositories would be valuable for future analysis of this process.

Although the findings reported in this chapter provide some useful information about depository item number distribution, and about some aspects of depository collection development, the inferences that can be made are limited in nature. These data provide information about broad patterns of document distribution and collection development, but the data can only be used in a limited fashion to provide information of a utilitarian nature for depositories, which are trying to improve collection development practices and priorities. What is needed is the development of an improved mechanism for document selection by depository libraries, including a subject context for the selection of item numbers. The next chapter provides a step toward this objective.

NOTES AND REFERENCES

1. Preliminary results were reported on this project at the First Annual Government Documents and Information Conference, held in Boston, May 4-5, 1981. The report has been published as: Peter Hernon and Gary Purcell, "Collection Development as Represented through the GPO Automated List of Item Numbers," in Peter Hernon (ed.), *Collection Development and Public Access of Government Information. The Proceedings of*

the *First Annual Government Documents and Information Conference*, 1981. (Westport, Conn.: Meckler Books, 1982).

2. *Guidelines for the Depository Library System*, as adopted by the Depository Library Council to the Public Printer, October 18, 1977. (Washington, D.C.: Government Printing Office, n.d.), p. 10.

3. Kay Schlueter, "Selection of Government Documents in Law School Libraries," *Law Library Journal* 71 (October 1976):479.

4. In conversation with Ms. Janet Erickson of the GPO Systems and Programs Division, Ms. Erickson indicated that only a handful of selective depositories (perhaps as few as 1-3) receive all item numbers.

5. George W. Whitbeck, Peter Hernon and John Richardson, Jr., "The Federal Depository Library System: A Descriptive Analysis," *Government Publications Review* 5(1978): 253-267.

6. Ibid., p. 257.

Chapter 4

Item Numbers of Potential Value To Academic Economists: A Theoretical Overview

Selective depository libraries select the categories of publications that they want to receive from among numerous categories designated by item numbers. The specific publications in any given item number category are defined by the Government Printing Office, and although many item numbers consist of a single title or series issued by the publishing agency, there are still many item numbers that represent artificial series and contain several unique titles. Although there is considerable flexibility in the choices available, depository libraries may receive titles within an item number that do not meet the library's collection development objectives.

The Superintendent of Documents Classification Scheme, which dates back to the late 19th century, reflects the archival heritage of government publications as public records. Since item numbers are derived from this classification scheme, organizational hierarchy and publication type are emphasized over subject content. In fact, similar subjects and works by the same author will often not be grouped together; they might be found in various places depending on the issuing agency and the type of publication.

Complicating matters for librarians is the fact that collection development *must* adhere to the structures of literature concept and view holdings within a subject context.[1] Consequently the significance of the findings derived from a comparison of item numbers to various variables (such as in the previous chapter) can be questioned. An examination of item numbers and a comparison of the numbers to specific variables will only be successful once the library profession has derived a generally agreed upon subject orientation from the item numbers. It should be empha-sized, however, that item numbers provide the basis for interaction be-tween the GPO and the depository community, and that they are not intended for collection development purposes. Still, it is beneficial for libraries to attempt to manipulate this information for developing their collections and improving inter-institutional cooperation. Even though the application may be imprecise, it may assist libraries in integrating government publications more effectively with other library resources and in identifying the array of library resources useful to a particular subject. The result, therefore, might be the type of administrative inte-gration for government publication collections that has been called for in the literature of documents librarianship.[2]

Since item numbers must be viewed in the context of specific govern-ment bodies (e.g., departments, agencies, and committees), it is neces-sary first to identify those bodies that have relevance to individual disciplines and then to focus on those item numbers that are appropriate. Building upon the previous chapter, this one attempts to make an initial estima-tion of those government bodies useful to members of one academic discipline, while the next chapter reports on the findings of a survey of documents use and suggests those government bodies as well as docu-ment types and titles most likely to be consulted by members of this academic discipline. Comparisons of selection and use patterns should be of value to libraries in developing collections of government publica-tions likely to meet the more frequent demands placed upon them. Since this book does not provide case study analyses of the institutions dis-cussed in the next chapter, no attempt will be made to draw conclusions about the collection development practices of the institutions surveyed.

This chapter focuses on academic economists due to the immense publishing output of the federal government for the discipline and to the fact that these faculty members have been previously investigated.[3] This analysis, therefore, builds upon previous research and incorporates data gathered from an examination of the *Monthly Catalog of United States Government Publications* and a survey of academic depository libraries.

The chapter is divided into three parts: (1) a listing of government bodies identified as issuing publications of value to academic economists; (2) identification of the bodies most frequently mentioned from the survey of depository libraries; and (3) examples of item numbers identi-fied in the *Monthly Catalog* as containing publications useful to econo-mists. It is our hope that the Depository Library Council to the Public Printer and the Government Documents Round Table (GODORT) of the American Library Association will refine the following, tentative listing. By investigating individual disciplines, libraries can identify the nucleus of appropriate government bodies, document types and titles. These

indings should suggest the nucleus of publications for a specific disci-
ply, interdisciplinary relationships, and the nucleus of resources for
proad areas such as the social sciences. The assumption is that a small
percentage of types, and perhaps even titles, account for a large per-
entage of the use of documents collections.[4]

GOVERNMENT BODIES PRODUCING PUBLICATIONS OF POTENTIAL VALUE TO ECONOMISTS

n order to identify the range of government bodies applicable to economists, the authors first examined entries in the *Monthly Catalog* from
1976 to 1981. Each entry for these years was scanned for subject head-
ings as well as Library of Congress or Dewey classification numbers
covering the discipline of economics. Whenever there was a match, the
authors recorded the government body and item number on the "List of
Classes of United States Government Publications Available for Selection
by Depository Libraries." Since the "List of Classes" records the government bodies, document series, and item numbers currently in GPO's
active file, it provides the basis from which to build an on-going subject
model. Consensus about the value of the information contained in this
source should advance collection development practices at the national
and subordinate levels. To assist in this effort, Appendix C reprints part
of a list arranged by item numbers and matching item numbers to series
and issuing agencies.

In addition to examining the *Monthly Catalog*, the authors selected fifty
academic depository libraries, on a random sample basis, and the seventeeen
institutions profiled in the next chapter. Librarians at the sixty-seven
institutions were sent question 10 from the questionnaire reprinted in
Appendix D and asked to identify those bodies from which they selected
publications for academic economists. The purpose of the survey was to
verify and supplement the list obtained from examining the *Monthly
Catalog*. Some forty-five, or 67.2 percent, of the libraries responded to
the mail survey.

Table 4.1 depicts the main government bodies identified as issuing
source material pertinent to the discipline of economics. It should be
emphasized that this table, as well as the others reported in this chapter,
focuses primarily on the publications coming through the GPO and its
depository program. The publications of other clearinghouses have not
been fully represented. Still, patterns should emerge concerning the use
of their publications.

Table 4.2 through 4.13 take subdivisions of selected government bodies and suggest those relevant to economists. In addition, it might be
noted that pertinent subdivisions of the Department of Energy include

Table 4.1. Government Bodies Publishing Information of
Potential Value to Economists

Action	Housing and Urban Development
Agriculture Department	Department
Arms Control and	Interior Department
Disarmament Agency	International Communication
Civil Aeronautics Board	Agency
Civil Rights Commission	International Trade
Civil Service Commission	Commission
Commerce Department	Interstate Commerce
Community Services	Commission
Administration	Judiciary
Congress	Justice Department
Defense Department	Labor Department
Education Department	National Academy of Sciences
Energy Department	National Aeronautics and
Environmental Protection	Space Administration
Agency	National Credit Union
Executive Office of the	Administration
President	National Foundation on the
Farm Credit Administration	Arts and the Humanities
Federal Communications	National Labor Realtions
Commission	Board
Federal Emergency Management	National Mediation Board
Agency	National Science Foundation
Federal Home Loan Bank	Office of the President
Board	Overseas Private Investment
Federal Maritime	Corporation
Commission	Personnel Management Office
Federal Mediation and	Railroad Retirement Board
Conciliation Service	Security and Exchange
Federal Power Commission	Commission
Federal Reserve System	Small Business Adminstration
Board of Governors	Smithsonian Institution
Federal Trade Commission	State Department (including
Foreign-Trade Zones Board	The Agency for International
General Services	Development)
Administration	Transportation Department
Health and Human Services	Treasury Department
Department	United Postal Service
	Veterans Administration

the Economic Regulatory Administration, Energy Information Administration, and Federal Energy Regulatory Commission. Economists might
also be attracted to the General Services Administration (the National
Archives and Records Service, Office of the Federal Register, and Consumer Information Center), the Judiciary (Court of Claims, Supreme
Court, Administrative Office of the U.S. Courts, and Tax Court), and the
Library of Congress (Copyright Office, Congressional Research Service,
and Processing Department—Cataloging Distribution Service Division).
As is evident, the potential list of government bodies providing source

Table 4.2. Agencies Reporting to Congress That Have Potential Value to Economists

Advisory Commission on Intergovernmental Relations
Advisory Council on Social Security
Commodity Futures Trading Commission
Congressional Budget Office
East-West Foreign Trade Board
Equal Employment Opportunity Commision
Export-Import Bank of United States
Federal Labor Relations Authority
Federal Paperwork Commission
Foreign Claims Settlement Commission
General Accounting Office
Government Printing Office
Library of Congress
National Advisory Council on Economic Opportunity
National Advisory Council on International Monetary
    and Financial Policies
Nuclear Regulatory Commission
Pension Benefit Guaranty Corporation
Tennessee Valley Authority

Table 4.3. Congressional Committees of Potential Value to Economists

Committee on Agriculture (House)
Committee on Agriculture, Nutrition, and Forestry (Senate)
Committee on Appropriations (House and Senate)
Committee on Armed Services (House and Senate)
Committee on Banking, Finance and Urban Affairs (House and Senate)
Committee on Budget (House and Senate)
Committee on Commerce, Science and Transportation (Senate)
Committee on Energy and Natural Resources (Senate)
Committee on Finance (Senate)
Committee on Governmental Affairs (Senate)
Committee on Interstate and Foreign Commerce (House)
Committee on Judiciary (House and Senate)
Committee on Labor and Human Resources (Senate)
Committee on Post Office and Civil Service (House)
Committee on Public Works and Transportation (House)
Committee on Small Business (House)
Committee on Ways and Means (House)
Joint Committee on Taxation
Joint Economic Committee
Select Committee on Congressional Operations (House)
Select Committee on Small Business (Senate)

Table 4.4. Segments of the Executive Office of the President Having
Potential Value to Economists

Central Intelligence Agency
Council on Environmental Quality
Council on Wage and Price Stability
Domestic Council
Economic Advisors Council
Foreign Broadcast Information Service
Management and Budget Office
Office of Special Representative for
    Trade Negotiations

Table 4.5. Segments of the Department of Agriculture Having
Potential Value to Economists

Office of the Secretary
Agricultural Marketing Service
Agricultural Research Service
Agricultural Stabilization and Conservation Service
Commodity Credit Corporation
Economic Research Service
Economics, Statistics and Cooperatives Service
Farmer Cooperative Service
Farmers Home Administration
Federal Crop Insurance Corporation
Foreign Agricultural Service
Forest Service
Rural Development Service
Soil Conservation Service
Statistical Reporting Service

Table 4.6. Segments of the Department of Commerce Having
Potential Value to Economists

Office of the Secretary
Census Bureau
Domestic Commerce Bureau
East-West Trade Bureau
Economic Analysis Bureau
Economic Development Administration
Environmental Data and Information Service
Export Development Bureau
Industrial Economics Bureau
Industry and Trade Administration
International Trade Adminstration
Maritime Administration
National Bureau of Standards
National Oceanographic Data Center
National Technical Information Service
Patent and Trademark Office
Resources and Trade Assistance Bureau
United States Travel Service

Table 4.7. Segments of the Department of Health and Human Services Having Potential Value to Economists

Aging Administration
Assistance Payments Administration
Center for Disease Control
Child Development Office
Children's Bureau
Consumer Affairs Office
Education Division
Education Office (reorganized)
Food and Drug Administration
Health Care Financing Administration
Health Resources Administration
Health Services Administration
Medicaid Bureau
National Center for Education Statistics
National Center for Health Services Research
National Center for Health Statistics
National Center for Social Statistics
National Clearinghouse on Aging
National Institute of Education
National Institute of Mental Health
National Institute on Alcohol Abuse and Alcoholism
National Institute on Aging
National Institute on Drug Abuse
National Institutes of Health
National Library of Medicine
Public Health Service
Public Services Administration
Social Security Administration
Youth Development Office

Table 4.8. Segments of the Department of Housing and Urban Development Having Potential Value to Economists

Federal Disaster Assistance Administration
Federal Housing Administration
Federal Insurance Administration
Federal National Mortgage Association
New Communities Administration

Table 4.9. Segments of the Department of Interior Having Potential Value to Economists

Bureau of the Mines
Fish and Wildlife Service
Geological Survey
Land Management Bureau
National Park Service
Outdoor Recreation Bureau

Table 4.10. Segments of the Department of Justice Having Potential Value to Economists

Drug Enforcement Administration
Federal Bureau of Investigation
Immigration and Naturalization Service
Law Enforcement Assistance Administration
National Institute of Justice

Table 4.11. Segments of the Department of Labor Having Potential Value to Economists

Office of the Secretary
Bureau of Labor Statistics
Employees Compensation Appeals Board
Employment and Training Administration
Employment and Standards Administration
International Labor Affairs Bureau
Mine Safety and Health Administration
Occupational Safety and Health Administartion
Unemployment Insurance Service
United States Employment Service
Veterans' Reemployment Rights Office
Wage and Hour Division
Women's Bureau
Workers Compensation Programs Office

Table 4.12. Segments of the Department of Treasury Having Potential Value to Economists

Alcohol, Tobacco and Firearms Bureau
Comptroller of Currency
Customs Service
Government Financial Operations Bureau
Internal Revenue Service
Public Debt Bureau
Savings Bond Division

Table 4.13. Segments of the Department of Transportation Having Potential Value to Economists

Office of the Secretary
Civil Aviation Security Service
Coast Guard
Federal Aviation Administration
Federal Highway Administration
Federal Railroad Administration
Motor Carrier Safety Bureau
National Highway Traffic Safety Administration
National Transportation Safety Board
Urban Mass Transportation Administration

material potentially useful for the *general* discipline of economics is indeed quite large. Undoubtedly, attempts to concentrate on specific subfields within the broad discipline (e.g., economic theory, econometrics and statistics, labor and human resources development, public finance, and urban economics) would reduce the potential range of government bodies.

GOVERNMENT BODIES MOST FREQUENTLY MENTIONED BY SURVEY RESPONDENTS

Examination of the responses from the forty-five institutions reveals distinct patterns as to the government bodies whose publications are selected for use by economists. Naturally the higher the degree offering the more government bodies identified. All responding libraries acquire publications from the Department of Commerce and Department of Labor. Still, within these departments they are most likely to draw upon the publications of certain agencies. In the case of the Department of Commerce, all respondents selected from the Bureau of the Census. Frequently they also drew upon the following agencies:

- Economic Analysis Bureau
- International Trade Administration
- Economic Development Administration
- Industry and Trade Administration
- Domestic Commerce Bureau
- Industrial Economics Bureau
- East-West Trade Bureau
- National Technical Information Service

As for the Department of Labor, all respondents selected from the Bureau of Labor Statistics. They also frequently acquired publications from the following agencies:

- Employment and Training Administration
- Wage and Hour Division
- Women's Bureau
- International Labor Affairs Bureau
- United States Employment Service

Some forty-one, or 91.1 percent, of the libraries selected Congressional publications for their economists. These publications comprise those from agencies reporting to Congress and Congressional committees themselves. The most frequently mentioned agencies are listed in order as follows:

- Congressional Budget Office
- Library of Congress (especially the Congressional Research Service
- Advisory Commission on Intergovernmental Relations
- Export-Import Bank of the United States
- Equal Employment Commission
- National Advisory Council on Economic Opportunity

Table 4.14, which depicts Congressional committees, shows that publica
tions from the Joint Economic Committee and Joint Committee on Tax
ation were most frequently mentioned. It might be noted that surve
respondents made only infrequent reference to the Committee on Agri
culture (House), Committee on Agriculture, Nutrition, and Forestry (Sen
ate), Committee on Armed Services (House), Committee on Armed Ser
vices (Senate), Select Committee on Congressional Operations (House)
and Committees on Post Office and Civil Service (House).

Table 4.14. Congressional Committees Whose Publications Are
Frequently Selected for Use by Economists*

Committee	Number	Percentage
Joint Economic Committee	35	77.8
Joint Committee on Taxation	35	77.8
Committee on Ways and Means (House)	31	68.9
Committee on Banking, Finance and Urban Affairs (House)	27	60.0
Committee on Banking, Housing and Urban Affairs (Senate)	27	60.0
Committee on Budget (Senate)	27	60.0
Committee on Budget (House)	27	60.0
Committee on Finance (Senate)	27	60.0
Committee on Interstate and Foreign Commerce (House)	27	60.0
Committee on Labor and Human Resources (Senate)	27	60.0
Select Committee on Small Business (Senate)	24	53.3
Committee on Small Business (House)	20	44.4
Committee on Appropriations (House)	17	37.8
Committee on Appropriations (Senate)	17	37.8
Committee on Commerce, Science and Transportation (Senate)	17	37.8
Committee on Energy and Natural Resources (Senate)	17	37.8
Committee on Governmental Affairs (Senate)	17	37.8
Committee on Judiciary (House)	14	31.1
Committee on Judiciary (Senate)	14	31.1
Committee on Public Works and Transportation (House)	14	31.1

Note: *Respondents could check as many as applicable

Following Congress and its publications, the next cluster of government bodies (thirty-eight, or 84.4 percent) covered the Federal Reserve System Board of Governors, Executive Office of the President, the Department of Health and Human Services, the General Services Administration, and the Department of Agriculture. For the Executive Office of the President, the most frequently mentioned agencies are listed in order as follows:

- Office of Management and Budget
- Economic Advisors Council
- Council on Wage and Price Stability
- Central Intelligence Agency
- Council on Environmental Quality

For the Department of Health and Human Services, the distribution of most frequently mentioned agencies is listed in order as follows:

- Social Security Administration
- National Center for Social Statistics
- National Center for Health Statistics
- National Center for Education Statistics
- Health Care Financing Administration
- Children's Bureau

Selections from the General Services Administration focus on the Office of the Federal Register, while for the Department of Agriculture they centered on the Economic Research Service, the Economics, Statistics, and Cooperative Service, and the Foreign Agricultural Service.

The final cluster of government bodies presented focuses on selections at the median number of responding institutions. Publications found here are from the Treasury Department, in particular the Internal Revenue Service; the Office of the President; the Department of Energy, especially the Energy Information Administration; the Environmental Protection Agency; the Federal Home Loan Bank Board; the Securities and Exchange Commission; the Department of Housing and Urban Development; the Interstate Commerce Commission; the Federal Trade Commission; the Small Business Administration; and the Department of Transportation and its Federal Aviation Administration, Urban Mass Transportation Administration, National Highway Traffic Safety Administration, and the National Transportation Safety Board.

ITEM NUMBERS CONTAINING PUBLICATIONS PERTINENT TO ECONOMISTS

An examination of the publishing history of an established item number and the documentation that the GPO distributes for new item numbers will suggest disciplines for which the publications might have appeal.[5] This does not guarantee that all the publications ever issued within a specific item number are pertinent to a given discipline. Nonetheless, the information has general value for collection development. It means that libraries can impose a subject orientation on the GPO automated item number file, which was described in the previous chapter, and use this data for developing documents collections responsive to the needs of their clientele. They can select item numbers with specific disciplines in mind as well as determine the degree to which clientele would want publications within a given item number. They could even inform academic departments about those item numbers that their faculty members and student population might find useful.

Widespread agreement on the subject orientation would enhance its reliability and validity. In the case of government publications available for distribution through the GPO depository program, the subject orientation is derived from examining government bodies, document series and types, and item numbers. Item numbers, therefore, are not viewed in isolation; the subject orientation is derived, first of all, by focusing on government bodies.

Table 4.15 presents a small fraction of the item numbers containing information of value to economists. Naturally more publications from the Bureau of the Census, Bureau of Labor Statistics, and other statistical reporting agencies have potential value. Even when all appropriate item numbers have been identified, it should not be assumed that they all have equal importance. Economists, as do other social scientists, rely on a few document types.[6] In other words, the number of government bodies producing publications of potential value to economists is indeed large. However, an examination of use patterns such as that performed in the next chapter indicates that academic libraries can be selective in the government bodies from which they select publications for their economists.

If libraries assume that any government publication or item number has potential value to their client groups, they might attempt to develop collections of record and to acquire all the resources necessary to meet any request, no matter how infrequent. To engage in such practices, however, is to dismiss the discussion of the first two chapters and the research conducted on collection development for other library resources.

Libraries should be able to acquire basic documents collections, which are likely to meet the more frequent demands of their client groups, without having to build collections containing astronomical title and volume counts. Both the physical and intellectual organization of documents collections requires the identification of relationships among subjects

Table 4.15. Examples of Item Numbers Specifically Identified As Containing Publications of Potential Value to Economists

Agriculture Department

A1.34:	(Statistical Bulletins, item 15)
A1.110:	(Agricultural Supply and Demand Estimates, item 11-F)
A67.26:	(Miscellaneous Series, Forest Agricultural Service, item 76-G)
A88.34:	(Tobaccco Stocks Reports, Agricultural Marketing Service, item 24-D)
A105.9/3:	(Prospective Planting, Economics, Statistics, and Cooperatives Service, item 20-B)
A105.17/2:	(Dairy Situation, Economics, Statistics, and Cooperatives Service, item 21-B)
A105.20/4:	(Rice Situation, Economics, Statistics, and Cooperatives Service, item 21-F)

Commerce Department

C1.57/4:	(Access, Office of Minority Business Enterprise, incorporating Outlook, item 126-C)
C1.72:	(Footwear Industry Revitalization Program, Annual Progress Report, item 126-D-9)
C3.24/2:	(Census of Manufacturers, general publications, item 135)
C3.145:	(State and Local Government Special Studies, item 148-A)
C3.191/2:	(Government Finances, item 146-E)
C3.211/5:	(Current Business Reports: Monthly Department Store Sales in Selected Areas, item 148-B)
C3.212:	(Technical Papers, item 151-A)
C3.254:	(Series FOF, item 131-J)
C3.259:	(Economic Research Reports, item 142-D)
C46.2:	(General Publications, Economic Development Administration, item 130-D)
C47.15:	(Summary and Analysis of International Travel to USA, United States Travel Service, item 271-A-4)
C59.14:	(Bureau of Economic Analysis Staff Paper, item 142-G)

Civil Aeronautics Board

CAB1.17:	(Air Carrier Financial Statistics, item 177-A-3)

Energy Department

E1.31/4:	(Demonstration Plants, item 474-A-13)
E3.9:	(Monthly Energy Review, Energy Information Administration, item 434-A-2)
E3.18/3:	(Statistics of Publicly Owned Electric Utilities in United States, Energy Information Administration, item 435-E-1)

Table 4.15. (Continued)

Environmental Protection Agency

EP1.23/2:   (Environmental Protection Technology Series, item 431-I-12)

Federal Mediation and Conciliation Service

FM1.1:   (Annual Report, item 433)

Federal Trade Commission

FT1.18:   (Quarterly Financial Report, Manufacturing Corporations, item 536-A

Interior Department

I28.27:   (Information Circulars, Mines Bureau, item 639-B)
I28.37/3:   (Mineral Commodity Profiles, Mines Bureau, item 639-B)
I49.15/3:   (Special Scientific Reports: Wildlife, Fish and Wildlife Service, item 614-C)

Labor Department

L2.3:   (Bulletins, Labor Statistics Bureau, item 768-A-1)
L2.6:   (Monthly Labor Review, Labor Statistics Bureau, item 770)
L2.61:   (Producer Prices and Price Indexes, Labor Statistics Bureau, item 771-B)
L2.71:   (BLS Reports, Labor Statistics Bureau, item 768-G)
L2.98:   (Special Labor Force Reports, Labor Statistics Bureau, item 768-R)
L2.104:   (Employment and Wages, Labor Statisitcs Bureau, item 754-B)
L36.9:   (Minimum Wage and Maximum Hours Standards Under Fair Labor Standards Act, Employment Standards Administration, item 780-A)
L36.11:   (Age Discrimination in Employment Act 1967, Reports Covering Activities under Act during fiscal year, Employment Standards Administration, item 746-C-2)

National Labor Reations Board

LR1.8:   (Decisions and Orders, item 826)

Executive Office of the President

PrEx2.20:   (Catalog of Federal Domestic Assistance, Management and Budget Office, item 853-A-1)
PrEx3.13:   (Economic Indicators Weekly Review, Central Intelligence Agency, item 856-B-12)

Table 4.15. (Continued)

PrEx3.14:	(Intelligence Energy Statistical Review, Central Intelligence Agency, item 856-B-13)

Small Business Administration

SBA1.30:	(SBIC Digest, the Equity Financing Arm of SBA, item 901-W)

International Trade Commission

TC1.33:	(Synthetic Organic Chemicals, U.S. Production and Sales, item 982-A)

and the extent to which patterns of knowledge overlap. According to James C. Baughman,

> Identifying overlapping subject areas indicates which subject areas are in communication. This communication needs to be determined since empirical relationships among associated subjects lay the foundation for present-day library collection development. Without an understanding of subject relationships, the librarian is lost in a sea of disjoint documents representing content from which selections must be made.[7]

Research into the structure of subjects as well as the structure of subject literatures is virtually non-existent in its coverage of the documents field. With further investigation of subject relationships among government bodies and item numbers, libraries can view collection development for government publications as a planning process. They can select document series of potential value to specific disciplines and inform client groups of subject relationships.

For the automated item number file to have practical collection development application, subject relationships for government bodies and item numbers must be determined. Given the importance of this file as a current reflection of selection patterns for over 1300 depository libraries, it is imperative that the research into subject relationships explored in this chapter be continued. Still, there are inherent weaknesses in any subject relationships derived from a file based on the archival heritage of the Sudoc Classification System. The value of a general subject orientation to the file, however, offsets these weaknesses.

NOTES AND REFERENCES

1. James C. Baughman, "Toward a Structural Approach to Collection Development," *College and Research Libraries* 38 (May 1977): 241-248.

2. Bernard M. Fry, "Government Publications and the Library: Implications for Change," *Government Publications Review* 4 (1977): 111-117; Charles R. McClure, "Indexing US Government Periodicals: Analysis and Comments," *Government Publications Review* 5 (1978): 409-421; and Charles R. McClure, "An Integrated Approach to Government Publication Collection Development," *Government Publications Review* 8A (1981): 5-15.

3. Peter Hernon, *Use of Government Publications by Social Scientists* (Norwood, N.J.: Ablex Publishing Corp., 1979).

4. For a discussion of literature scattering see: Samuel C. Bradford, *Documentation* (London: Crosby Lockwood, 1948).

5. If research for this book had been subsidized by the federal government or a funding organization, the authors could have explored other methods for identifying relevant government bodies. For example, they might have used the Sudoc search key for the OCLC data base. Further studies might investigate such data bases, presuming the cost of searching could be covered. Researchers might also use indexes such as the *American Statistics Index* to identify government bodies and item numbers relevant to specific disciplines.

    For our purposes, we wanted to see if discernible patterns would emerge in the identification of government bodies producing source material relevant to a specific discipline. Our methodology indicated that patterns do emerge and that future studies can build from our initial work.

    As future studies explore other disciplines, a more complete picture of government bodies consulted will emerge. The range of government bodies most often selected and used in the social sciences may be relatively small. Specific bodies may have appeal to a variety of disciplines and specialties within disciplines. Undoubtedly Bradford's law of scattering pertains to the documents field.

6. Hernon, *Use of Government Publications by Social Scientists*.

7. Baughman, "Toward a Structural Approach to Collection Development," p. 245.

Chapter 5

Document Use Patterns
of Academic Economists

Selection and retention decisions for depository collections must be based on a variety of factors, including use patterns of the clientele. With this in mind, this chapter reports on a study of one client group, academic economists, and examines those federal entities (e.g., departments, agencies, and committees), types of documents, serial titles, and life spans of documents that they are most likely to consult for information. Use, as discussed in this chapter, is not restricted to that which is found in libraries; user-need studies must "focus on what people do, wish they could do if they could just figure out how to get the necessary information."[1] As Herb White of Indiana University points out,

> Meaningful effectiveness studies aren't easy to do. They can't be completed simply by asking people whether the library usually has the books they want, whether it is open the hours they like, or whether interlibrary loan is helpful. We already have the answers to these questions— we've been putting them into our users' minds since they were children. However, reassuring as the answers may be, they don't help us in dealing with the real problems: the relatively low use of library resources for solving information problems and the emphasis on support for library collections rather than librarians. More in-depth user needs assessment studies should address these concerns.[2]

In the complex dynamics of the information-seeker's decision making processes lay the reasons for the neglect of libraries and the patterns of information seeking, which involve the use of other information resources. This chapter will examine information seeking for one discrete user group.

On the basis of the few user studies that have been conducted, it would seem that government publications that are related to the social sciences generate the widest use. Undoubtedly certain publications within the health sciences as well as selected disciplines in the sciences and humanities also receive extensive use; however, this has not been documented in the existing literature.[3] Two studies of social scientists and their information-seeking strategies have documented the importance of government publications to economists. One study, conducted in England during the 1960s, noted that "economists stood apart from others users, as they did not use monographs and theses as frequently as others [social scientists], but were much more likely to use government publications."[4] The other study, conducted at academic institutions in the United States in the late 1970s, discovered that economists and political scientists reported more frequent use of government publications than did sociologists and historians.[5] Because of this evidence, which suggests heavy use of government publications by economists, it was decided to select academic economists for further investigation about their document use patterns.

RESEARCH DESIGN

This chapter builds upon a recent dissertation in which the author investigated use of government publications by social scientists at seventeen academic institutions. The following survey examines the same institutions and incorporates that research design and sampling frame. These institutions selected represent schools that are both public and private in nature and have varying highest degree offerings. Geographical coverage is of colleges and universities in the state of Illinois, Indiana, Michigan, and Ohio.[6]

The same institutions selected for the recent dissertation were used here so that survey results of the two studies could be compared. It is the authors' belief that collection development surveys of a specific nature, such as the one reported here, should follow and not precede general user surveys. Librarians need to identify user perceptions, the reasons for documents use and non-use, as well as information-seeking patterns prior to determining the more frequently needed government bodies, document types and titles. With these observations in mind, the objectives of the study are:

1. To depict the patterns of general library use in comparison to specific use of the government document collection

2. To depict the reasons for use and non-use of government publications

3. To relate the patterns of document use to institutional variables (e.g., highest degree offered)

These objectives suggest six hypotheses that relate to economists and their use of government publications and have implications for collection development for document collections. The hypotheses can be stated as follows:

H1: *Document users fall into similar areas of teaching specialties*

H2: *There is no statistically significant difference in regard to highest degree offered as to the levels of government that publications are used*

H3: *There is no statistically significant difference, in regard to highest degree offered, as to the reasons economists consult or use government publications*

H4: *Regardless of highest degree offered, economists are most likely to consult government publications conveying statistical data, to consult a recognizable group of document titles, and to rely upon the resources of a small group of government bodies*

H5: *There is no statistically significant difference, according to highest degree offered, as to the age of the government publications most frequently consulted*

H6: *The variables of frequency of library and documents use, and highest degree offered, are not statistically significant factors for determining whether or not an economist is currently engaged in, or completed within the past year, a scholarly activity intended for publication that cited a government publication(s) in the bibliography or footnotes*

METHODOLOGY

The authors contacted each college and university and obtained a list of all full-time economists who taught during the Spring 1981 term. A thirteen item (eight page) questionnaire was developed and sent to the 214 economists in March 1981 (see Appendix D). One month later, non-respondents were sent a second copy. Data gathering extended through June 1981.

Table 5.1, which depicts the number of economists at each institution and the response rate, shows that 150 (70 percent) of the economists responded. Except for John Carroll University and Case Western University, the institutional response rate was at least 50 percent. Table 5.2, which illustrates the response rate by institutional control and highest degree offered, indicates that 7.3 percent of the respondents were from baccalaureate institutions, 29.3 percent from master's-granting institutions, and 63.3 percent from doctoral institutions.[7] Together economists from baccalaureate and master's-granting institutions accounted for more than one-third (36.6 percent) of the responses.

Table 5.1. Number of Responses by Institution

Institution	Number of Full-Time Economists		
	Total	Respondents	(%)
Hanover College	3	2	(66.7)
Ohio Wesleyan University	5	3	(60)
Principia College	3	2	(66.7)
Indiana State University, Evansville	2	2	(100)
Indiana University, Kokomo	2	2	(100)
Butler University	4	3	(75)
John Carroll University	10	4	(40)
Valparaiso University	4	2	(50)
Central Michigan University	18	11	(61.1)
Eastern Illinois University	13	11	(84.6)
Western Illinois University	17	13	(76.5)
Case Western Reserve University	8	3	(37.5)
Northwestern University	19	14	(73.7)
Notre Dame University	19	13	(68.4)
Indiana University, Bloomington	26	17	(65.4)
Michigan State University	42	32	(76.2)
Southern Illinois University, Carbondale	19	16	(84.2)
Total	214	150	(70.1)

Although each grouping according to institutional control and highest degree offered is not proportional, the participation of economists from baccalaureate institutions is sufficient for the purpose of analysis, that is, if analysis examines highest degree offered by the institution and does not differentiate between public and private institutions. The concept of institutional control (e.g., whether public or private) therefore will not become a study variable. The authors realize that a relatively small number of responses to specific questions by faculty members at baccalaureate institutions influences the results of a test for significance of relationships between variables and that a small sample may not reflect the true value. Because of this, analysis of use patterns by highest degree offered will draw primarily upon a comparison of rankings.

The Statistical Package for the Social Sciences (SPSS) was used for the purpose of analyzing questionnaire responses. The chi square test was used to test for significance of relationships between the two variables being investigated in each relationship. The Spearman Rank Order Correlation Coefficient was used for a comparison of rankings of institutions by highest degree offered. This measure of association required that the data be ranked in order of magnitude. For the purposes of testing the significance of relationships between variables, the level of significance was set at 0.05. Nonstatistically significant relationships were also identified and certain ones presented in this chapter.

Table 5.2. Response Rate by Institutional Control and Highest Degree Offered

Institutional Control	Highest Degree						
	Baccalaureate	(Number)	Master's	(Number)	Doctorate	(Number)	Row Total
Public	Indiana State University, Evansville	(2)	Central Michigan University	(11)	Indiana University, Bloomington	(17)	
	Indiana University, Kokomo	(2)	Eastern Illinois University	(11)	Michigan State University	(32)	
			Western Illinois University	(13)	Southern Illinois University, Carbondale	(16)	
	Subtotal	4		35		65	Row Total 104
Private	Hanover College	(2)	Butler University	(3)	Case Western Reserve University	(3)	
	Ohio Wesleyan University	(3)	John Carroll University	(4)	Northwestern University	(14)	
	Principia College	(2)	Valparaiso University	(2)	Notre Dame University	(13)	
	Subtotal	7		9		30	Row Total 46
	Column Total	11		44		95	150

89

GENERAL CHARACTERISTICS
OF RESPONDING ECONOMISTS

Previous studies concerned with the use of government publications have not attached statistical significance to such variables as professorial rank, the number of years at the institution, involvement in sponsored research, and class levels taught (e.g., undergraduate and graduate). Consequently, this survey did not incorporate similar variables into the questionnaire. Instead, it focused on teaching specialties, frequency of library and documents use, level of government consulted, and the reasons for documents use and non-use. Each of these variables is described below very briefly with an indication of its usefulness for this study.

Teaching Specialities

The discipline of economics was subdivided into standard, component parts reflecting various teaching options, and economists were asked to select from among the specified categories those areas of specialty reflected in their teaching. The authors supplied the categories in an effort to control against a proliferation of specialities and against varying terminology. Since faculty members often have more than one teaching specialty, a tally of the combinations will not necessarily equal 150, the total number of respondents.

Table 5.3 depicts the teaching specialties of respondents. Half of the economists (50.7 percent) marked economic theory as a specialization. International economics was next in frequency of mention (24.7 percent). As expected, the higher the degree offered by the institution, the greater the diversity of teaching specialties represented by faculty members of that institution.

Use of the Library

In order to place utilization of the library's documents collection into perspective, economists were asked to estimate the number of times that they used the resources of the college or university library during the previous year. For purposes of hypothesis testing and statistical analysis, respondents were classified as heavy, moderate, and limited users, as well as non-users of the library. Because the questionnaire had nine fixed categories specifying frequencies of use ranging from zero to more than fifty, the assignment of respondents to a grouping was based on response distribution. Approximately half of the respondents (47.3 percent) went to the library, for whatever reason(s), more than thirty times and therefore comprise the heavy users. Since no faculty members admitted a lack of need for the library, there are no respondents classified

Table 5.3. Teaching Specialties of Responding Economists

Specialty	Number*
Economic Theory	76
International Economics	37
Econometrics and Statistics	30
Labor and Human Resource Development	30
Public Finance	24
Industrial Organization	22
Comparative Economic Systems	22
Money and Banking	14
Economic History	14
Urban Economics	13
Planning	10
Demography	9
Public Utility	8
Economic Development	6
Economics of Natural Resources	5
Other (e.g., Economic Education, Health, Economics of Nutrition, Industrial Relations, and Radical Political Economy	16

Note: *Respondents could check as many specialties as applicable

as library non-users. Limited users (10 percent) consulted the library no more than ten times, while moderate users (42.7 percent) had used it between eleven and thirty times during the previous year.

The frequency of library use was examined from another perspective. Each questionnaire was coded so that there would be a record of respondents and non-respondents. Questionnaires for those responding without a follow-up reminder were compared to those who received a reminder. There was no statistically significant difference between the two groups ($\chi^2(1,2) = 0.15, p < .05$). It seems that frequent library users were not more likely to participate without a reminder; this finding supports the validity of the survey.

Use of Government Publications

Respondents were classified as heavy, moderate, and limited users, as well as non-users of the government publications located in their college or university library. The assignment of faculty to each grouping was also based on the distribution of their estimated use of the documents collection. Since faculty members who used the collection fewer than six times per year were queried further about their reasons for infrequent use, non-users became those economists who did not use the collection at all, and limited users were those consulting the collection one to five times. The assignment of respondents to the groups of heavy and moderate users was based on the distribution of the remaining 106 response (70.7 percent). Since the midpoint for these responses falls in the category "sixteen to twenty," heavy users become those using documents more than fifteen times and moderate users comprised the range six to fifteen times.

Table 5.4, which compares library and documents use, reflects a statistically significant difference among economists whose library use was heavy, moderate, or limited, and those who either did not use documents or whose use was heavy, moderate, or limited ($\chi^2(2,3) = 51.86$, p > .05). This finding adds support to the particular groupings employed for heavy, moderate, and limited users as well as non-users of the library and documents collection. Heavy library users account for 47.3 percent

Table 5.4. Comparison of the Frequency
of Library and Documents Use

| | Documents Use | | | | |
| | Heavy (Number) | Moderate (Number) | Limited (Number) | Non-Use (Number) | |
Library Use					Total
Heavy	41	19	6	5	71
Moderate	14	31	11	8	64
Limited	—	1	9	5	15
Total	55	51	26	18	150

of the documents use; 74.5 percent of the heavy documents users are also heavy library users. It might be useful to repeat that frequencies of library and documents use are based upon faculty estimates. Undoubtedly, some document users have their secretaries, or student or research assistants gather needed information. In such cases, estimating frequency of use provides an underestimation of actual use. Further, distinctions between heavy and moderate users may, in some case, be arbitrary.

As with the frequency of library use, questionnaires for those responding without a follow-up reminder were compared to those receiving one. The assumption that more frequent document users are more likely to participate without a reminder, however, cannot be discounted; there is a statistically significant difference ($\chi^2(1,3) = 8.11$, p > .05). This finding can probably be accounted for by the skewing of responses.

Overwhelmingly, economists are either heavy or moderate document users (106 or 70.7 percent); only forty-four (29.3 percent) can be labeled as either limited users or non-users. Thus, due to the fact that such a high percentage of economists are heavy or moderate users of documents, frequency of documents use does not become a meaningful variable for data analysis. The hypotheses therefore will be analyzed on the basis of the highest degree offered by the institution; neither institutional control nor frequency of documents use become study variables.

Use of Documents

When government publications were consulted, it was primarily for activities relating to research or scholarly writing (107 faculty) or teaching (106 faculty). Secondary reasons pertained to consulting (42 faculty) and recreational reading matter (16 faculty). Incidentally, two respondents mentioned that they referred to government publications in public speaking, including radio and television interviews.

Limited Use and Non-Use of Documents

A total of forty-four, or 29.3 percent, of the respondents consulted the government publications collection of their college or university library five or fewer times the previous year. In fact, eighteen of these economists did not use the documents collection at all.

One questionnaire item probed the reason(s) for infrequent use and non-use of documents. The three reasons cited most frequently were as follows:

* obtain personal copies (21)

* do not need this type of resource on a regular basis (19)

* believe that government publishes little or nothing of value in their particular fields (19)

The following reasons were mentioned less frequently:

* reliance on secretary, student or research assistants to gather needed government publications (5)

* the amount of time expended in trying to find relevant information in government publications is out of proportion to what I find (3)

* unfamiliar with arrangement of the government publications collection (3)

* unaware of the existence of such materials at the library (1)

* government publications provide more detailed information than is needed (1)

- reliance on a departmental collection of government publications (1)

Economists who indicated that they obtain personal copies of documents, rely on support staff to gather needed government information, or use documents located in their department are, in fact, more extensive users of government information than the question concerning frequency of documents use reveals. These faculty members use government publications, but not always those located in their college or university library. Therefore, by omitting from consideration those faculty members who checked one or more of these special reasons, the major reasons for infrequent use and non-use become twofold: they believe the government publishes little or nothing of value in their particular field, and they do not need documents on a regular basis. The other reasons are much less important. This findings appears to be true regardless of highest degree offered.

TESTING THE HYPOTHESES

This section of the chapter focuses on the specific faculty hypotheses already described. Because of the exploratory nature of this study, the objective behind these hypotheses was to examine findings on the basis of institutional characteristics (specifically highest degree offered). In order to compare institutions, patterns and exceptions are reported among institutions having similar highest degree offerings. In addition, overall frequency distributions are reported for individual questionnaire items. However, no distinction is made on the basis of institutional control (public or private affiliation).

Since previous research has not focused on specific factors associated with collection development for government publications, there is an insufficient basis upon which to predict the expected direction that the findings would take. It should be noted that the high response rate to our questionnaire (70 percent) suggests that faculty members will, indeed, respond to survey instruments trying to elicit document use patterns (assuming the questionnaires are well-designed and adhere to basic conventions of survey research).[8]

H1: *Document users fall into similar areas of teaching specialities*

Table 5.3 depicts the teaching specialties of responding economists. Heavy and moderate use of government publications is spread out among all the categories, including economic theory. Because of this distribution, document use does not cluster into any recognizable pattern by eaching specialty; the hypothesis therefore cannot be accepted. Apparently, government publications comprise an information resource of potential value to any teaching specialty within the discipline of economics. Variation within each specialty may be due to such factors as the nature of the specific projects in which the respondent is involved, the extent of the teaching load, the availability of desired information in other formats, and ease of access to desired information. At any rate, further research should probe this topic.

H2: *There is no statistically significant difference in regard to highest degree offered as to the levels of government of which publications are used*

One questionnaire item asked for an identification of the levels of government in which publications are used. To aid in the determination, the authors defined a government publication as informational matter that has been published as an individual document at government expense, or as required by law. It should be noted that although the publications of one level of government received a certain number of checks, this does not indicate the relative frequency with which respondents use them.

Publications of the United States government were identified as used by the largest number of faculty members (136), while those of the United Nations and other international agencies were next (69), and those of state governments were third (54). Publications of foreign (46) and municipal governments (22) were used by the fewest number of faculty members. The Spearman Rank Order method was used to test for a difference among highest degree offerings of the institutions (see Table 5.5). The results indicate that the relationship between baccalaureate and master's-granting institutions is the strongest (rho = .875). This means that economists at these two types of institutions indicated most frequent use of United States government publications. At baccalaureate institutions, publications of state governments as well as the United Nations and other international agencies were tied for second position. Municipal publications placed next and foreign publications last. In the case of master's-granting institutions, state publications placed second and United Nations and other international agencies third. The position of the other two levels of government was reverse that of the baccalaureate institutions.

The document use pattern relationship between master's and doctoral granting institutions is moderate (rho = .7). Federal publications still received the most interest. The ranking for publications of all the other levels of government, however, differed, with the exception of municipal publications, which placed last in both instances. For the doctoral

Table 5.5. Comparison of Levels of Government
Consulted and Highest Degree Offered

| | Levels of Government | | | | |
Institutions	Federal (Number)	State (Number)	Municipal (Number)	Foreign (Number)	International Agencies (Number)
Baccalaureate	10	6	3	2	6
Master's	39	23	11	12	22
Doctorate	87	25	8	32	41

institutions, publication of the United Nations and international agencies were placed second; publications for foreign governments were placed third and those of state governments were placed fourth.

The document use pattern relationship between baccalaureate and doctoral institutions is also moderate (rho = .625). The main differences among baccalaureate, master's and doctoral-granting institutions are twofold: (1) economists at doctoral institutions are least likely to mention state publications, and (2) economists at baccalaureate institutions are least likely to indicate use of foreign government publications (it is interesting to note that local government publications were least frequently mentioned at the other types of institutions). Since the Spearman rho relationships were all moderate to strong, highest degree offering did not produce statistically significant differences as to the levels of government in which publications are consulted.[9]

Only thirteen responding economists (8.7 percent) indicated that they do not consult government publications at all. These faculty members represent nine institutions, primarily public doctoral institutions; this finding is not surprising since 43.3 percent of the respondents are associated with institutions having this type of control and level of degree program. The teaching specialties of the thirteen economists are as follows:[10]

- economic theory (8)
- comparative economics (2)
- econometrics and statistics (2)
- managerial economics (1)
- energy economics (1)
- economic history (1)

As noted in the section on "Use of Government Publications," eighteen respondents never use the documents collection located in their college or university library. Naturally thirteen of them are the previously mentioned non-users. The remaining five consult documents, but they do not visit the depository collection. Instead, they frequently obtain personal copies of needed government publications. If, by chance, they need something from the depository collection, they send a secretary, student or research assistant to borrow the title or to obtain the needed information.

H3: *There is no statistically significant difference, in regard to highest degree offered, as to the reasons economists consult or use government publications*

Table 5.6, which depicts the reasons for consulting government publications, underscores the importance of statistical data and research and technical reports generated and distributed by government agencies. As might be expected, faculty members at doctoral-granting institutions are most likely to consult government publications for grant information (69.6 percent).[11] Regardless of highest degree offered, there is strong agreement in the ranking of the reasons for consulting government publications (rho = .89, baccalaureate to master's-granting institutions; rho = .92, master's to doctoral institutions; and rho = .80, baccalaureate to doctoral institutions); therefore, the null hypothesis cannot be rejected. It is interesting to note that economists at baccalaureate institutions suggested the first three reasons depicted in Table 5.6 as having equal importance. These three reasons, however, may not necessarily comprise discrete categories. Economists, for example, might consult government publications covering current events and issues of interest for the statistical data contained therein.

Table 5.6. Reasons for Consulting Documents

Reasons	*Number*
Statistical Data	122
Research and Technical Reports	90
Current Events and Issues of Interest	76
Resources That May Be of Value to Students	69
Information of Historical Value	38
Grant Information	23
General Interest Reading	17
Legal Material	16

H4: *Regardless of highest degree offered, economists are most likely to consult government publications conveying statistical data, to consult a recognizable group of document titles, and to rely upon the resources of a small group of government bodies*

Types of Documents Consulted

One questionnaire item asked economists to identify, from among predetermined categories, the type(s) of government publications they are most likely to consult.[12] Table 5.7, which displays the types, confirms the first part of the hypothesis; subsequent sections confirm the rest of the hypothesis. Economists draw most extensively upon statistical data and periodicals. Next in overall importance are annual reports, reports of investigation and research, and committee and commission reports. It should be noted that not all categories comprise discrete or mutually exclusive entities. For example, agencies and committees may distribute newsletters, which, in fact, contain bibliographies or lists of publications.

Table 5.7. Types of Government Publications
Consulted by Highest Degree Offered

	Highest Degree Offered			
Types	*Baccalaureate (Number)*	*Master's (Number)*	*Doctorate (Number)*	*Total*
Annual Reports	7	28	39	74
Bibliographies or Lists	—	11	16	27
Bills and Resolutions	—	2	7	9
Committee and Commission Reports	1	11	31	43
Decisions and Opinions (e.g.,) from the Supreme Court)	—	3	11	14
Directories	—	6	5	11
Films and Other Audiovisual Aids	2	—	—	2
General Information Pamphlets	1	5	10	16
Hearings	—	10	17	27
Journals and Proceedings (e.g., *Congressional Record*)	—	5	20	25
Laws and Statutes	—	5	15	20
Periodicals	10	32	56	98
Press Releases	1	5	9	15
Reports of Investigation and Research	4	20	36	60
Rules and Regulations	—	7	13	20
Statistical Reports (e.g., census publications)	11	34	67	112

The relationship between responses from baccalaureate and master's-granting institutions is moderate (rho = .58, so too is the relationship between faculty members at baccalaureate and doctoral institutions, rho = .55). On the other hand, economists at master's and doctoral institutions show the strongest agreement (rho =.86). Regardless of highest degree offering, there is similiarity in the rankings of the major types consulted. Of greatest importance are statistical reports, periodicals, annual reports, and reports of investigation and research. Variations occur in the rankings of the remaining document types. Surprisingly to the authors, respondents infrequently mentioned hearings, laws and statutes, rules and regulations, and bibliographies. Economists at master's and doctoral institutions rely on a wider range of types than do their colleagues at baccalaureate institutions. For example, only faculty members at baccalaureate institutions do not consult hearings. Economists at doctoral institutions are most likely to consult journals and proceedings as well as committee and commission reports. Only faculty members at baccalaureate institutions, however, use films and audiovisual aids. The fact that variations exist in the types of documents used among economists at institutions that offer different degrees is a particularly interesting finding and is probably associated with the way faculty members use the information in teaching, research, grant proposals, and so on.

Document Titles Consulted

Economists were asked to select from among a list of document titles the one(s) they are most likely to use. The list contained *Statistical Abstract of the United States, Historical Statistics of the United States, County and City Data Book, Code of Federal Regulations*, and eleven other standard titles.[13] Table 5.8, which depicts the sources mentioned according to highest degree offering, underscores the overall importance of the *Economic Report of the President*, the *Survey of Current Business, Federal Reserve Bulletin, Statistical Abstract*, and *Economic Indicators*.

The Spearman Rank Order Coeffcient test indicates that rankings by highest degree offering are similar. There is strong agreement between baccalaureate and master's-granting institutions (rho = .81), master's and doctoral institutions (rho = .79), and baccalaureate and doctoral institutions (rho = .82). Economists at baccalaureate institutions most frequently mention the *Federal Reserve Bulletin*. Next in importance are the *Monthly Labor Review, Economic Report of the President*, and *Survey of Current Business*. These faculty members are the least likely to consult *Statistical Abstract*. Regardless of highest degree offering, the *Code of Federal Regulations* and the *Federal Register* are infrequently consulted; however, in the case of baccalaureate institutions they are not used at all.

Table 5.8. Frequently Used Titles by Highest Degree Offered

	Highest Degree Offered			
Titles	Baccalaureate (Number)	Master's (Number)	Doctorate (Number)	Total
Business Conditions Digest	4	9	12	25
Code of Federal Regulations	—	3	6	9
Consumer Price Index (CPI Detailed Report)	7	23	39	69
County and City Data Book	3	15	12	30
Current Population Reports	3	17	30	50
Economic Indicators	6	26	41	73
Economic Report of the President	8	28	65	101
Employment and Earnings	4	17	25	46
Federal Register	—	5	6	11
Federal Reserve Bulletin	9	28	47	84
Historical Statistics of the United States: Colonial Times to 1970	2	16	30	48
Monthly Labor Review	9	17	28	54
Statistical Abstract of the United States	4	32	47	83
Survey of Current Business	8	32	59	99
Treasury Bulletin	1	5	12	18
Other	2	12	27	41

Economists at master's-granting institutions most frequently marked *Statistical Abstract* and the *Survey of Current Business*. Next in importance are the *Economic Report of the President* and the *Federal Reserve Bulletin*. Except for the *CPI Detailed Reports* and *Economic Indicators*, all other titles are infrequently used. In the case of doctoral institutions, the *Economic Report of the President* ranks first; following it are the *Survey of Current Business, Federal Reserve Bulletin,* and *Statistical Abstract.*

It might be noted that the "other" category attracted forty-one responses. Of the sources listed, twenty-eight, or 68.3 percent, are statistical publications; seventeen, or 60.7 percent, of these are publications from the U.S. Bureau of the Census (e.g., the *Census of Population and Housing, Census of Government* and *Census of Manufacturers*). Examples of the non-statistical publications mentioned include *World Energy News, Congressional Record, Minerals Yearbook,* and reports of the Federal Communications Commission and Interstate Commerce Commission. Future research might probe whether economists receive personal copies of the most frequently consulted titles, or whether they consult departmental copies or library holdings.

Government Bodies Consulted

The "List of Classes of United States Government Publications Available for Selection by Depository Libraries" (Government Printing Office) identifies government bodies (e.g., departments, agencies, and committees) for which Superintendent of Documents classification numbers have been assigned. Since previous research has not explored those government bodies that economists, or other social scientists, are likely to consult, the authors, following the recommendations of several economists, selected from the master list those government bodies of potential interest to academic economists. The list was shown to several other economists for comment prior to submission to the study sample.

Reproducing the entire "List of Classes" would have resulted in a bulky questionnaire, one which probably would not have been throughly examined and would not generate an acceptable return rate. Consequently the list of government bodies was reduced and numerous "other" options inserted; still the final list of choices was extensive. As will be discussed later in the chapter, the analysis *assumes* complete and accurate self-reporting. It should be emphasized that the authors regard self-reporting questionnaires as but one method for identifying patterns of documents use. Whenever possible, additional means of data collection should be used.

As shown in Table 5.9, responding economists indicated a preference for publications from the Department of Commerce. Next in importance were those from the Department of Labor, Congress, Federal Reserve System Board of Governors, Executive Office of the President, Department of Agriculture, and the Department of Health and Human Services. Publications of the judiciary and the remaining executive departments, commissions, and independent agencies were checked by no more than twenty-seven economists.

Spearman rho indicates moderate agreement between baccalaureate and master's institutions (rho = .69) as well as baccalaureate and doctoral institutions (rho = .64). The agreement between master's and doctoral institutions is stronger (rho = .85). It might be noted that comparison of baccalaureate to other degree offerings is complicated by the fact that economists at baccalaureate institutions do not consult a wide range of government bodies; many of the categories went unchecked. In the case of master's-granting institutions, all but eight categories were marked. Although faculty members at doctoral institutions gave some support to all categories, twenty options received four or fewer responses. This

Table 5.9   The Seven Most Frequently Consulted Government Bodies
by Highest Degree Offered*

Government Bodies	Highest Degree Offered			
	Baccalaureate (Number)	*Master's (Number)*	*Doctorate (Number)*	*Total*
Department of Commerce	10	33	63	106
Department of Labor	6	26	45	77
Congress	2	26	46	74
Federal Reserve System Board of Governors	8	24	41	73
Executive Office of the President	2	20	45	67
Department of Agriculture	3	15	26	44
Department of Health and Human Services	2	14	22	38

Note: *Appendix E provides the complete list of government bodies consulted.

finding suggests that the higher the degree offering, the more likely any specific category will be marked. Still, variations occur on an institutional basis, and use appears to be concentrated in a comparatively small number of government bodies.

Regardless of highest degree offering, publications from the Department of Commerce are most likely to be consulted. The Federal Reserve System Board of Governors ranks second for baccalaureate institutions, but ranks fourth for master's, and ranks fifth for doctoral institutions. Publications of the Department of Labor are also important in regard to highest degree offering, while those of the Executive Office of the President, Congress, Department of Agriculture, Department of Health and Human Services, and the Department of Energy are least important at the baccalaureate level. It might be noted that economists at doctoral institutions are more likely to consult publications of the National Science Foundation and the Environmental Protection Agency than are economists at the other institutions.

In addition to identifying government bodies, economists also suggested the agencies within the larger organization that they are most likely to consult. Tables 5.10 through 5.16 present the most frequently mentioned agencies and Congressional committees. Publications of statistical reporting agencies such as the Bureau of the Census and the Bureau of Labor Statistics comprise major resources for economists. Within the Executive Office of the President, responding economists focus on publications of the Economic Advisors Council, Office of Management and Budget, and Council on Wage and Price Stability. In the case of Congress, the high ranking of the Government Printing Office is undoubtedly due to its role as printer of agency publications rather than as a compiler of indexes, bibliographies, and catalogs. When the economists consult the publications of other agencies reporting to Congress, they most likely do so for the Congressional Budget Office and General Accounting Office. The Joint Economic Committee is the most frequently consulted Congressional committee. Next in importance are the committees for Banking (House and Senate), Budget (House and Senate), and Finance (Senate). It might be noted that when publications of the Department of Energy are consulted, it is for those of the Energy Information Administration (17), Federal Energy Regulatory Commission (11), and Economic Regulatory Administration (7).

Table 5.10. Ranking of Most Frequently Mentioned Agencies from the Department of Commerce

Agencies	Number*
Bureau of the Census	92
Economic Analysis Bureau	35
International Trade Administration	20
Economic Development Administration	19
Environmental Data and Information Service	17
National Technical Information Service	8
East-West Trade Bureau	8
Domestic Commerce Bureau	8
Industrial Economics Bureau	8
Export Development Bureau	5
Industry and Trade Administration	4
Other	11

Note: *Respondents could check as many categories as appropriate

Table 5.11. Ranking of Most Frequently Mentioned Agencies from the Department of Labor

Agencies	Number*
Bureau of Labor Statistics	65
Employment and Training Administration	17
International Labor Affairs Bureau	15
Wage and Hour Division	14
Unemployment Insurance Service	11
United States Employment Service	9
Occupational Safety and Health Administration	6
Employment Standards Administration	4
Women's Bureau	4
Other	6

Note: *Respondents could check as many categories as appropriate

Table 5.12. Ranking of Most Frequently Mentioned Agencies within the Executive Office of the President

Agencies	Number*
Economic Advisors Council	45
Office of Management and Budget	23
Council on Wage and Price Stability	22
Central Intelligence Agency	11
Council on Environmental Quality	10
Office of Special Representative for Trade Negotiations	6
Other	4

Note: *Respondents could check as many categories as appropriate

Table 5.13. Ranking of Most Frequently Mentioned Agencies from the Department of Agriculture

Agencies	Number*
Economic Research Service	21
Economics, Statistics, and Cooperative Service	15
Statistical Reporting Service	14
Foreign Agricultural Service	10
Agricultural Research Service	8
Forest Service	4
Rural Development Service	4
Agricultural Stabilization and Conservation Service	4
Soil Conservation Service	3
Farmers Home Administration	3
Agricultural Marketing Service	3
Farmer Cooperative Service	3
Other	9

Note: *Respondents could check as many categories as appropriate

Table 5.14. Ranking of Most Frequently Mentioned Agencies from the Department of Health and Human Services

Agencies	Number*
Social Security Administration	20
National Center for Social Statistics	12
National Center for Education Statistics	5
Consumer Affairs Office	5
National Center for Health Statistics	4
Aging Administration	4
Other	14

Note: *Respondents could check as many categories as appropriate

Table 5.15. Ranking of Most Frequently Mentioned Agencies Reporting to Congress

Agencies	Number*
Government Printing Office	23
Congressional Budget Office	22
General Accounting Office	18
Export-Import Bank of United States	12
Advisory Commission on Intergovernmental Relations	10
East-West Foreign Trade Board	7
Advisory Council on Social Security	7
National Advisory Council on International Monetary and Financial Policies	4
Equal Employment Opportunity Commission	4
Other	10

Note: *Respondents could check as many categories as appropriate

Table 5.16. Ranking of Most Frequently Mentioned Congressional Committees

Committees	Number*
Joint Economic Committee	42
Banking, Finance and Urban Affairs (House)	20
Banking, Housing, and Urban Affairs (Senate)	19
Budget (House)	13
Budget (Senate)	13
Finance (Senate)	13
Joint Committee on Taxation	9
Energy and Natural Resources Committee (Senate)	9
Labor and Human Resources (Senate)	9
Ways and Means (House)	8
Small Business (House)	7
Interstate and Foreign Commerce (House)	7
Judiciary (Senate)	5
Commerce, Science and Transportation (Senate)	5
Agriculture (House)	4
Agriculture (Senate)	4
Appropriations (House)	4
Appropriations (Senate)	4
Judiciary (House)	4
Governmental Affairs (Senate)	3
Select Committee on Small Business (Senate)	3
Other	5

Note: *Respondents could check as many categories as appropriate

Because use patterns vary by the highest degree offering of the institu
tion as well as among schools with the same level of degree offering
profiles of the major government bodies, agencies, and Congressiona
committees that are of value to economists at a particular institution car
be constructed. In this way, librarians can select and retain those gov
ernment publications that are likely to generate the most use in thei
own institutions. Additional research should explore other discipline
and identify similiarities and dissimiliarites in use patterns.

H5: *There is no statistically significant difference according to highest degre*
offered as to the age of the government publications most frequentl
consulted

Previous research has suggested that social scientists, excluding histo
rians, and public library users frequently rely upon documents issuec
within the past three years. In the case of economists, a majority (62.5
percent) consulted documents issued within this time frame.[14] Giver
these findings, it could be assumed that respondents to the presen
survey would have similar use patterns and that the null hypothesi:
cannot be rejected.

Table 5.17 depicts the ages of the documents consulted by highes
degree offering. The chi square test indicates a statistically significan
difference between degree program and respondents who use document:
not older than three years and those reporting other use pattern:
($\chi^2(2,1) = 9.37$, p > .05). Some ninety-seven, or 70.8 percent, of the re
spondents use documents up to three years of age, while few economists
seven, or 5.1 percent, consult older documents; almost one-fifth of the
respondents, however, suggest that there is no set pattern to the docu
ments used. The previous study of social scientists from these same
institutions found that interview subjects (other than historians), whc
checked no set pattern as to the age of the government publications the
seek, draw mainly upon current materials, three years old or younger
When they need older information, it is primarily for time series and
statistical data.

Section 9 of the 1962 Depository Library Act provides for discretionary disposal of documents after retention for five years and is testimony
to the perceived short life span of the average government publications
The findings of this study suggest that the five year retention requirement should be relaxed or at least reexamined in relationship to specific document types (e.g., statistical data and Congressional hearings)
and titles. In any case, with the proliferation of source material available for depository distribution and the need for zero growth for many
collections maintained by both partial and regional depositories, it is

Table 5.17. Age of Documents Used by Highest Degree Offered

Highest Degree Offered	Less than a year Number(%)	1-3 years Number(%)	4-5 years Number(%)	Age 6-10 years Number(%)	Over 10 years Number(%)	No set pattern; age varies Number(%)	Row Totals
Baccalaureate	5 (50)*	5 (50)	—	—	—	—	10 (7.3)
Master's	8 (20)	25 (62.5)	—	1 (2.5)	—	6 (15)	40 (29.2)
Doctorate	28 (32.2)	26 (29.9)	3 (3.4)	—	3 (3.4)	27 (11)	87 (63.5)
Column Totals	41 (29.9)	56 (40.0)	3 (2.2)	1 (0.7)	3 (2.2)	33 (24.1)	137

Note: *Row percentages

time that further research be devoted to the life span of government publications.

H6: *The variables of frequency of library and documents use and highest degree offered are not statistically significant factors for determining whether or not an economist is currently engaged in, or completed within the past year, a scholarly activity intended for publication which cited a government publication(s) in the bibliography or footnotes*

One questionnaire item asked if the economist is currently engaged in, or has recently completed within the past year, a scholarly activity intended for publication, which cites a government publication(s) in the bibliography or footnotes. Of the eighty-eight (58.7 percent) who had cited a government publication, approximately one-fifth (20 or 22.7 percent) mentioned a publication that had not been specified in relation to the previous questionnaire item eliciting the document title(s) they are most likely to use. Comparison of the data with highest degree offering did not produce a statistically significant difference ($\chi^2(2,1) = 1.5$, p<.05). Since economists citing government publications in their scholarly writings come from all degree programs, the null hypothesis cannot be rejected.

The list of titles supplied by respondents was supplemented with a search of the monographic and periodical literature published since 1978. The names of all responding economists who use government publications were checked in such sources as *Books in Print, Cumulative Book Index*, and *Social Sciences Index*, and the writings of those listed were then scrutinized for references to government publications. The resulting pool of titles was used as a validity check on survey responses.[15] The written responses did, in fact, coincide with the government bodies and document types actually listed by individual respondents. For example, there were references to publications of the Advisory Commission on Intergovernmental Relations, the Bureau of the Census, the Central Intelligence Agency, the Department of Energy, the Department of Labor, Federal Communications Commission, Interstate Commerce Commission, and the Joint Economic Committee. In addition, there were references to statistical data, periodicals, court cases, and other types of government publications. To be expected, there was variation among the document titles reported on the questionnaire and the full range of those cited in the literature.[16]

LIMITATIONS OF THE STUDY AND ALTERNATIVE RESEARCH METHODS

Certain limitations arise with a survey of this type, but is is hoped that their impact can be minimized. Since not all the academic institutions from the states of Illinois, Indiana, Michigan, and Ohio could be surveyed, stratified random sampling procedures were used. Still, the survey represents academic depository institutions from four of the more populous states and is reflective of economics programs offered by various types of institutions.

The authors realize that they are describing utilization patterns based upon self-reporting. It is assumed that the self-reporting is accurate and complete;[17] presumably faculty members can differentiate government publishing from other types of publishing and distinguish among the various types of government publishing. Given the high response rate and the completeness of responses, the authors believe that a self-reporting questionnaire can play a useful role in collection development for government publication. However, such questionnaires provide only one means for data gathering. Other methods can be used to examine use patterns in general as well as those for library resources. For example, librarians can explore sales patterns at nearby GPO bookstores, monitor circulation records and documents waiting reshelving, conduct citation analyses as well as maintain a record of reference questions asked and those unanswerable from the immediate collection.[18]

Even though it is outside the scope of the present survey and the findings cannot be merged into a general picture of information seeking for Midwestern academic economists, the authors would still like to illustrate the type of data that can be gathered from conducting citation analyses and monitoring the sales patterns of nearby GPO bookshores.

Citation Analysis

The benefits of citation analysis are evident from a perusal of the annual summary statistics on periodicals and their rate of obsolescence contained in the *Social Sciences Citation Index*.[19] Two government periodicals are listed as cited by economists: the first, the *Monthly Labor Review*, was consulted by responding economists; the second, *Problems of Communism*, was not. The half-life for the *Monthly Labor Review* is 4.9 years, while for *Problems of Communism*, it is 3.6 years.[20] As Table 5.18 illustrates, 75 percent of the citations from 1979 journals to articles in the *Monthly Labor Review* are to articles published between 1970 and 1979. Almost 90 percent of the citations to *Problems of Communism* are to articles published during the same period. Combining the chronological distritution of citation counts with other data (e.g., those gathered from self-reporting questionnaires), librarians can make decisions regarding retention. They might retire the pre-1970 volumes of the *Monthly Labor Review* and *Problems of Communism* to subordinate shelf space or discard infrequently needed volumes. They might even store or discard some of the volumes for the early 1970s. Selective holdings combined with an active weeding program frees a large amount of shelf space while still meeting the majority of user requests. After all, the more depository libraries try to acquire and retain source material to meet single and infrequent requests, the more publications they must acquire and retain. The more items acquired, the higher the cost for processing, storage, and service. Consequently libraries need to determine what percentage of demand for government publications they will meet internally and then rely on resource sharing for lesser-used titles and infrequent requests.

Table 5.18.   Cumulative Percentage of Citations from the 1979 Journals to Articles Published during Previous Years in Two Government Periodicals*

	Monthly Labor Review (%)	Problems of Communism (%)
1979	5.42	7.06
1978	23.10	20.10
1977	35.66	40.76
1976	42.93	54.34
1975	50.49	64.12
1974	59.76	73.91
1973	65.76	79.34
1972	69.18	83.69
1971	72.46	88.03
1970	75.17	89.67

Note: *SSCI *Journal Citation Reports* (*Social Sciences Citation Index*). 1979 Annual, Volume 6. Philadelphia, PA: Institute for Scientific Information, 1980.

Earlier findings that overall use is concentrated on source material issued in the past three years has been further substantiated by the present survey. The five year retention policy mandated by the Government Printing Office should be relaxed so that selective depositories have greater flexibility in developing selection and retention policies that reflect local needs. For example, data concerning the half-life of the *Monthly Labor Review* and *Problems of Communism* suggest that a five or even a three year retention policy should not be applied uniformly across document types and titles. Libraries might require extensive backfiles for only selected titles, ones suggested by a needs assessment.

Use of GPO Bookstores

Twenty-seven GPO bookstores scattered throughout the United States provide a sales outlet for the purchase of government publications, a means for people to browse among a variety of different titles (ranging from general information pamphlets to highly technical treatises), and a mail-order house for document titles not held locally in stock. An examination of these bookstores, their clientele and sales patterns, offers insights into the information requirements of various groups and suggests titles that they deem important enough to purchase.

The following comments build upon the findings of a study into the sales patterns for the bookstore located in Boston, Massachusetts.[21] Although this study did not deal with the same population as the self-reporting survey discussed in this chapter (e.g., it examines purchasing by New England, rather than Midwestern, academic economists), nevertheless it illustrates another means of monitoring the information requirements of the academic community.

In 1980, the Boston bookstore has sales totaling $330,615 and was seventh among all the bookstores outside the Washington D.C. area in profit margin.[22] Economists from nearby academic institutions regard the bookstore as one means for acquiring needed government publications. They periodically visit the bookstore and browse through the stock or call in requests for specific titles. The following list contain titles that might appeal to economists:

- *A Basic Guide to Exporting* (Department of Commerce, 1979)
- *Business Conditions Digest*
- *Business Statistics*
- *Directory of Companies Required to File Annual Reports with the Securities and Exchange Commission* (Securities and Exchange Commission, 1980)
- *Economic Indicators*
- *Economic Report of the President*
- *Monthly Labor Review*
- *U.S. Industrial Outlook*
- *The World Factbook* (National Foreign Assessment Center, 1981)

Economists might also want various trade (exporting) publications and newly issued census publications. The bookstore manager suspects that once issued the 1980 census publications covering the state of Massachusetts and the city of Boston will be good sellers. He notes that newly issued budget publications also sell well; examples of these include the *Budget of the United States Government, An Analysis of President Reagan's Budget Revision for Fiscal Year 1982* (Congressional Budget Office, March 1981), and *Additional Details on Budget Savings* (Office of Management and Budget, April 1981).

SUMMARY

Libraries incorporate the information requirements of their clientele into decision making regarding the selection and retention of government publications. In order to do this, documents librarians can employ a variety of methods for data collection. For example, they can experiment with self-reporting questionnaires (user and use surveys), conduct citation analyses of writings by faculty and students, examine circulation records and lists of document reference questions,[23] and peruse the collections of GPO bookstores and monitor sales patterns. Research on questions relating to government publications may not always result in problem solving or abate disagreement, but as in other areas, it does place opinions and assumptions in perspective, clarify issues, and create an awareness of unforeseen areas which merit further investigation.

Collection development should be based on an awareness of information-seeking patterns and the fact the the library is but one information source provider. Faculty members often prefer information gathered from interpersonal sources (e.g., colleagues) and resources held in their own personal collections.[24] In order to improve the delivery of needed information, librarians need to determine perceptions and expectations about the depository collection. Research would reveal use patterns for source material held in the depository collection as well as the circumstances under which the collection is consulted.

Librarians need to develop functional documents collections, ones that meet a large percentage of recurring demands from the immediate collection, and to rely on inter-institutional cooperation for titles in less demand.[25] This chapter has shown the overall government bodies, document types and titles that academic economists are likely to consult. Economists at individual institutions might not use all those bodies, types, and titles listed as consulted by institutions having a particular degree program. Institutional variations therefore should be taken into account when libraries develop document collections for economics, and other programs. Still, it should be observed that a small number of government bodies, documents types and titles account for the majority of use for a depository collection. Economists, for example, rely heavily upon statistical data and seek out government bodies and titles that convey the needed data. Further, if libraries engage in retrospective purchasing for the discipline of economics, they might well concentrate upon time series, in particular those containing census data.

This chapter has presented general study findings and has shown that faculty members will respond to collection development surveys. Additional studies should examine documents use by other disciplines and explore the role of personal collections. Studies of general documents use (such as the one reported in this chapter) should be compared to those describing use of specific depository collections. The research would show if there is a statistically significant difference between the government bodies, document types and titles consulted in the depository collection, and those which social scientists gather from other channels. As is evident, much remains to be learned about use of government publications held in depository collections. The next chapter, which places documents use in the context of general library selection practices, examines the implications of the survey findings.

NOTES AND REFERENCES

1. Herb White, "Library Effectiveness—The Elusive Target," *American* Libraries 11 (December 1980): 683.
2. Ibid.
3. See Peter Hernon, *Use of Government Publications by Social Scientists* (Norwood, N.J.: Ablex Publishing Corp., 1979), pp. 22-26.
4. *Investigation into Information Requirements of the Social Sciences*, Reserach Report No.1, Volume 1. Text by Maurice B. Line, Project Head (Bath, England: Bath University of Technology, University Library, May 1971), p.55.
5. Hernon, *Use of Government Publications by Social Scientists*, p. 9.
6. Ibid., pp.27-32, 131-134.
7. Percentages are subject to rounding.
8. See Dale R. Potter, et al., *Questionnaires for Research*, USDA Forest Service Research Paper (Portland, OR: U.S. Department of Agriculture, Forest Service, Pacific Northwest Forest and Range Experiment Station, 1972); and Douglas R. Berdie and John F. Anderson, *Questionnaires: Design and Use* (Metuchen,N.J.: Scarecrow, 1974).
9. For a discussion of statistical significance see: Sidney Siegel, *Nonparametic Statistics for the Behavioral Sciences* (New York: McGraw-Hill, 1956), pp.212-213.
10. Respondents could check as many specialties as applicable.
11. The ranking of the reasons depicted in Table 5.6 is identical to that reported by Hernon in his earlier study of economists at the same institutions: *Use of Government Publications by Social Scientists*, p.51.
12. The list of categories was adopted from those specified in Rae Elizabeth Rips, "Reference Use of Government Publications," *Drexel Library Quarterly* 1 (October 1965): 3-18.
13. Previous research indicates that these might be basic titles for economists. See Hernon, *Use of Government Publications by Social Scientists*.
14. Hernon, *Use of Government Publications by Social Scientists*; and Gary R. Purcell, "The Use of Tennessee State Government Publications," *Tennessee Librarian* 32 (Spring 1980): 26-27.

15. Survey respondents were asked to list citations to government publications from writings completed within the past year. The literature search, on the other hand, extended back to 1978 and could not take into account manuscripts submitted for publication, those currently in the publication process, and those recently published. Consequently the validity check could not be expected to produce an exact match of document titles. Further, the survey did not fully attempt to identify the range of monographic documents consulted and cited.

16. Since readers might be interested in some of the titles cited, the following represents a partial listing:
    * *Annual Housing Survey* (Bureau of the Census).
    * *Community Cost Plant Closings: Bibliography and Survey of the Literature*. By Rick Carlisle and Michael Redmond (Federal Trade Commission, July 1975).
    * *East European Economics: Post-Helsinki: A Compendium of Papers* (Joint Economic Committee, 1977).
    * *Municipal Government Wage Survey* (Bureau of Labor Statistics).
    * *National Income and Product Accounts of the United States, 1929-74* (Bureau of Economic Analysis, 1976).
    * *1967 Input-Output Structure of the U.S. Economy*. Vol. 1: *Transactions Data for Detailed Industries* (GPO, 1974).
    * *Petroleum Refineries in the United States and Puerto Rico* (Bureau of the Mines).
    * *Revisions of Tariff*. Federal Communications Commission, No. 260, Private Line Services, Series 5000, Docket 18128. 61 *FCC* 2d 606 (November 26, 1976).
    * *Rules to Govern the Assembling and Presenting of Cost Evidence*. Docket 34013, 337 Interstate Commerce Commission 298 (July 30, 1970).
    * *Social Indicators* (Department of Health, Education and Welfare)

17. For a discussion of other study limitations see: Hernon, *Use of Government Publications by Social Scientists*.

18. For a discussion of additional data collection methods see: William C. Robinson, "Evaluation of the Government Documents Collection: An Introduction and Overview," *Government Publications Review* 8A (1981): 111-125.

19. *SSCI Journal Citation Reports (Social Sciences Citation Index)*, 1979 Annual, Volume 6 (Philadelphia, PA: Institute for Scientific Information, 1980).

20. Half-life is defined as "the number of journal publication years from the current year back whose articles have accounted for 50 percent of the total citations received in a given year." *SSCI Journal Citation Reports*, 1978 Annual, Volume 6 (Philadelphia, PA: Institute for Scientific Information, 1979), p. 1A

21. Peter Hernon, "Use of GPO Bookstores," *Government Publications Review* 7A (1980): 283-299.

22. U.S. Congress, House, *Legislative Branch Appropriations for 1982*. Hearings before a Subcommittee of the Committee on Appropriations, Part 2 (Washington: GPO, 1981), p. 910. The authors wish to thank Mr. Manuel Martin, manager of the Boston Bookstore, for his assistance in identifying the information requirements of economists.
    The following discussion examines the general discipline of economics and does not differentiate among teaching and research specialties. Undoubtedly some of the following titles have broader appeal than do others.

23. See Peter Hernon, "State 'Documents to the People'," *Government Publications Review* 3 (1976): 259-260, 265-266.

24. Mary Ellen Soper, "Characteristics and Use of Personal Collections," *The Library Quarterly* 46 (October 1976): 397-415.

25. See Peter Hernon, "Functional Documents Collections," *Microform Review* 9 (Fall 1980): 209-219.

Chapter 6

Selection and Use

The purpose of this chapter is to analyze the findings of the previous chapters and to show the relationship between the selection of government publications by libraries and patterns of documents use by client groups. In addition, there is a discussion of community analyses, "information overload," and methods for increasing citizens' access to government publications housed in libraries.

Since libraries select from the universe of available government publications those of current and potential use to their client groups, collection development for most depository libraries ought to center on those item numbers that will receive the most use. Publications that are not used or are used very infrequently should neither be selected nor retained. Focusing on the portrait of collection development that this book has painted, this chapter examines the use of documents in relationship to selection and hypothesizes that further explorations into the subject relationships will produce a recognizable group of government bodies, document types and titles able to meet a high percentage of the demands on any collection.

Practicing librarians may opine that they lack the time, resources, and expertise to conduct the type of analysis portrayed in this book. It is true that documents departments are frequently understaffed, that the person in charge of the collection might be a nonprofessional staff member or assigned to the position on a part-time basis, that routine tasks (processing and servicing the collection) consume staff time, and that staff members feel ill-equipped to conduct research and community analysis. These possibilities suggest that there should be research to examine the staffing of depository libraries and to identify the variety of tasks performed by the professional and nonprofessional staff. The results of this research might suggest alternatives to the staffing patterns of depository libraries. After staffing has been explored, discussion should focus on collection development. Collection development should become a planning process whereby a collection policy, reflecting user needs, is formulated, tested, and refined. The policy therefore is not an end in itself; it represents the commitment of a library to make selection, acquisition and retention decisions based upon an evaluation component. To assist libraries in conducting the necessary community analysis upon which to base collection policies, this chapter suggests studies that can be adapted to meet local needs.

SELECTION

Now that the Government Printing Office has automated its item number file, there is a machine-readable record of categories that depository libraries are currently selecting. Updated on a regular basis, this file has potential benefit for researchers and others interested in collection development for government publications. There is a potential for libraries to receive printouts listing the items selected by other depositories in the area and to use this information to further inter-institutional cooperation. This file offers the possibility for libraries to determine which other depositories currently receive a particular item number; however, they can neither determine when a depository began selecting the item number nor how extensive the holdings within the item number are. The file can also suggest which item numbers have potential appeal to various types of depositories. Profiles of depositories can therefore be constructed. For example, it can be shown not just what academic libraries select but, more specifically, selection patterns by institutional control (public and private) and highest degree offered (arts associate, baccalaureate, master's, and doctoral). The file, as is evident, has collection development application, especially if a subject orientation can be imposed on it. Unless item numbers take on a subject orientation, libraries must base collection development largely upon the content of the categories rather than subject relationships.

In this book, one user group, academic economists, was selected to demonstrate the relationship between information requirements of users and the selection of item numbers by libraries. As shown in Chapter 4, potentially a large number of government bodies produce source material of value to academic economists. In order for academic libraries to identify the government bodies from which selections should be made, these libraries must take into account factors such as curriculum and institutional mission. To prevent these factors from being abstractions, actual decision making should be based on an examination of college catalogs, course syllabus, and interaction with client groups through user requests, visits to the offices of faculty members, and so on. It may be that most depository libraries do not undertake this type of formal examination. A probable scenario for the selection of new item numbers is that the depository receives notification that new item numbers will appear and then a staff member responsible for the documents collection reads the descriptive note and decides whether or not the content has potential value to client groups. Where such practices occur, depositories are making the judgements on source content and perceived needs, rather than subject relationships and documented current or potential needs. For example, Chapter 4 indicates that depository libraries perceive the Office of the Federal Register, General Services Administration, as producing source material of value to academic economists. However, the use survey reported in Chapter 5 suggests that publications from this Office do not comprise a significant resource for these faculty members.

Government publication collections contain a wealth of source material of value to almost any discipline. The problem, however, is to integrate this material administratively with other collections. Librarians and client groups should not have to associate information needs, first of all, with resource types (e.g., monographs, periodicals, and government publications). If required to do so, additional steps are required of clients in order to locate desired information. For example, when clients have identified government publications as an appropriate resource, they must next discover the appropriate format (e.g., hardcopy, microform, or machine-readable) and its specific location within the library. All of these decisions involve barriers to use and should be recognized and addressed through administrative integration of the collection.

The retention of more government publications than the client groups require presents problems in gaining access to needed source material. Shelves overcrowded with publications of varying quality have a negative impact on users in their search for pertinent source material. Research relevant to this problem indicates that a major reason for limited use of government publications is that the time and effort required for locating needed source material is out of proportion to the value of what is found.[1] The problems involved in making documents available when needed by library users may be different by an order of magnitude from those associated with providing other library materials for users. The factors that create greater problems in providing documents are the high rate of obsolescence for many documents, the ephemeral nature of a substantial proportion, the extensive number of separate titles, and the marginal quality of many bibliographic access resources. For these reasons documents librarians must keep use patterns in mind when making selection and retention decisions. To recap, libraries should concentrate their holdings on document types and titles that will be used most commonly by the clients they serve. At the same time, they should seek to improve their ability to acquire needed source material from outside the institution.

The findings reported in Chapter 3 merit some additional comments. First, selective depositories do not choose all the titles that both the GPO and the Depository Library Council believe should be common to all depository collections. This perhaps should not be surprising because these titles were not determined on the basis of research into use patterns and needs assessments. It is questionable whether the GPO and the Depository Library Council should suggest that all libraries receive specific items since not all libraries collect the same subject areas or have similar collection needs. More realistic suggestions of titles to be collected could be based on the construction of profiles by library type.

Table 3.2, which reported the fifty most frequently selected item numbers, shows that titles such as the *U.S. Government Manual* and the *Congressional Directory* are not common to all depository collections. However, these are titles that one might expect all depositories to find useful. Surprisingly, the *Publications Reference File*, which is a microfiche catalog of those publications in the active sales file of the Superintendent of Documents, only ranked 25th (selected by 1,098 depositories). It is also surprising that *Selected U.S. Government Publications*, a free catalog of new sales publications, ranked 40th (selected by 1,050 depositories). These findings underscore the value of research into the characteristics of depository libraries not selecting significant item numbers. Such profiles, combined with other data such as the fact that many depositories are not actively engaged in deselection, have serious implications for collection development as well as the depository library program as an interlocking network.

Each year, a vast amount of source material becomes available for depository distribution. Many libraries, however, are highly selective in what they acquire; over 30 percent of the depositories take less than the 25 percent of item numbers recommended in the *Guidelines*.[2] Presumably these libraries believe that a majority of their information needs can be addressed from a small collection of depository publications. If a high percentage of item numbers have limited value to most libraries, perhaps even including regional depositories, one can question whether it is necessary to make them available for depository distribution. It might be time for a reexamination of distribution decision making. The identification of the universe of government publications and depository distribution need not be thought of necessarily as synonymous concepts.

The structure of the depository library program and the document delivery capability of the program should also be probed. It may be that there are, in fact, too many depositories and public access to government publications/information could be enhanced from a smaller program, one that is able to deliver needed source material promptly through an interlocking computerized network.[3] Another matter should be considered. Noting that libraries comprise only one area of government generated information, some librarians have argued for a merging of Federal Information Centers under the auspices of the depository library program. Prior to pursuing alternative structural arrangements, there should be a further identification of the strengths and weaknesses of the depository program. For example, research should investigate the ability of staff members serving documents collections to handle reference questions. Unobtrusive or hidden testing such as that employed by Crowley and Childers may show that documents librarians, like general reference librarians, can only answer correctly slightly more than half of the questions requiring bibliographic and factual data.[4] If patterns in the quality of service do emerge, can variations be accounted for by type of depository library? Where are the weak links in the depository library program? How widespread are the problems? At present questions such as these must be posed in the abstract. Further research will answer these questions and point the way to rectifying structural and other weaknesses in the depository library program.

USE

Functional Collections

Chapter 5 reports on exploratory efforts to identify high use government publications for the discipline of economics. It underscores the importance of statistical data and periodicals to these faculty members. Following these types in overall importance are annual reports, reports of investigation and research, and committee and commission reports. Further, academic economists are most likely to consult a few document serials (e.g., the *Economic Report of the President*) and to rely upon the publications of selected government bodies (e.g., the Bureau of the Census and the Bureau of Labor Statistics). By examining use by economists in terms of highest degree offered by the institution in which they teach, the chapter reflects the basic government bodies, documents types and titles used by economists at baccalaureate, master's, and doctoral institutions. Librarians at academic institutions can use these data to explore and compare use patterns for faculty members at their own institutions.

Identification of subject relationships for the humanities as well as the social, behavioral, and physical sciences would expand the number of government bodies producing potentially useful source material. However, there would be a large degree of overlapping, with some government bodies having appeal to a variety of subject disciplines. An examination of use patterns would also produce recognizable patterns and undoubtedly show heavy concentration upon a few document types. For example, social scientists most often consult government publications for statistical content; therefore the publications of statistical reporting agencies as well as annual reports of various government bodies take on increased importance. Since the *American Statistics Index* and the *Statistical Reference Index*, both produced by the Congressional Information Service, offer statistical publications of the federal government and state governments, libraries can improve access to statistical data needed by their client groups. Thus, depository libraries ought to actively and aggressively promote the strengths of the depository collection and how it supplements library holdings in other formats.

A relatively small group of government bodies, document types, and perhaps even document titles will account for a large percentage of the most heavily used literature. Attempts to develop comprehensive or extensive collections will add titles at an exponential rate, but it may be that a basic concentration of government bodies, document types and titles comprise part of the nucleus, or core, of all fields. In other words, there may not be as many different core government bodies, document types, and document titles as there are special fields. Core resources, as has been found to exist with journal literatures, have appeal to a variety of fields. For example, the *Monthly Labor Review*, which is a periodical covering labor and public policy, appeals to faculty members in fields such as business and economics, demography, history, law, public administration, and sociology. *Problems of Communism* is cited in fields such as economics, history, political science, and sociology.[5]

Community Analysis

A library that operates without a general collection development policy works under a serious handicap in terms of establishing a sound and well-developed collection to meet the needs of its users. Efforts to generate data useful for determining the appropriateness of the policy or the extent to which it is being followed fall into two general categories: user oriented techniques and collection oriented techniques. Since user oriented techniques are useful for determining the information needs of client groups, this part of the chapter focuses on these techniques.[6]

Community analysis implies a study of the client groups, actual and potential, which the library serves. It is difficult to understand how successful collection development can take place without access to information obtained about the characteristics and information needs of the client groups served by the library. Basing a collection policy on supposition or fragmented experience may be misleading and inadequately represent the information needs of the entire user community. In *Developing Library Collections*, G. Edward Evans has described the process of conducting a community analysis.[7] Libraries must collect information about the actual and potential users of the library as well as identify their information needs and information gathering behavior. In this way, they can see the potential role for the institutional library as an information provider. Knowledge of user population information needs is necessary to serve as a base point against which the major provisions of a collection development policy can be judged and priorities established, and against which individual selection decisions can be made. In addition, the holdings of other information resources within the institution or the geographical area should be identified to reduce costs by avoiding unnecessary duplication and to increase the speed of access to materials.

There are several sources available to assist libraries in devising and refining collection development policies for depository collections. For example, the next chapter discusses the elements essential in formulating a collection policy. Appendix A reprints collection policies in use at seven institutions. Further, libraries wanting to undertake a community analysis might consult *Use of Government Publications by Social Scientists* and Appendix D, the faculty questionnaire, of that book.[8] This questionnaire can be modified to meet local needs. In addition, Appendix D of this book reprints the use survey employed to generate the data for Chapter 5. This questionnaire could also be modified to meet local needs. Libraries may even want to survey client groups about the information formats they consult (e.g., hardcopy/paper, microform, machine-readable, and audiovisual), willingness to use government publications appearing in a microformat, and the types of government publications they would use in a microformat. Such information would be useful in making selection and retention decisions, especially since the GPO now regards microfiche as the principal format for distribution to depository libraries.

Documents librarians do not have to investigate the information needs of all client groups simultaneously and to the same depth. It is important, however, that community analyses be undertaken and that they be conducted on a regular basis. Documents use patterns can be considered in a large context—use of the library and its resources. If this is done, documents staff members can work with librarians in other departments to integrate administratively various library genre.

Information Overload

User/use studies will reflect the information needs of client groups and, in the case of faculty members, their preference to use information that is the most physically accessible. For both teaching and research they draw extensively upon materials that they have added to their personal collections or upon materials within their department. According to one author,

> ...a seeker of information, for whatever purpose, will go first to a source he perceives to be the most accessible to him. In spite of the possibility that the information he needs may exist in a more authoritative form elsewhere, even in a form more intellectually accessible to him than that closer to hand, he will tend to be satisfied with what he finds nearest and not search further. The cost to the user of going beyond his immediate environment may outweigh the cost of using sources that are judged inferior by other knowledgeable people.[9]

Personal collections are perhaps "easier to use because they are smaller and not as complex as institutional libraries."[10]

User/use studies will reflect that social scientists, for example, rely heavily upon their subject literature and interpersonal sources (e.g., colleagues) for awareness of source material. They do not make extensive use of indexing and abstracting services and bibliographies housed in libraries. In fact, libraries may not comprise a major resource in their information gathering. Further, social scientists may be satisfied with their present information gathering strategies and believe that awareness of additional information may overburden them with information. Consequently they may question the value and quality of information for which they must undertake a sustained search. Faculty members at baccalaureate institutions having to teach a number of different courses may be generalists, who seek capsulized information rather than the detail contained in government publications. Faculty members at other academic institutions may have access to the small body of heavily used public documents from other channels.

Studies building upon the research contained in Chapter 5 might examine how economists gather those serial titles in demand and their receptivity to other document titles and types. In that economists work with the publications of specific government bodies over time, they become familiar with the publishing programs of these bodies and do not always seek ways to gain access to new source material. Consulting bibliographic aids and library collections may not be an effective means for gaining access to government publications.

If government publications housed in depository collections are not utilized to their potential, what are the implications of an acquisition policy that encourages the selection of a vast number of public documents, many of which will not be heavily used? The findings of this book suggest that libraries should carefully select the levels of government, government bodies, and document types and titles needed, regardless of the formats in which source material appears. Format should not dictate selection. Government publications should not be acquired in a microformat if the major reasons for doing so are reducing processing time, saving space, and reducing costs. The relationship of the source material to user needs, current and potential, is the overriding consideration. By subjecting a microform package to the scrutiny of a needs assessment as well as prioritizing collection needs, library staff members can determine the importance of the package to the total library collection and to client groups.

To encourage greater use of government publications, reference service and "outreach" programs should increase client awareness of what the government publishes, while at the same time making it easier for client groups to gain access to potentially useful source material. Libraries might devise current awareness and selective dissemination of information services by which faculty members can peruse new titles and select ones meriting duplication, in microfiche or paper copy, for personal collections. Libraries might also purchase and make available portable microform viewing equipment for home and office use, as well as circulate microforms for which replacement or duplicate copies are available. Profiles reflecting faculty interests could be constructed and a table of contents service initiated. As an alternative, libraries could circulate lists of item numbers containing source material for specific fields and could encourage faculty members to browse collections for pertinent source material. It should be remembered that browsing comprises an important means by which social scientists, and presumably other client groups, locate source material.[11] Consequently the identification of subject relationships among item numbers could be used to encourage browsing and additional use of depository collections. The insights gained from an active outreach program would reflect the needs of the community served by the library. It would also provide a means for keeping the results obtained from a community analysis current and accurate.

Collection development, as a planning process, is an ongoing activity, taking into account changing information requirements of client groups. It is recommended, therefore, that many depository libraries concentrate their holdings on the more frequently needed source material. Each depository library will have to determine how many demands it wants to meet internally and to rely on resource-sharing for lesser-needed document types and titles. Focusing on collection development in these terms, with proper attention given to goals, objectives, and cooperative relationships, depository libraries within each state can formulate the type of state plan[12] that encourages libraries to develop collection policies and to look at the depository program as an interlocking network.

NOTES

1. See Peter Hernon, *Use of Government Publications by Social Scientists* (Norwood, N.J.: Ablex Publishing Corp., 1979).
2. George W. Whitbeck, Peter Hernon, and John Richardson Jr., "The Federal Depository Library System: A Descriptive Analysis," *Government Publications Review* 5 (1978): 258.
3. For a discussion of the depository library program as a network see: Peter Hernon, *Microforms and Government Information* (Westport, CT: Microform Review, Inc., 1981); and Peter Hernon (ed.), *Collection Development and Public Access of Government Information. Proceedings of the First Annual Library and Government Documents Conference* (Westport, CT: Meckler Books, 1982).
4. Terence Crowley and Thomas Childers, *Information Service in Public Libraries* (Metuchen, N.J.: Scarecrow, 1971).
5. *SSCI Journal Citations Reports (Social Sciences Citation Index)*, Volume 6, 1980 Annual. Eugene Garfield (ed.). Philadelphia, PA: Institute for Scientific Information, 1981, pp. 592 and 611.
6. For a discussion of user orientation and collection oriented evaluation see: William C. Robinson, "Evaluation of the Government Documents Collection: An Introduction and Overview," *Government Publications Review*, 8A (1981): 111-125. Also see: William C. Robinson, "Evaluation of the Government Documents Collection: A Step by Step Process," *Government Publications Review* 9 (1982): 131-141.
7. G. Edward Evans, *Developing Library Collections* (Littleton, CO: Libraries Unlimited, 1979).
8. Hernon, *Use of Government Publications by Social Scientists*.
9. Mary Ellen Soper, "Characteristics and Use of Personal Collections," *The Library Quarterly* 46 (October 1976): 401.
10. Ibid., p. 414.
11. Hernon, *Use of Government Publications by Social Scientists*.
12. The Depository Council to the Public Printer has endorsed the development of state plans, in which depository libraries delineate their responsibilities and address the following points:

- collections
- service
- bibliographic access (depositories must know what the others collect)
- communication among state plan participants
- financial responsibility
- goals
- review and evaluation mechanism
- signed agreement among participants
- approval by state library agency or other designated body
- other considerations (e.g., staff training and publicity)

Recognizing the value of better coordination of the depository library program in individual states, the GPO has encouraged those states in need "of such plans to undertake them."

Chapter 7

Model Collection Development Policy

This chapter provides a model collection development policy that can be used by selective U.S. document depositories. The model is concerned with non-depository government publications as well as those distributed through the GPO depository system. It is limited to publications of the U.S. government because this level of government comprises the central theme of this book. However, elements of the policy can be adapted to other levels of government as well.

In order that the model collection development policy be more realistic, it has been written for a specific library. The "library" for which it was written is a composite of existing academic depository libraries with which the authors are personally acquainted, and thus it is not based on any one library. Through the use of this technique, it is possible to illustrate, in a concrete fashion, the patterns to be found in a collection development policy.

The intent of the authors is to demonstrate in this model how the basic elements of a collection development policy, as noted in Chapter 1, can be applied to a specific library. It is hoped that the model policy can thus be used as a point of departure for the creation, revision, or augmentation of document collection development policies. The model can be used in conjunction with the actual policy statements reproduced in Appendix A. Although oriented toward selective depositories, parts of it are also applicable to non-depositories as well.

U.S. government publications do not comprise a separate, distinct "format" as argued by some authors. Government agencies publish in a variety of intellectual formats such as monographs, periodicals, annuals, and pamphlets. In addition, publishing occurs in several physical formats such as paper copy, microforms, art reproductions, and filmstrips. Yet, though published in various formats, they are treated in the majority of selective depositories as if they were a distinct format. The decision

125

by depositories to treat documents in a separate fashion stems from three basic reasons: 1) the GPO, the distributor, has established a coherent system of organization for depository items based on the concept of provenance. Many of the bibliographic resources that provide intellectucal access to documents utilize this system, hence there are certain advantages for depositories to use this system; 2) the volume of separate publications distributed through the depository system makes it convenient and economically feasible for libraries to use the system; and 3) depository distribution, by its nature, requires a central point for receiving and verifying the receipt of publications, and this in turn makes it logical for libraries to treat the documents separately.

Because libraries tend to provide separate treatment for public documents, typically, government publications are also treated separately in collection development policies, and the model policy presented here does this too. However, an attempt should be made to prepare a collection development policy that integrates all types of materials by subject area. A policy of this nature will show the subject relationship between government publications and other resources in the collection. The GPO has called on depositories in each state to participate in the creation of a state plan for resource sharing. Because public documents do not exist in a vacuum among state resources, consideration of resource sharing should extend beyond government publications alone. An integrated collection development policy, as advocated here, is an important step in establishing a local base for statewide resource sharing.

The institution for which the model policy is designed is a composite institution, as noted above. This composite institution is described prior to the text of the policy statement in order to provide a context into which the policy statement can be placed. Some of the information found in this introduction is typical of that which would be included in the overview, or introductory section, of the entire library collection development policy, but this is not intended to serve that purpose. Rather, it is only to provide a context for the model documents policy.

GOVERNMENT PUBLICATIONS
COLLECTION DEVELOPMENT POLICY:
OAKWOOD STATE UNIVERSITY

Introduction

Oakwood State University was established in 1902 as Oakwood Normal School, with its primary objective being the preparation of elementary and secondary school teachers. In 1924 the school was designated as

Oakwood State College, and finally in 1955 it was renamed Oakwood State University. It is located in the city of Oakwood, which is a regional population center of 125,482 (1980 Census of Population). Oakwood is in an area of the state in which the primary industries are agriculture, forestry, forestry products, and paper mills. At present the university is a multipurpose regional university with eight colleges, twenty-five departments, seventeen master's-level programs, and seven doctoral level programs. The colleges of the university are: Arts and Sciences, Education, Home Economics, Communications, Agriculture, Engineering, Business, and Nursing. Doctoral programs exist in Education, Forestry, Paper Science, Biology, Economics, Business, and Agricultural Economics. The 1981-1982 student body size is 12,481 and the faculty size is 842.

The mission of the university, as established by the State Higher Education Commission, designates its primary purposes as teaching, public service and research, in that order. In those areas where doctoral programs are offered, it is expected that the colleges and departments will place a higher priority on research.

The library of the university has a collection of 645,000 items (including bound periodicals but excluding government publications), and it is a selective depository for GPO government publications. It has been a depository since 1925. The library is organized on a divisional basis and the collection is divided among the three major divisions, which are humanities, social sciences, and sciences. In addition, there are separate public service departments for circulation, reserve, and educational media, as well as the technical service departments. Both the depository and map collections are located in the social science division. The on-line bibliographic search facility, which is located in this division as well, provides access to Lockheed DIALOG and System Development Corporation ORBIT. For convenient access to microform collections held by the library, microforms are divided by subject among the three divisions. However, all microforms of government publications, regardless of subject, are located in the social science division.

Community Served

The Oakwood State University library serves the faculty and students of the university as its primary constitutency. In addition, non-university people can use the library on site without charge, and guest borrowing privileges are available for a fee of $25 per year. The library provides reference and documents service to all who walk in. Also, telephone reference service is provided without regard to the caller's association with the university. The primary constituency, however, consists of the 10,542 undergraduate students and the 1,939 graduate students, in addition to the faculty. An extensive community analysis of the on-campus users served by the library was undertaken during the 1979-80 academic year, and the information derived from that analysis provides the basis for the collection development policies presented here. Available, but not reported here, is a breakdown by undergraduate and graduate student major as well as by faculty specialty.

Collection Parameters

In general, the collection reflects the curriculum areas of the university. Those areas of the collection that are strongest are those where doctoral or master's degrees are offered. Subject fields that are represented strongly in the collection are paper science, forestry, business, economics, agricultural economics, educational administration, curriculum and instruction, botany, microbiology, advertising, and journalism.

The library has established few limits on the types of formats that can be collected, although guidelines have been established for particular subject fields. For example, in education, a complete set of ERIC microfiche documents is available. In addition, a collection of films, filmstrips, audio and video tapes, LP recordings, K-12 textbooks, and curriculum materials is also available. Similar non-book collections are available where appropriate for other areas. The guiding principle in their selection is the application of the materials to the curriculum and research needs of the university's academic programs.

The priorities established for the collections are determined on a department by department basis and are arrived at by consultation between the collection development librarian, division librarians, specialists (such as the documents librarian), and faculty representatives from the academic units. Retrospective collections have been developed in those areas where doctoral study is available, but primary emphasis is placed on current materials in the undergraduate and master's programs. Limited duplication of materials is required because the entire library is housed in a single building, and there are no departmental libraries. All reference work is performed in one of the three divisional libraries. Duplicate copies for books placed on reserve are ordered, when appropriate, at a ratio of one book per ten students.

Cooperative Collection Development

The Oakwood State University library is the largest library within a 125 mile radius. As a consequence, it serves as a center to which other libraries in the region of the state can turn for assistance. The library is part of a statewide consortium of academic and public libraries, which are members of OCLC through a regional utility, and which have their own separate cooperative exchange agreement. One of these libraries, the state library, is the regional depository for U.S. government publications. The university library strongly subscribes to the notion of interlibrary cooperation, and the director and division heads meet every six months with their counterparts from other academic and large public libraries in the state, which are part of the consortium. At these meetings they discuss methods of furthering cooperative services. One area in which cooperation has been particularly successful is in the depository library program.

COLLECTION DEVELOPMENT POLICY FOR U.S. GOVERNMENT PUBLICATIONS

Introduction

Consistent with the general collection development policy statement, the priorities for the collection of government publications are to meet the instructional needs of undergraduate and graduate students as well as the teaching and research needs of the faculty. In addition, as a federal depository, it is required to be open to use by the public, and the needs of the general public are considered when depository collection development decisions are made. The library attempts to comply with *Instructions for Depository Libraries* and *Guidelines for the Depository Library System*.

U.S. government documents are physically and administratively located within the social science division of the library. One professional staff member is designated as the documents librarian and, in addition, one full-time clerical assistant and three part-time student assistants are assigned to work with documents.

The recently conducted user study demonstrated a need for statistical information sources. Consequently the microfiche collection intended to accompany the *Statistical Reference Index* (CIS, 1980-) has been acquired. In addition, the library intends to acquire the index and similar microfiche package when the *International Statistical Index* (CIS, 1983-) is published. However, limited effort is expended to acquire other local, foreign, or intergovernmental publications on a systematic basis. Requests from faculty or students are the primary means for initiating purchase of local or foreign government publications.

Reference assistance for the documents collection is provided primarily by the documents librarian, but also by the four other members of the social science division staff. The documents librarian also has responsibility for a modest map collection, and for on-line searching of government document bibliographic data bases. On-line searching of government document data bases is provided as a service on a strict cost recovery basis.

The U.S. documents collection consists of the depository collection in paper copy and microfiche. The library has selected paper or microfiche copies only for those items for which there is a continuing demand. Because the user study demonstrated that there was a consistent demand for statistical information and for Congressional hearings, these are all acquired and maintained as depository items. All hearings are acquired in paper copy when that option is available.

Non-depository items are acquired on an ad hoc basis from the publishing agency, when requested by faculty members or graduate students. Exceptions to this are important non-depository series concerned with statistics, which are acquired through the CIS non-depository microfiche collection. However, wholesale purchase of non-depository items is not undertaken. Requests for non-depository items not held by the library are met through interlibrary loan. Technical reports are acquired from ERIC and NTIS. All ERIC documents are received automatically on microfiche. NTIS documents are acquired on a selective basis using the *Selective Research in Microfiche* (SRIM) program, with the subject profiles for this service corresponding to those areas where doctoral programs are offered by the university. Other NTIS documents can be acquired on demand, upon request of a faculty member or graduate student. Usually these are acquired in microfiche unless a compelling reason is made for paper copy (such as assignment of an item for reserve reading). Ad hoc orders for microfiche copies are also placed on-line now that this service is available through commerical on-line vendors.

Depository publications are organized using the Superintendent of Documents Classification System (SuDocs), and all paper copy items are housed in the social science division except selected reference titles, which are shelved in the reference collection of the appropriate divisional library. A shelf list and series check-in file are maintained in the social sciences divisional library by the documents librarian. Records of depository and non-depository items are maintained there. Microfiche copies of depository items are filed by SuDocs number and microform copies of CIS, ERIC, and NTIS documents are filed as appropriate to the respective systems. Non-depository items acquired by the library are recorded as being received, and although the record is retained by the documents librarian, the items are cataloged and housed in the general collection.

Subject Parameters for the U.S. Documents Collection

The depository collection represents about 45 percent of the item number categories currently distributed by the Government Printing Office. Subject emphasis for item numbers received through depository distribution is based on the teaching and research needs of the academic programs on campus, and the strengths correspond to those areas of the curriculum with graduate programs. Depository documents that do not fall into these areas, and consequently are not selected, can be acquired through interlibrary loan from the regional depository, as needed. There are several broad areas in which emphasis is placed, based on the results of the community survey as listed below.

Agriculture. Publications of the Department of Agriculture are acquired, with particular emphasis on forestry, paper science, agricultural economics, and home economics. Publications of the Department of Commerce and other governmental units that pertain to these areas are also acquired in depth (e.g., the *Census of Agriculture*).

Business and Economics. Publications of the Department of Commerce and the Small Business Administration are acquired to support the curriculum of the College of Business, the doctoral program in Economics, and the MBA program. In addition, a full range of statistical publications is acquired. The *American Statistics Index* (ASI) non-depository microfiche collection is received and items included here are generally not duplicated in hardcopy. However, selected publications are duplicated for use in reference (e.g., the *Handbook of Labor Statistics*). The list of duplicated statistical publications is reviewed annually to evaluate the need for continued duplication.

Education. All publications of the Department of Education are acquired as well as publications from agencies that deal with adult and children's needs such as the National Center for Child Abuse and Neglect. In addition, a complete file of ERIC documents is acquired and maintained.

Publications of Congress. Congressional publications are received from the GPO, whenever possible, in paper copy, because there is a heavy faculty and student demand for committee prints, hearings, the serial set, and other publications. Items are not duplicated unless found to be useful for reference service in one of the divisional libraries. The list of duplicated items is reviewed annually.

Bibliographies and Indexes. As a result of the user survey, the high interest subjects were determined, and bibliographic sources that meet the information requirements of users have been given high priority. Among these are the *American Statistical Index, Congressional Information Service (CIS) Index,* and the *Index to U.S. Government Periodicals.* Materials included in these bibliographic sources, but not found to be present in the collection, can be obtained through interlibrary loan from the regional library.

Method of Selection

The method followed for the selection of depository items is to identify agencies that publish materials related to specific subjects and to select item numbers from those agencies that relate to the subjects. A list of subject areas has been constructed, with appropriate agencies and series titles for each subject. The list is available in machine-readable form and consequently can be updated and revised easily. It is maintained in the social science divisional library and copies are printed and maintained in each of the other divisional libraries. A sample of the list is shown below. In order to ensure full coverage for every subject area, all agencies, series, and item numbers are listed under each subject to which they apply. Although this results in the duplication of series titles under several subjects, it means that series titles appropriate to each subject are easily identified for that subject.

Subject List of Item Numbers

Economics

Agriculture Department
A1.34:   Statistical Bulletins, item 15
A67.26:   Miscellaneous Series, Forest Agricultural Service, item 76-G

Commerce Department
C3.14/2:   Census of Manufacturers, item 135
C3.191/2: Government Finances, item 146-E
C3.259:   Economic Research Reports, item 142-D

Labor Department
L2.3:   Bulletins, Labor Statistics Bureau, item 768-A-1
L2.6:   Monthly Labor Review, item 770
L2.104:   Employment and Wages, item 754-B

Current and Retrospective Selection

Items for current selection emphasize the instructional needs of the curriculum as well as faculty research needs. These are supported by the

cquisition of commercially produced indexes such as *CIS* and *ASI*. Paper
ppy indexes will be augmented by the microfiche index *Publications*
eference File and on-line access to indexes such as the *Monthly Catalog*,
IS, ASI, GRA/I(NTIS), and *RIE(ERIC)*. Current acquisition of non-
epository items can be initiated upon request from faculty members or
raduate students. Requests will be evaluated for purchase on an ad hoc
asis by the documents librarian. Additional non-depository items may
e selected by the documents librarian or other professional staff mem-
ers, in line with curriculum and research needs of the library.

Retrospective selection will occur on a very selective basis, and then
argely in areas where it is required by graduate level study or faculty
esearch. Usually retrospective items not held will be acquired through
iterlibrary loan from the regional depository. Existing retrospective
ollections will be maintained in microform or paper copy in the follow-
ig areas: Congressional publications, statistics, agriculture, and com-
ierce and business.

Microforms. Microforms will be acquired in lieu of paper copy publi-
ations in the instances specified elsewhere in this policy statement, namely
ublications unavailable in paper copy, selected non-depository micro-
orms that are indexed in *CIS* and *ASI*, and microfiche received from
RIC and NTIS. Microform acquisition is subject to this general caveat:
f an item is not important enough to acquire in paper copy, it will not be
cquired in microform. Microforms will be selected only when they re-
ate to functional areas of the documents collection and to the curricu-
um and research needs of the university. Cost and space savings alone
re not a valid reason for the selection of microforms.

Discarding and Replacement. Discarding of depository items will be
onducted in accordance with the policy outlined by the Government
'rinting Office as stated in *Instructions to Depository Libraries*. The proce-
lure by which this will be done is for the documents librarian to examine
ll series titles annually and approximately 10 percent of the items on
he shelf each year in order to identify items that can be retired from the
ollection. Permission will then be requested of the regional library for
he deselection of the titles. This will be done either on an item number
)r individual title basis, depending on the librarian's judgment of the
)erceived needs of the users of the library.

Replacements for missing items will be judged individually to deter-
nine if a title needs to be replaced. It will only be replaced under the
`ollowing circumstances: 1) if there is a perceived demand for the item;
2) if it is needed to complete a series judged to be important to the major
:urriculum or research areas of the library; or 3) if the cost of replace-
nent is commensurate with the perceived value of the document. Items

which are considered worthy of replacement will be replaced. Micro forms, in most cases, will be the medium of preference for replacemen However, when necessary, an item will be purchased through the out-o print book market.

Duplication Policy. U.S. government publications normally will no be duplicated. Exceptions to this policy will be made on an ad hoc basi and the decision will be based on consultation between the document librarian and the head of the divisional library that requests the duplica tion. The normal circumstance in which duplication will occur will b with publications that have reference value in two or more division Another circumstance will be for publications that have value to non public service units of the library. A third circumstance will be for item requested for reserve reading assignments. Other circumstances tha arise will be judged on the merits of the individual case. The final deter mination will be made by the division library head.

Purchase of Non-depository Materials. Non-depository items require for purchase fall into these categories: 1) publications issued by individ ual agencies, commissions, Congressional committees, and so on; 2) pub lications distributed by NTIS; 3) ERIC documents; 4) GPO non-depositor items distributed on microfiche. As noted above, all ERIC documents ar received on an automatic basis. Selected NTIS documents will be re ceived through the SRIM microfiche distribution program for selected areas. The profile for SRIM microfiche documents, designed by the documents librarian in consultation with the faculty, is subject to annua review. Additional NTIS documents will be acquired if requested by a faculty member or graduate student.

Conclusion

The collection development policy will be evaluated on a continuing basis. Selected parts of the policy will be subjected to review on an annua basis. Each annual review will be based on a user study, which will focu on one segment of the user population and will supplement the majo user study conducted in 1979-80. Through this mechanism, there will be a continuous review of user information requirements and a continuous evaluation of the relevance of the collection development policy to mee the information requirements of the clientele served by the library.

APPENDICES

Appendix A

Collection Development
Policies in Use

A committee of the Government Documents Round Table (GODORT),
the American Library Association, has gathered collection development
policies from various libraries housing document collections. Those college, university, and law school libraries responding to the committee's
inquiry were contacted and asked if they would be willing to have their
collection development policies reprinted as an appendix item. Except
for Carleton College (Northfield, Minneosta), those institutions responding to our inquiry are reported below. Carleton College is not represented because its policy can be found in Bruce Morton's "Toward a
Comprehensive Collection Development Policy for Partial U.S. Depository Libraries," *Government Publications Review*, 7A (1980): 41-46.

   I. Arizona State University
  II. University of California, Irvine
 III. Central Washington University
 IV. State University of New York at Buffalo
  V. Kearney State College
 VI. University of Iowa
VII. Stanford University

I. COLLECTION POLICY GOVERNMENT
DOCUMENTS COLLECTION:
ARIZONA STATE UNIVERSITY[1]

Federal Documents

    Introduction. Government documents, organized in a separate col-
lection and served by a specialized staff, are a "form" collection, rather

than a subject collection. The department contains within itself, department ments of selection, acquisitions, serial records, "cataloging", maintenance and reference. Subject matter in the collection ranges from art and ar history to highly technical scientific research reports. The Department acts as a library within a library, specializing in one type of publisher rather than one subject area.

Because government publications are a form or format, rather than a subject collection, the collection cannot be described in terms of a collec tion policy statement based on a subject area. The collection is more logically described in terms of "institutional" objectives as outlined in the ALA "Guidelines for the Formulation of Collection Policies," 1979, sec tion 2.2.1, A-F.

As a result of discussion with the chair of Collection Development and the Associate University Librarian, the "institutional" guidelines rather than the "subject" guidelines will be used for the Federal Government publications collection.

Purpose. To collect, organize and provide access to the publications of the U.S. Government, thus supporting the current and anticipated instructional, research and service programs of the University, and provid ing for the needs of the community at large.

A. Clientele to be served.

The collection is a resource for student programs and research needs, and for the highly technical and specialized research pro grams of the University. The clientele ranges from undergraduate and graduate students, to ASU faculty and staff.

In addition to the academic community, Government Documents has a direct responsibility to the local, state and national commu nity through the U.S. Government Depository Library Program (see. F, below for description of this responsibility). Clientele in the non-academic area ranges from private citizens, other libraries, to large business concerns in the valley and state government offices.

B. General subject boundaries of the collection.

The collection is as comprehensive as possible in the areas needed for academic teaching and research, both current and anticipated. Strong emphasis is placed on materials in the areas of:

1. Statistics, economic and social, including a responsibility to aid in the acquisition and use of machine-readable data available from the U.S. Government.
2. Energy research, emphasizing alternative energy sources, solar energy being the most prominent.
3. Congressional documents both retrospective and current, supporting the departments of Political Science and History.
4. All materials dealing with Arizona and the Southwest, including such publications as housing data, weather records, the environment, economics, water quality and supply, geological reports, and vital and demographic statistics.

C. Kinds of programs or user needs supported.

If appropriate to the publications of the U.S. Government, all programs and needs of the University are supported within the collection. Major emphasis is placed on those subject areas growing out logically from Government emphasis and interest (as outlined in B above). However, when publications exist, and programs in the University use or will use the material, those items are selected and received. The Department selects in these areas as comprehensively as possible, in spite of the lack of publication activity (arts and humanities are particular subjects where this is the case, also sports, religion and philosophy). In all of these subject areas the Government has done some major work and continues to publish some relevant reports and studies, but these publications are a very small percentage of the total Government output.

The collection also supports the administrative needs of the University as well as the academic programs, by providing information on research grants and contracts, agency rules and regulations governing the programs, and statistical data used for support or emphasis in University administrative actions. Particular types of material relating to administrative support includes government standards, grants and contracts indexes, and some agency administrative handbooks for managing grant proposals.

Non-academic user needs are filled as a result of filling the academic and administrative needs of the University. Although no specific items are selected for the non-academic community, ASU Library is the major research library in the area and thus is the primary resource for this type of information for government and private use.

D. General priorities and limitations governing selection, including:

(1) Degree of continuing support for strong collections.

Current selection—Areas of particular strength and emphasis in the collection will continue to be supported (see B, above, nos. 1-4) in selection of documents through the Depository Library System.

Indexes and reference works from the commercial press supporting the collection and facilitating its use will be purchased as funds allow. Emphasis will be placed on those items that add an alternative or totally new approach to a particular body of material, rather than those items that in substance duplicate indexing already available.

Indexes for current material will be considered in light of on-line facilities and availability of access. Current "literature search" publications that in part duplicate a data base already in the library will not be purchased.

Non-depository material will be sought and added to the collection, whenever possible, through the current subscription to Library of Congress' Documents Expediting Service, mailing lists, and purchase of microfilm collections which supplement the Depository holdings (for example, ASI Non-Depository Microfiche Collection).

Retrospective selection—Areas of particular strength and emphasis in the collection will continue to be supplemented with retrospective purchasing and acquisitions of gift material.

Out of print catalogs and exchange lists are searched regularly for materials needed in the collection. Particular emphasis is placed on material not offered in microformat, or which is difficult to use in microformat:

    a. Bureau of American Ethnology publications (because of heavy use, and illustrations and maps are difficult to use in microformat).
    b. Geological Survey publications (because of maps).
    c. Bureau of Indian Affairs (heavy use).
    d. National Bureau of Standards (reference use).
    e. Material relevant for research on Arizona.

Microform collections of retrospective materials for strong collections are purchased for items which meet one of the following criteria:

a. Material is well indexed and lends itself to use in microformat.
b. Material is not logically (because of cost or scarcity) available in hardcopy.
c. Material is available in microformat only (i.e., U.S. Congress, Committee Prints Microfiche Collection to 1970).
See also D, 2 below for full policy on microformat.

(2) Forms of material collected or excluded.

    a. Microformat collection policy.
    Microforms are purchased or procured in lieu of hardcopy materials in the following cases:

      1. Replacement of bulky, but not heavily used materials that are necessary to the library collection. i.e., *Congressional Record, Federal Register, Congressional Serial Set*, etc.

      2. Materials which are closely indexed (item, volume, page no.) which are of great importance to the collection and can be purchased in a set on microform—thereby saving space and not losing convenience and volume of use because of the caliber of indexing; i.e., *CIS Index/Microfiche Collection* (indexes and abstracts all Congressional hearings, reports, and documents), *ASI Non-Depository Microfiche Collection*, etc.

      3. Materials that are extremely expensive in hardcopy, or so rare that they would be impossible to get in hardcopy, but are necessary for the teaching and research of the University. i.e., *Defense R & D of the 60's, Censuses of 1790-1940, First—Fifteenth Census of the United States, Non-Decennial Census Publications 1820-1945, U.S. Congress Committee Prints 1917-1969*, etc.

      4. Indexes and reference tools available in no other format, or easier to use in the microformat. i.e., *Indexes NTIS Technical Reports (except Subject and Title) 1958-1972, U.S. Patent Classification Index* (all patents issued as of Dec. 1978, *Checklist of U.S. Public Documents 1789-1976, CFR Cumulative Subject Index* (not purchased as of 1-80), etc.

      5. Periodicals or long runs of serials which would complete our present holdings. i.e., *Monthly Labor Review, U.S. Geological Survey Monographs*, etc.

6. Technical reports, because of their narrow field and limited use, will be ordered in microformat only Exceptions to this policy are:

a) Technical reports needed in hardcopy for reference purposes in any one of the reference areas. i.e., *Medical Tree Structure*, etc.
b) Items difficult or impossible to use in micro format.
c) Items needed for reserve for relatively large groups of people.
d) Reports available only in hardcopy.

b. Machine-readable data base collection policy.
Although not collected or serviced by the Department data bases of the government are a source of research material necessary to the University. Government Documents Service will not collect machine-readable data, but will collect:

1. All information on data bases available through government sources.
2. All available code books for government tapes housed at ASU Computer Center through the State Data Center.
3. As much information as possible on the Census Bureau services through the State Data Center at Arizona Department of Economic Security.

(3) Languages, geographical areas collected or excluded.

Languages—Material will not be excluded from the collection becaue of language, however, the major language of the collection is English. Other languages included in the collection are mainly Spanish and Native American languages. Translations of foreign press (FBIS) and technical reports (JPRS) are collected extensively. Bilingual education materials and studies are collected as they become available.

Geographical areas—Statistical data are collected extensively for the Southwest and Western United States, with summary data collected for the whole U.S. (i.e., *Climatological Data*, Water Resources Reports). Data needed for statistical comparisons and models are collected for all areas (i.e., Census data, Federal program funding information). World data, international studies and foreign economic, political and demographic studies are collected as they meet the collection guidelines of particular subject areas (See Collection Development subject guidelines by LC classification number).

(4) Chronological periods collected or excluded—Not applicable, no particular periods emphasized or excluded.

(5) Other exclusions.

    a. Maps.
All sheet maps will be sent directly to Map Service, except those used with an accompanying text or table (i.e., *Census Block Statistics* with *Census Metropolitan Map Series*). Atlases, unless needed for reference purposes by another department (see (6) below), will be housed and serviced as other materials in the Department.

    b. Administrative documents.
Unless useful for research or to support the administrative needs of the University, federal administrative documents will not be selected or collected (i.e., *Qualified Products List*, U.S. Department of Defense, *Master Cross Reference List*, U.S. Department of Defense, *Federal Specifications*, U.S. General Services Administration).

    c. Posters and general advertising brochures will not be selected or collected.

(6) Duplication of materials.

    a. Reference materials.
All Federal documents are housed and serviced in Government Documents Service. Only those documents used as reference sources in a reference location will be cataloged and shelved in that reference area outside Documents Service. Duplication of these reference sources depends on their relevance to the Documents Collection.

        1. Reference works produced by the Government and naturally a part of that collection will be duplicated for the outside site (i.e., *Statistical Abstract*, *Industrial Outlook*, *United States Government Manual*, *STAR*).

2. Reference works produced by the government, but indexing or abstracting non-government materials, and not needed within the Documents Department for access and use of the collection, can be cataloged and shelved in a reference area for use in that area without duplication (i.e., *Personnel Abstracts, Index Medicus, Research in Education*).

b. Materials that are heavily used, and in demand within the department will be duplicated as the need arises/or use indicates, and as funds are available (i.e., Arizona Census materials, *Dictionary of Occupational Titles*, etc).

c. Materials used for class reserve will be duplicated if the demand is high, or if the items are also needed for reference use in the Documents area.

E. Regional, national or local cooperative collection agreements which complement or otherwise affect policy.

(1) Depository Collections are necessarily part of a local/regional, and national network. Items or series offered on Depository from the U.S. Government may or may not be selected by ASU Library for addition to its collections, but Regional Depositories will receive all Depository items, and are under obligation to make these items available for use within the region they serve. Thus any item not selected by ASU Library, and which is a Depository Item, is available for use (and perhaps interlibrary loan) from U of A Library and the State Library and Archives (both regional depositories).

Items of little interest to the academic community (i.e., administrative publications, or posters and charts), and not selected, are available for use in the area.

(2) Center for Research Libraries (CRL) holds some large collections of U.S. Government documents in microformat. The older *FBIS Reports, Greenwood Press Hearings, Witness Index,* and the *Readex Non-Depository Microprint Collection*, are all items which can be readily borrowed from CRL.

ASU Library, Government Documents Service, makes a constant effort to keep current with CRL acquisitions, and not to duplicate these acquisitions unless the material is of high use to the University. i.e., National Archives Material is purchased on request by CRL for member libraries. ASU Library does not purchase any NARS material, except those items of vital research importance (NARS Arizona Territory Census Schedules, 1880, 1900).

(3) U of A and NAU Libraries both have extensive documents collections in some areas. As a result of these collections ASU Documents Service is able to borrow items on interlibrary loan, and use funds to purchase other collections not owned by a library in Arizona. Examples of these non-duplicated collections which are available to ASU on interlibrary loan are:

a. U of A
NASA Reports, 1969- (all high numbered series identified by * in STAR)
DOE Reports, 1976- (all depository reports indexed in ERA)
NTIS Technical Reports, 1979- (all AD and PB accession numbers indexed in GRA/I)

b. NAU
Congressional Serial Set 1938-1970.

F. Legal, regulatory, or policy requirements.

(1) *Federal Government Requirements*—ASU Library is a Selective Depository, and as such is subject to the Federal laws regarding Depository libraries, 44 USC 1901-1916, and to the U.S. Government Printing Office, *Instructions to Depository Libraries.*

Both of these documents and other compiled guidelines and administrative rules are on file in the Government Documents Service office.

(2) *ASU Library Policy*—The Department follows all Library rules and procedures, unless in conflict with the Federal requirements for Depository libraries.

Collection Development policies for specific subject areas are followed by the Department whenever possible. Subject Specialists are consulted when questions arise regarding collections or acquisitions. The Department, as a member of the Acquisitions Committee, keeps informed with collection policies and aids in the assessment of subject areas through direct contac with the subject specialists involved.

NOTE

1. This collection policy for Arizona State University Library, Tempe, was suplied b Donna R. Larson, Head of Documents Service. The library also has separate policie for its state and local government documents collections.

II. SELECTION POLICY FOR THE GOVERNMENT PUBLICATIONS DEPARTMENT: UNIVERSITY OF CALIFORNIA, IRVINE[1]

Introduction

The primary mission of the Government Publications Department is to meet the information and research needs of its users, support specific academic programs and meet its responsibilities as a depository collection for United States and California publications. All technical processing functions of the Department, such as collection development, acquisitions, cataloging, etc., are directed toward this end. In addition to its role as a separate unit within the library, the Department seeks to coordinate its public service programs and collection development policies with other library departments in order to insure consistent and effective growth of both the departmental collection and that of the General Library.

The Department develops and maintains a collection of materials, both serial and monographic, published by the governments of the United States, California, Canada, and from selected international organizations such as the United Nations, International Monetary Fund, The Organization of American States, etc. The Department also develops and maintains an Orange County Public Affairs Collection which provides materials on local issues and interests, from both governmental and non-governmental sources. The Department has been a selective depository for the United States since 1964 and for California since 1966. In addition, the Departement is a depository for materials issued by the Southern California Association of Governments. The average acquisitions rate of the Department is approximately 33,000 publications per year.

In addition to the collections developed by the Government Publications Department, there are many other government publications housed in the general stacks and the Medical Sciences Library. These are acquired by the appropriate subject bibliographers in order to support a ariety of curriculum and research needs. On-going consultation between he subject bibliographers and the Government Publications Department s an important aspect in the acquisitions of these materials.

As a designated depository library for both U.S. and California government publications, the Government Publications Department must meet certain mandatory operational standards and performance requirements which have been established by the Federal and State governments. The collection development effort of the department is obligated to take into account these external forces, beyond the concerns of the library.

The type, level, quantity, quality, and subject matter of the publications collected by the Department are also influenced by other external variables. These variables are primarily the result of the publishing program of the various government entities. Some of these influencing factors include:

1. The amount of publishing done and the topics included vary by level of government entity, federal, state, local, etc. The financial picture of these entities at any given time has a strong affect on the amount and type of publishing done by the entity.
2. The extent of the coverage of the material published by a government entity is determined by its nature and mission.
3. Not all material published by every government entity is available to libraries. The U.S. government especially publishes a large number of materials, both classified and unclassified which are not available.

The one constant in the above unknown variables is the need for the material collected to support all levels of research and teaching on the campus and to provide information to the University community and the general public. Thus, the degree of comprehensiveness of the various subject areas of material collected by the Department is influenced by the interrelationship of these variables. The assignment of levels of collection emphasis to subject fields in government publications is very intricate and requires careful assessment of the variables discussed above as they apply to each section of the collection, such as U.S., California, International, etc. The importance of each factor varies from government to government and is not easily predictable for a particular subject area. Therefore, in the selection policies which follow, the level of compehensiveness for each subject area has not been included but wherever possible, an approximate percentage of all materials collected from each government entity is indicated.

General Purpose

To support all levels of research and teaching on campus, to provide information on public affairs to the University community and the general public, and to make the collection available to local citizens and industries engaged in research activities. Emphasis is on the research and teaching program on the campus.

In order to achieve this purpose the Department collects available materials published by the legislative, judicial and executive branches of the U.S. government through the Federal Depository Library System and through individual requests and orders of non-depository publications. In order to provide access to this collection by the users, bibliographical tools published by both governmental agencies and commercial publishers are systematically collected.

Languages
English

Geographical areas
U.S.

Chronological limits
Emphasis on current materials. A designated library since 1964. Retrospective materials are collected to fill in gaps in existing holdings or in response to specific requests.

Types of material collected
Printed material of all types
Microforms

Types of material excluded
Patents
Maps from agencies which have their own depository arrangements
Maps not accompanied by textual materials
Military specifications
Reports done under contract to a government agency, except those which are distributed by the Government Printing Office

Subjects and Collecting Levels

The Federal Government plays an active role in society, supports a growing percentage of basic and applied research in all fields, concerns itself with more and more of the activities of its citizens, and issues reports and other publications on its work. Therefore, the subject matter of its publications is of such great extent, variety, and complexity that it would be a very difficult task to try to list all of the topics which are published by the Federal Government.

In meeting the need of this Campus within the realm of U.S. government publications, the Government Publications Department collects over 70 percent of U.S. publications which are offered through the Depository System. The Department also makes a special effort to collect nondepository items with the emphasis on social sciences and technical publications with social implications.

The following list attempts to cover only the major fields of knowledge:

> Agricultural Science
> Biological Sciences
> Computer Science
> Earth Sciences
> Engineering and Technology
> Health Sciences
> Physical Sciences
> Social Sciences
> Anthropology
> Business
> Economics
> Education
> Geography
> History
> Law
> Political Science
> Psychology
> Sociology
> Statistics
> Social Ecology

California State Government Publications

General Purpose. To support all levels of research and teaching on campus, to provide information on public affairs of the State of California to the University and the general public, and to make the collection available to local citizens and industries engaged in research activities.

In order to achieve this purpose, the department has been a Selective Depository Library since 1966. However, a large percentage of California State publications are not covered by this depository arrangement and must be selected on an individual basis.

Languages
English (some Spanish)

Geographical areas
California

Chronological Limits
Emphasis is on current materials. Retrospective materials to fill in gaps in existing holdings, or in response to specific requests.

Types of material collected
Printed materials and microforms

Types of material excluded
University of California Publications
State University and college publications (except those few documents which are sent as depository items)
Maps
Reports done under contract to a government agency, except those which are obtainable through the LDA (Library Distribution Act) program.

Subjects and Collecting Levels. The Department attempts to obtain a comprehensive collection of California State publications. This objective is achieved through the following methods.

First, as a designated Selective Depository Library the Department obtains on a gratis basis all publications designated for Selective Depository Libraries and all documents sent to it on a depository basis. It has no discretion as to subject matter.

Second, the Department augments its depository collection by individual selections. The Department collects about 85 percent of the publications listed in *California State Publications*. Since the *California State Publications* list is not comprehensive, additional sources must be checked for publications of particular relevance. The Department is especially concerned with State publications in the following areas:

Criminal Justice
Economic Conditions
Education
Energy Issues
Environment
Government Processes
Health Services
Housing
Law
Minorities and Affirmative Action

Recreation
Social Services
Statistics
Transportation
Urbanization
Water Resources

International Government Publications

General Purpose. To support undergraduate and graduate teaching and research needs for publications of international government organizations. This objective is achieved through a number of different acquisition arrangements: selective standing orders, serial subscriptions, and individual monographic orders. The collection is limited to international organizations which are composed of the governments of three or more countries.

The Department has comprehensive standing orders for sale publications from a number of international organizations:

Food and Agriculture Organization (FAO)
Organization for Economic Cooperation and Development (OECD)
Organization of American States (OAS)
United Nations (UN)
United Nations Educational, Scientific, and Cultural Organization (UNESCO)
World Health Organization (WHO)

In addition, it selectively acquires publications from such organizations as:

Council of Europe
European Communities
International Bank for Reconstruction and Development (World Bank)
International Labor Organization (ILO)
International Monetary Fund (IMF)

Languages
English is the preferred language, if used by the organization.
French, Spanish.

Geographical areas
International

Types of material collected
Printed and microform materials

Types of material excluded
Any material issued by a non-government organization. *The Yearbook of International Organizations* is used as the authority for defining whether an organization is governmental or non-governmental.

Subject and Collecting Levels. For some international organizations it is possible to arrange for comprehensive standing orders. In these instances the subject emphasis follows the mission or missions of the organization as reflected in its publication program. For other international organizations publications are selected on an individual basis. In these instances the selected publications will reflect the mission of the organizations with emphasis on obtaining those materials which support or supplement the key subject areas of the departmental collections.

Orange County Public Affairs Collection

General Purpose. To support graduate and undergraduate programs and general public inquiry in the pertinent fields by making selected acquisitions, both government and non-governmental, in the field of public affairs within Orange County:

A) Governmental.

Orange County and selected city governments. Emphasis is on budgets, plans and key department publications which supply social, political and economic data regarding the area which would not be available otherwise. In addition, SCAG has designated the Department as one of its depositories for its public review documents.

B) Non-governmental.

Materials published by: (1) "special interest groups" operating within the county such as Friends of Newport Bay; (2) chapters of national organizations which direct their energies to local concerns, e.g., Orange County League of Women Voters; (3) the business and industrial communities, such as Chambers of Commerce, The Irvine Company, the major banks of Southern California, etc.

Languages
English

Geographical areas
Orange County, California
Regional or "Southern California Basin" area concept

Chronological limits
Emphasis on current materials with 1960 as the cut off date for inclu-

sion in GPD as opposed to inclusion in Special Collections, in most instances.

Types of materials collected
Printed materials only

Types of materials excluded
Codes and ordinances
Local historical society publications

Subjects and collecting levels

A) Economic Conditions
Education
Environment
Government and Politics
Health Services
Housing
Land Use
Minorities
Recreational and Resources
Social Services
Statistics
Transportation
Urbanization
Water Resources

B) Other publications are acquired as comprehensively and extensively as their availability to the public by the issuing agency permits.

Canadian Government Publications

General Purpose. To collect mainly monographic studies or special reports which supplement key subject areas in the major collections of U.S., California, and International Organizations.

The criteria followed by the Government Publications Department in developing its Canadian collection do not necessarily conform to other acquisition programs within the Library.

Languages
English

Geographical areas
Canada

Chronological limits
Emphasis on current materials. Retrospective material may be collected in response to specific requests.

Types of materials collected
Printed materials

Subject and collecting levels
Material which supplement and/or complement the main collections of U.S., California, and International publications. Emphasis is on monographic publications of current status.

NOTE

1. Collection development policy for the government publications collection at the University of California, Irvine. The policy statement, supplied by Judy Horn (Head, Government Publications Department), "is part of a larger collection development policy for the entire library. Although it can be utilized as a seperate policy, its format and content were dictated by the larger policy document."

III. GOVERNMENT PUBLICATIONS COLLECTION DEVELOPMENT POLICY: CENTRAL WASHINGTON UNIVERSITY[1]

I. Service objectives

  A. To provide a strong comprehensive collection of government publications in order to provide materials to support the reference and information needs of the library clientele.

   1. The students and faculty of Central Washington University.
   2. The citizens of the community and region.

II. Selection policies

  A. To support the academic programs of Central Washington University.
  B. To meet the obligations of a federal depository library, as specified by Title 44, *U.S. Code*.

Procedural Guidelines

I. Depository Programs.

The largest bulk of materials acquired for the government publications collections is through the depository programs. Central Washington University is a depository library on a selective basis for the United States Government publications, and a full depository library for the State of Washington publications.

A. Selection of Federal Documents.

The Government Printing Office is the distributing agency for the United States Government Publications. Generally every three or six months a revised *List of Classes Available for Selection by Depository Libraries* is issued by GPO. As government reorganization frequently takes place, there are continuous additions and deletions on this list. New additions are offered to depository libraries through "Surveys" issued frequently. Depository libraries are invited to select from these surveys which categories they wish to receive on a regular basis. Computer printouts of the *List of Items Selections* are issued quarterly. Two copies of the list are sent each time to each depository library showing the item numbers selected by that particular library. The depository libraries are requested to compare the printout with their records and correct errors. Each quarter the Depository Libraries may make desired additions or deletions. New items are offered by frequent surveys. The documents librarians do the selecting with the aid of library colleagues and other faculty. Weeding is a big part of the operation. The government stipulation is that material selected remain a part of the collection for five years. Many categories are broadly inclusive, which requires broad selection and severe weeding on a regular basis. Selection of items of permanent value is determined by the same priorities as those established by the library as a whole.

B. Selection of Washington State Publications.

The Washington State Library, Documents Center, is the distributing agency for the Washington State documents. A monthly checklist is distributed. Although CWU is a full depository, approximately only two-thirds of the publications issued by Washington State agencies are actually received. In many instances the state agencies do not request enough copies to be printed for full distribution to all depository libraries. Other ways of obtaining such needed items should be explored. Alternatives are: (1) requests for complimentary copy sent directly to agencies, (2) purchasing hardcopy or microform (if available), (3) depend upon interlibrary loan.

II. Purchasing Government Publications.

There are several situations which necessitate the purchase of government publications. The different categories are outlined below:

A. United States Publications.

1. Replacement of lost items.
2. When second copies of the depository item are needed:

   a. for reference (Ex.: *Statistical Abstract, Resources in Education*)
   b. on popular topics (Ex.: Child Abuse)
   c. of local interest (Ex.: Mt. St. Helens eruption)

3. Items not received on depository program (Ex.: NTIS publications)
4. Replacement of hardcopy to microform (Ex.: *Federal Register*)

B. Washington State Publications.

1. Replacement of lost items
2. When second copies of the depository item are needed.

   a. for reference
   b. on popular topics
   c. of local interest

3. Items not received on depository program (Ex.: WAC, Washington State Register)
4. Replacement of hardcopy to microform.

C. States other than Washington (State).
Publications issued by agencies of other states than Washington state should be acquired to meet curriculum needs. The procedure should be to first request a copy. If this does not bring results, the usual order procedure should be applied.

Suggested items to be selected according to availability:

1. Pocket data books
2. Blue books
3. Statistical abstracts
4. School directories
5. State Geographical Survey publications
6. Special interest subjects
7. Checklists of publications

D. Foreign countries, international organizations and United Nations. Publications should be acquired as needs arise, with priority given to curriculum needs. Foreign country publications of a popular, general informative nature may be obtained from the established embassies or consular offices in the United States. International organization publications such as some of the series issued by OECD and the United Nations should be placed on standing order. Others should be selected item by item according to interest and need. Faculty should be consulted in cases where need has not been previously established or changes in curriculum anticipated.

E. Indexes and Bibliographies.

Indexes and bibliographies are indispensable tools in dealing with government publications retrieval for users. Some are available as selected items through the depository programs. Others have to be purchased. Extremely useful indexes such as *CIS, ASI, Andriot, Undoc*, etc., should be placed on standing order. Other indexes and bibliographies should be selected upon determination of their appropriate usefulness as tools of retrieval or selection.

F. Microforms.

The policy for selection of microforms by the Documents Department is limited to those dealing with government publications and maps. The Government Printing Office has since the fall of 1977 issued certain categories of the U. S. government publications in microfiche for selection by depository libraries. Series such as the Congressional documents and reports, the *Congressional Record*, appropriation hearings, and *Code of Federal Regulations* are offered either in hardcopy or in microfiche. Depository libraries may choose either but not both.

1. Guidelines for the purchase of government documents in microform:
   a. early historical documents available in no other form
   b. back runs of continuations such as *U.S. Reports, U.S. Statutes at Large*, etc.
   c. replacement of bulky hard copies necessary to keep permamently
   d. current state documents needed but not available in hard copy

G. Maps.
   A separate paper.

III. General Guidelines.

The Acquisitions Department should be aware of possible duplication of government publications through the approval program, faculty requests, reprints, etc. Publications such as those issued by the Smithsonian Institution (as an example) are often times Federal depository items, but may also appear in the general market place. Commercial publishers often reprint government publications, sometimes under disguised titles, making it difficult to recognize them as government publications. All categories of government publications may be available from the issuing agencies. The government documents librarians and staff members learn by experience which agencies are most likely to send requested items. Such possibilities should be tried before purchases are made. Some United States government agencies offer to place libraries on their mailing lists for certain series or categories of their publications. Some states, foreign countries, and international organizations are willing to do the same. Advantage should be taken of such offers whenever useful publications can be obtained this way. Some examples are:

World Bank	Annual Development Report. . Annual
	World Bank Atlas. . Annual
Canada	*Agriculture Abroad.* . Monthly
United Nations	United Nations Fund for Population Activities
	Population Facts at Hand. . Annual
	Populi, Journal of UNFPA. . Quarterly

Budgetary allowances should be provided to accommodate the needed purchases in order to meet the service objectives. The sum allotted to the disposition of the Documents Department should be determined according to how the purchasing of general publications, indexes, series, etc., are handled by the Acquisitions Department.

MAP LIBRARY: COLLECTION DEVELOPMENT POLICY[2]

The collection development policy of the Map Library is expressed in two goals:

1. Acquisition and maintenance of a viable Washington State and Pacific Northwest regional map collection, including both standard map series and thematic maps, closely related to the University's curricular offerings.
2. Acquisition and maintenance of a basic reference set of maps providing worldwide coverage.

These two goals best fulfill the purpose of the Map Library, which is to provide map materials to support academic programs at CWU. The Map Library will not attempt to become a comprehensive research-oriented map collection for areas outside the Pacific Northwest region. Rather, effort will be directed to building and maintaining a world-wide map collection serving a reference, as opposed to a research, function.

Procedural Guidelines

I. Introduction.

The collection development policy of the map library is expressed in two goals:

1. Acquisition and maintenance of a vital Washington State and Pacific Northwest regional map collection including both standard map series and thematic maps, closely related to the University's curricular offerings.
2. Acquisition and maintenance of a basic reference set of maps providing world-wide coverage.

These two goals best fulfill the purpose of the Map Library, which is to provide map materials to support all academic programs at CWU. They also are suited to the needs and desires of the primary users of the map library, which are those students, faculty, and members of the community needing Washington State thematic and topographic quadrangles and general maps of the region, other states of the U.S., foreign countries, continents and the world for a variety of purposes. The several depository programs go far in contributing to the accomplishment of these goals, but, alone, cannot attain them.

II. Description of Depository Programs.

The overwhelming majority of maps acquired by the Map Library come via depository programs.

1. U.S. Geological Survey (U.S.G.S.)
   Just under 4,000 U.S.G.S. maps were received last FY 78-79. These include primarily topographic quadrangle maps of the 50 states at scales 1:1M, 1:250,000, 1:65,500 and 1:24,000. Special maps, for example, National Park maps, are also received. The depository contract states that lost, stolen, or damaged maps will be replaced free of charge. The U.S.G.S. is the Map Library's principle map source.
2. National Ocean Survey. (NOS)
   Domestic nautical and aeronautical charts are issued by NOS. The Map Library receives all aeronautical charts and has se-

lected only those nautical charts of the west coast, Alaska and Hawaii.

3. Defense Mapping Agency, Topographic Command (DMATC)
   About 75 maps per year are received from this agency, mostly nautical and aeronautical charts of foreign areas. Once a great source for 1:1M maps of the world and 1:250,000 scale maps of many countries, the DMATC (old Army map service) now has only a slim 8-page sales catalog from which the public and map libraries can purchase selected map series. We continue our depository contract with DMATC in the hopes that they will offer more to depositories in the future.

4. U.S. Government Printing Office.
   Bureau of the Census, Central Intelligence Agency, and the Forest Service regularly issue maps. These are routed to the Map Library.

III. Purchase of Maps issued by Federal Agencies.

At times maps need to be purchased from federal agencies. No hierarchical arrangement or prioritized listing is implied in the following series of government agencies. From the:

1. U.S. Geological Survey.
   a. Older special maps published before 1962, the year Central became a depository.
   b. Duplicate copies of Washington State topographic maps.

2. Defense Mapping Agency, Topographic Command.
   a. Topographic map series of the world at 1:1M or larger.

3. U.S. Government Printing Office.
   a. CIA maps not received on depository
   b. Replacement of lost copies of Census and Forest Service maps.
   c. Obtaining second copies of local forest service maps.

4. Bureau of Land Management.
   a. Planimetric maps at 1:100,000 of Washington and Pacific Northwest.
   b. Special series maps of Washington (State) & Pacific Northwest.

Before purchasing any of these maps every attempt will be made to obtain the map free of initial charge from the agency, arguing from our depository library status.

IV. Washington State government maps.

Very few maps are received from state government agencies on the depository program. Maps produced by state agencies are usually seen by those agencies as special items and ideally as self-supporting. Furthermore, these maps are sometimes difficult to track down. When discovered, the Map Library requests copies. If maps cannot be obtained in this fashion they must be purchased.

V. Governments other than the U.S. and Washington State. (see VI)

VI. Commercial Publishers, Learned Societies, and Scholarly Associations.

Acquiring maps published by the private sector and other governments, domestic and foreign, should be governed by geographical priorities. Prioritized list with subject and scale parameters are listed after each area:

1. Washington State	— All scales and subjects.
2. Pacific Northwest	— All subjects available.
3. Western U.S.	— All subjects of area as a whole; thematic maps of states as a whole.
4. U.S.	— Thematic maps of the U.S. as a whole; sectional maps; base, topographic and thematic maps east of the Mississippi River as required.
5. Canada, Latin America	— General and thematic maps of countries as a whole; topographic maps at 1:250,000; larger scales as requested and as budget allows.
6. Europe	— General and thematic maps of the continent and of individual countries. Topographic maps as required or requested and as budget allows.
7. World	— General and thematic maps of the Earth as a whole. International Millionth Map of the World (IMW) series complete.
8. Africa, Asia, Australia, Oceans	— General and thematic maps of each continent and country. Topographic maps as requested or required and as budget allows.

VII. Atlases.

A responsibility of the Reference Dept.

VIII. Budget.

A separate budget with adequate funds should be established for the Map Library in order to move realistically toward achieving its stated goals.

NOTES

1. Collection development policy for the documents collection at Central Washington University, Ellensburg. The policy statement was supplied by Ruth Hartman, Head Documents Librarian.
2. The Central Washington University Library services and operates documents, maps and microforms as one unit or department.

IV. SELECTION POLICY: SUNY—BUFFALO[1]

Scope

These selection policies are an adaptation of the Law Library's overall collection development policies specifically designed to facilitate the decision process for official government publications and related material. Selection is the impetus which determines future workload levels implicit in all of the other procedures of the department. Selection governs the size of the documents collection as well as the government jurisdictions and subject areas covered. Close coordination is necessary between the selection of government documents and the selection of trade publications for the Law Library. In addition, the Documents Department has certain university wide responsibilities, particularly in the area of international documents, which must be coordinated with selection of documents in other unit libraries.

Summary

The selection policies include determinations as to which governments are represented, which types of documents are desired, and what subject areas are covered, as well as considerations of cost, format, space requirements, and workload factors which impinge on the selection decision.

Significance

The selection policies outlined here are essentially a codification of past practice and do not yet represent a rational and consistent philosophy for the development of an ideal documents collection.

Policies

1. GOVERNMENT JURISDICTIONS. Although the Documents Department has no objection to dealing with any government to obtain special requests, ongoing selection is concentrated on the following jurisdictions:

1.1 *International Organizations*

1.1.1 United Nations—comprehensive—select everything available on standing order except the following five periodical subscriptions:

> Monthly Bulletin of Statistics
> Commodity Trade Statistics
> Statistical Indicators...
> Industrial Research...
> Monthly Bibliography:Books

Order Readex microprint as money is available to relieve pressure of mimeographed documents on filing cabinet space. Negotiate with Lockwood concerning the category "Economic Publications," which is costing us $500-600 per year.

1.1.2 Organization of American States—comprehensive—have standing orders for the Informational and Technical Publications of the General Secretariat of the O.A.S. and the Official Records of the O.A.S.

1.1.3 Council of Europe—extensive—have the law library standing order plan through Manhattan Publishing Company, which includes publications in catalogue sections I, II, III, IV, V, VI and on subjects of human rights, law, legislation, and criminology, including the European Court of Human Rights, Series A and Series B.

1.1.4 International Labor Office—extensive—have standing orders for the following:

> International Labour Review
> Legislative Series
> Minutes of the Governing Body
> Official Bulletin. Series A
> Social and Labour Bulletin
> Documents of the International Labour Conference

Order the Yearbook of Labour Statistics every few years. Order miscellaneous monographs, reports, etc., as needed.

1.1.5 International Court of Justice—extensive—having a standing order for publications through the UN Sales Section.

1.1.6 GATT (General Agreement on Tariffs and Trade)—comprehensive—have a standing order through UNIPUB.

1.1.7　International Civil Aviation Organization—comprehensive—have a standing order paid from a deposit account which must be replenished periodically.

1.1.8　European Community—Lockwood is a depository. Law Library has selected titles cataloged in the *INT* collection. Decision needs to be made on what to duplicate.

1.1.9　International Atomic Energy Agency—selective—we seem to be on a mailing list for some series. Order miscellaneous publications from IBID.

1.1.10　International League for Human Rights—selective—we pay membership dues to receive certain periodicals.

1.1.11　International Monetary Fund—selective—cancelled our "combined subscription" in 1978.

1.1.12　Organization for Economic Cooperation and Development—selective—Cancelled our comprehensive standing order in 1975. We are still getting:

> Guide to Legislation on Restrictive Business Practices
> Nuclear Law Bulletin
> News from OECD

Other miscellaneous monographs from *IBID*. Lockwood maintains an overall standing order.

1.1.13　UNESCO—selective—We are currently receiving:

> Copyright Bulletin
> General Conference Proceedings and Records
> Nature and Resources
> Report of the Director General

Order the Statistical Yearbook every few years. Order miscellaneous monographs from *IBID*.

1.1.14　World Bank—selective—Have a standing order for the "Occasional Papers."

1.1.15　World Intellectual Property Organization—selective—Currently receiving updates for the:

> PCT Applicant's Guide
> Copyright Law Survey

1.1.16　Other International Organizations—selective—Order pertinent items upon request, from catalogs, or from *IBID*.

1.2　*National Governments*

1.2.1　United States—selective—We select less than 20% of the items available to depositories, including items selected for UGL and other ampus libraries. Scan the Shipping Lists for other titles which should be rdered. Lockwood Library is also a depository. Order technical reports rom NTIS upon demand. We have deposit accounts with both GPO and ITIS.

1.2.2   Canada—selective—Order very selectively from the *CALL News-*tter, Documents to the People, Government Publications Review*, and every-thing from the Law Reform Commission. Lockwood is a depository and ends us some primary legal materials. The local office of the Canadian Consulate and Trade Commission is also a potential source of docu-ments. (See also Canadian Provinces under 1.3 State Governments.)

1.2.3   Great Britain—selective—We maintain standing orders for the House of Commons Papers and the Command Papers through Blackwell. At the present time the payments are through Acquisitions not Docu-ments. We occasionally order from the HMSO catalog.

1.2.4   Other National Governments—Sometimes order things from New Zealand and Australia.

1.3   State Governments

1.3.1   New York State—extensive—We have been a depository since 970, but depositories receive very few publications automatically. Order verything interesting from the *Checklist of Official Publications of the State f New York* as well as from newspapers, *Newsvane* and other current istings. Get on agency mailing lists for decisions and opinions, etc. Order urrent Bills from the Legislative Record and Index Company. Get the ound volumes of Bills from Lockwood. Lockwood is also a depository nd they subscribe to the microfilm put out by Research Publications, nc.

1.3.2   Core States—selective—The Law Library collects most heavily rom the following states:

> California
> Connecticut
> Florida
> Georgia
> Illinois
> Indiana
> Massachusetts
> Michigan
> Minnesota
> Missouri
> New Jersey
> Ohio
> Pennsylvania

Texas
Washington
Wisconsin

1.3.3 Other States—very selective—For core states and other state select from LC's *Monthly Checklist of State Publications*, CSG's *State Govern ment Research Checklist*, and Merriam Library's *Recent Publications on Gov ernment Problems*.

1.3.4 Canadian Provinces—very selective—We are on the mailing lists for a number of annual reports. Order very selectively from the *CALL Newsletter*.

1.4 Local Governments

1.4.1 Cities—Have a small collection but would like more, especially from the City of Buffalo and the Town of Amherst. Buffalo and Erie County Library is a depository for Buffalo documents. Lockwood Li brary subscribes to "Current Urban Documents" on microfiche. We re ceive Charters of the Cities of the State of New York from the NYS Department of Audit and Control. Need an aggressive program for collecting local documents. Requires regular trips to City Hall. Newspa pers are also a source of information.

1.4.2 Counties—Top priority is to keep the Charters of New York State counties up-to-date. For previous correspondence see the file la beled NYS COUNTY CHARTERS in the Document Librarian's desk. "Current Urban Documents" includes some counties. Buffalo and Erie County Library collects from Erie County. We are especially interested in the Erie and Niagara Counties Regional Planning Board.

1.5 Associations

1.5.1 Council of State Governments—comprehensive—Standing order.

1.5.2 American Enterprise Institute—extensive—Have standing or ders for AEI Studies and for Legislative Analyses. Order miscellaneous publications selectively.

1.5.3 International Commission of Jurists—Have a special standing order from the American Association for the International Commission of Jurists for United Nations Human Rights materials, which are mailed directly to Prof. Leary. Other orders are handled through acquisitions.

1.5.4 Vance Bibliographies—Order very selectively. The architecture series is available at AED.

1.5.5 Other Associations—The Acquisitions Department relies on us to order from:

International Association of Chiefs of Police
National Association of Attorneys General

Association of Family Conciliation Courts
Legal Services Corporation
Society for the Right to Die

Do not order from other associations without checking acquisitions first.

2. TYPE OF PUBLICATION

2.1   *Annual Reports*—extensive—especially for federal agencies and New York State agencies. Continue those already in kardex and select new ones according to subject guidelines.

2.2   *Decisions and Opinions*—extensive—especially for federal level and New York State. It is hard to find out whether NYS agencies are issuing mimeographed opinions.

2.3   *Bibliographies and Catalogs*—selective—use judgment as to usefulness. Comprehensive lists are to be preferred to agency lists. Publications catalogs for international organizations are extremely desirable. Likewise, catalogs of associations are useful bibliographical tools.

2.4   *Blue Books, Manuals, Directories*—extensive

2.5   *Commission Reports*—selective

2.6   *Comparative Legislation*—comprehensive

2.7   *Judicial Publications*—comprehensive

2.8   *Legislative Histories*—comprehensive

2.9   *Legislative Studies*—selective

2.10   *Miscellaneous Publications*—very selective

2.11   *Popular Explanations of the Law*—very selective

2.12   *Proceedings*—selective

2.13   *Rules and Regulations*—select only full administrative codes and for core states only.

2.14   *Statistical publications*—very selective

3. SUBJECT AREAS

administrative law
arbitration
banking
British legal issues
Canadian legal issues
coastal zone management
commercial law
comparative law
constitutional revision
consumerism
copyright and patents
criminal justice

international law
labor issues
legal history
legislatures
local government
medical/ethical issues
military justice
minorities
multinational corporations
negotiation
regulation
school law

economic problems	securities
environment	social issues
family law	social security
human rights	state government
insurance	taxation

4. FORMAT

4.1 *Hardcopy*—Prefer paper copies whenever possible.

4.1.1 Congressional Bills—select in paper as long as we have students to file them. Lockwood Library has Bills on microfiche from GPO beginning with the 95th Congress.

4.1.2 *Congressional Record*—select in paper, fill in missing volume in paper. If it becomes necessary to switch to microform, retain paper indexes.

4.1.3 *Code of Federal Regulations*—select in paper. We have a microform copy from a commercial publisher as backup.

4.1.4 Congressional Reports—select in paper copy

4.1.5 Congressional Serial Set (reports volumes)—select in paper copy

4.1.6 General Accounting Office—request selected reports from agency in hardcopy. Do not select microfiche from GPO.

4.1.7 NTIS—order paper copies unless outrageously expensive.

4.2 *Microform*—if a publication is not available in paper we have no objection to microforms. Prefer negative polarity for transparent microforms.

4.2.1 Congressional Hearings—we are presently buying CIS microfiche because of space limitations and ease of use of the CIS Index Abstracting system. When GPO offers all hearings on microfiche, switch to GPO.

4.2.2 Congressional Documents—select on microform.

4.2.3 UN Publications—buy Readex Microprint as money is available.

4.2.4 New York Local Laws of Cities, Counties, Towns and Villages— no longer being printed. Buy the microform each year.

4.2.5 Congressional Bills—replace those stored in the basement with CIS fiche if money becomes available.

4.3 *Loose-Leaf Services*—select very carefully keeping in mind the time and staff required for filing updates.

5. LANGUAGE—think twice about foreign language publications.

Evaluation

No statistics are kept on selection decisions. Evaluation of selection is possible by monitoring what was and was not selected in certain catalogs, depository items selected and not selected or by monitoring requests for information and determining what percentage is filled using the available collection and how many must be referred elsewhere.

GOVERNMENT DOCUMENT POLICY[2]

Official government publications are the heart, if not the soul, of a law library. Statutory law, administrative law, and case law are all the result of governmental action even though the printed documentation of that action may be distributed by commercial publishers. Primary material such as statutes and court reports will be acquired by any law library whether or not it has an active documents program. Secondary materials such as annual reports and legislative studies are found in the best law libraries.

Acquisition Policy

In the Charles B. Sears Law Library the Documents Department assists in the acquisition of primary materials when those materials are not available through a vendor, but its main function is to seek out and acquire the secondary materials which are only available from government agencies directly. The collection of such documents enhances the ability of the Law Library to support the research and educational programs of the Law School and in particular the State and Local government program, the Sea Grant Program, the Buffalo Legislation Project, and the Buffalo Law Review.

As a federal depository we are required to make our documents accessible to the general public, but we are not obligated to tailor our selections to meet the needs or tastes of the general public. Our clientele includes the entire university community since we have collections such as New York Legislative Documents and United Nations materials, which are unique within the library system. Because we have a $10,000 budget for buying documents we attempt to satisfy *any* special request which is brought to our attention.

Individual documents are routinely selected when they fall within the subject parameters of the Law Library collection: state and local government, constitutional law, environmental law, coastal zone management, medical/ethical issues, school law, labor law, arbitration, negotiation, commercial law, taxation, criminal justice, family law, legal history, social issues, government regulation, administrative law, economic issues, human rights, comparative law, international law, multinational corporations and Canadian and English legal issues. Particular care is taken to acquire those materials which lend themselves to the study of legislative history Every subject has legal aspects; no subject is, per se, outside the scope of the collection.

The following sources are regularly perused for items to be ordered:

> Depository Shipping Lists
> New York State Checklist
> Monthly Checklist of State Publications
> State Government Research Checklist
> Recent Publications on Governmental Problems
> IBID
> CALL Newsletter

In addition we have depository arrangements with the federal government and New York State, and maintain a comprehensive standing order for United Nations publications.

Processing

Bibliographic control over documents is maintained through the kardex for continuations and through the order file for monographs. The kardex contains 2,005 active titles but we have a backlog of 12 linear feet of documents which need to be added to the file. The order file contains one card for every monograph received since 1976, arranged by issuing agency

Location and Cataloging Policy

Government documents are located throughout the library. Approximately 65% of the document kardex items are routed to the stacks after check-in. A few cataloged sets are located on the 5th floor in the Documents Department so users will be near other legislative history materials. These sets are the *Congressional Record*, the New York Legislative Documents, the New York Senate and Assembly Journals and the New York State Bills. The size of the cataloged collection on the 5th floor is 5,086 bound volumes and 690 unbound issues.

New continuations and monographs are sent to cataloging as the workload there permits. Documents relating to the Sea Grant program have the highest priority for cataloging, followed by State and Local Government materials. Lower priority documents and ephemeral materials are kept in the Documents Department on the 5th and 6th floors of the library.

Uncataloged documents are of the following types:

A) voluminous series which are self arranging by numbers printed on them—examples are bills, congressional committee reports, and UN mimeographed documents.
B) documents from a jurisdiction with a recognized classification scheme such as the United States, New York State, Canada, and the United Nations.
C) miscellaneous documents from other jurisdictions, primarily the other states, Canadian provinces, local governments and international organizations.

Type C, the miscellaneous documents, need to be cataloged to provide adequate access. The size of this cataloging backlog is 1,066 bound volumes and 18,673 unbound documents. Since Type B documents can be found through indexes and checklists, cataloging is not so crucial. The size of the Type B collection is 2,435 bound volumes and 48,462 unbound documents.

Public Service Policy

Reference service for documents is provided by the Reference Librarian on duty at the 2nd floor Reference Desk, Monday-Thursday 9-9 and Friday-Saturday 9-5. The Documents Department on the 5th floor is staffed by two clerks and a technical assistant (.85 FTE) during regular working hours and by student assistants in the evening from 5-9 and on Saturdays from 9-5. The Documents Librarian is available for reference assistance 13 hours per week.

A "New Acquisitions List" is prepared and distributed on a monthly basis. Unbound documents circulate. Bound volumes do not.

Depository Policy

The Law Library became a federal depository in January 1979. At last count we had selected 723 (17.8%) of the 4,055 items available. Some of the items were selected for and are routed to the Undergraduate Library (72 items) or other libraries on campus (9 items). We do not select congressional hearings because we lack the space to store them. Instead, we subscribe to the CIS microfiche which serves as a backup for Lockwood's hardcopy collection.

Depository publications are treated in the same manner as non-depository publications. Some are integrated into the cataloged collection and others are arranged by SuDoc number in the Documents Collection. We do maintain two additional files for depository monographs—one file by title and one by SuDoc number. We use the depository system to obtain documents we would acquire anyway. We rely on Lockwood Documents to provide the comprehensive federal document collection for the University.

The New York State depository program is rather rudimentary. We receive approximately 50 documents per year automatically, just the double starred items on the Checklist. Anything else we must order, usually from the agency. Here again we rely on Lockwood Documents to have the comprehensive collection of New York State Documents although the Law Library has the most extensive collection of legislative materials, including the bound volumes of Bills.

NOTES

1. The policy statement for Charles B. Sears Law Library, State University of New York ar Buffalo, was supplied by Karen F. Smith, documents librarian.
2. This policy statement was also developed at the Charles B. Sears Law Library. The two policy statements for this library, reported here, were written at different times and for somewhat different purposes. Still, they complement each other.

UNITED STATES

	Copies	Classifi- cation	Responsi- bility	Cost	Format
Primary Material					
Statutes at Large	1)Tan	Law	Docs	Deposit	paper
	2)Tan	"	"	$50/vol	paper
U.S. Code	1)Tan	Law	Acq	$20/vol	paper
	2)Red	"	Docs	Deposit	paper
Journals	none				
Federal Register	1)Tan	Law	Docs	Deposit	paper
	2)Red	"	"	$50/yr	paper
	3rd	"	Acq	$200/yr	fiche
CFR	1)Tan	Law	Docs	Deposit	paper
	2)Red	"	"	$450/yr	paper
	3rd	"	Acq		film
U.S. Reports	1)Blue	Law	Acq	$15/vol	paper
	2)Red	"	"	"	paper
	3)Blue	"	Docs	Deposit	paper

	Copies	Classifi- cation	Responsi- bility	Cost	Format
U.S. Reports	1)Yellow	Law	Docs	Deposit	paper
(Preliminary)	2)Red	"	"	$50/yr	paper
	3)Yellow	"	"	"	paper
Secondary Material					
Bills	1)Wine	VF	Docs	Deposit	paper
Slip Laws	1)Yellow	VF	Docs	Deposit	paper
Committee Reports	1)Wine	SuDoc	Docs	Deposit	paper
	2)Wine	SuDoc	"	"	paper
Reports Documents CIS Hearings Prints	1st	Law	Acq	$2,750	fiche
Congressional Record Daily edition	1)Wine 1)Wine	Law "	Docs "	Deposit "	paper paper
agency decisions, annual reports, basic reference material, indexes, periodicals	one	Law	Docs	Deposit	paper + fiche
regulatory agencies, looseleafs, presidential material, miscellaneous docs	one	mixed	Docs	Deposit	paper

NEW YORK

	Copies	Classifi- cation	Responsi- bility	Cost	Format
Primary Material					
Laws of New York	1)Blue	Law	Docs	Deposit	paper
	2)Blue	"	"	LML	paper
	3)Tan	"	"	gift	paper
	4)Tan	"	"	"	paper
Local Laws...	1)Tan	Law	Docs	Deposit	paper
	2)Red	"	"	LML	paper

Copies	Classifi-cation	Responsi-bility	Cost	Format
3)Wine	"	"	gift	paper
one	"	"	$75/yr	film
compiled laws	seven	"	Acq		paper
NYCRR	two	Law	Acq		paper
NYS Register	1)Yellow	Law	Docs	$40/yr	paper
New York Reports	three	Law	Acq		paper
Appellate Reports	three	Law	Acq		paper
Miscellaneous	three	Law	Acq		paper
Senate Journal	1)Wine	Law	Docs	Deposit	paper
Assembly Journal	1)Wine	Law	Docs	Deposit	paper
Attorney General	1)Tan	Law	Docs	Deposit	paper
Opinions	2)Red	"	"	$10/vol	paper
	3)Tan	"	"	"	paper

Secondary Material

	Copies	Classifi-cation	Responsi-bility	Cost	Format
Bills	1)Wine	VF	Docs	$469/yr	paper
Legislative Manual	1)Blue	Law	Docs	Deposit	paper
	2)Wine	"	"	$10/vol	paper
Legislative Documents	1)Wine	Law	Docs	Deposit	paper
Bill Jackets	one	Law	Acq		fiche
NYS Checklist	1)Wine	Law	Docs	Deposit	paper
	2)Blue	"	"	Gift	paper
agency decisions,	1)Brown	Law	Docs	Deposit	paper
gubernatorial material,				+ Gift	
annual reports					
legislative committee	one	NY	Docs	Deposit	paper
reports, miscellaneous docs				+ Gift	paper

OTHER STATES

	Copies	Classifi-cation	Responsi-bility	Cost	Format
Primary Material					
...ession laws	all	Law	Acq		micro
...ompiled laws	all	Law	Acq		paper
...ules & regs	some	Law	Acq		paper
...ourt reports	all	Law	Acq		paper
...egislative journals	none				
...ttorney General	all	Law	mixed		paper
Secondary Material					
...ills	none				
...egislative manuals	all	Law	Docs		paper
...egislative studies	some	mixed	Docs		paper
...hecklists	all	Law	Docs		mixed
...nnual reports	some	mixed	Docs		paper
...iscellaneous docs	all	mixed	Docs		paper

CANADA

	Copies	Classifi-cation	Responsi-bility	Cost	Format
Primary Material					
...tatutes of Canada	1)Grey	Law	Docs	LML	paper
...anada Gazette	one		Docs	LML	paper
...ederal Court Reports	1)Grey	Law	Docs	LML	paper
...upreme Court Reports	1)Grey	Law	Docs	LML	paper

	Copies	Classification	Responsibility	Cost	Format
Dominion Law Reports	1)Grey	Law	Acq		paper
Statutory Orders & Regulations	none				
Secondary Material					
Bills	no longer receiving				
Debates of the House of Commons & Senate	no longer receiving				
Canadiana	no longer receiving				
Treaty Series	one	Can	Docs	LML	paper
Canadian Government Publications	one	none	Docs	$24/yr	paper
miscellaneous docs	one	Can	Docs		paper

CANADIAN PROVINCES

	Copies	Classification	Responsibility	Cost	Format
Primary Material					
Ontario Revised Statutes					
Ontario Revised Regulations	1)grey	Law	Docs	$40	paper
Ontario Gazette	1)Grey	Law	Docs	$30/yr	paper
Ontario Reports	1)Grey	Law	Acq		paper
Secondary Material					
catalogs	one	none	Docs		paper
miscellaneous docs	one	none	Docs		paper

GREAT BRITAIN

	Copies	Classifi-cation	Responsi-bility	Cost	Format
Primary Material					
Halsbury's Laws of England		Law	Acq		paper
Halsbury's Statutes		Law	Acq		paper
Statutory Instruments		Law	Acq		paper
All England Law Reports		Law	Acq		paper
Secondary Material					
Bills	none				
Parliamentary Debates	none				
Command Papers	one	none	mixed	$ 800	paper
House of Commons Papers	one	none	mixed	$2000	paper
House of Lords Papers	none				
Treaty Series	one	Law	mixed	$ 150	paper
Government Publications	one	none	mixed		paper
Miscellaneous docs	one	mixed	Docs		paper

UNITED NATIONS

	Classifi-cation	Responsi-bility	Cost	Format
Standing Order				
Mimeographed Documents	UN-VF	Docs	$ 350	paper
General Publications	UN	Docs	$ 204	paper
Economic Publications	UN	Docs	$ 593	paper

	Classification	Responsibility	Cost	Format
Social Publications	UN	Docs	$ 45	paper
International Law	UN	Docs	$ 119	paper
Political and Security Council	UN	Docs	$ 14	paper
Transport and Communications	UN	Docs	$ 25	paper
Disarmament	UN	Docs	$ 19	paper
Narcotic Drugs	UN	Docs	$ 26	paper
Demography	UN	Docs	$ 108	paper
Human Rights	UN	Docs	$ 19	paper
Unitar Studies	UN	Docs	$ 22	paper
Public Finance	UN	Docs	$ 9	paper
International Statistics	UN	Docs	$ 278	paper
Treaty Series	Law	Docs	$ 120	paper
Official Records	none	Docs	$ 824	paper

Subscriptions

UNDOC	UN	Docs	$ 80	paper
UN Monthly Chronicle	none	Docs	$ 10	paper
Objective Justice		Docs	$ 3	paper
Bulletin on Narcotics		Docs	$ 10	paper
Population & Vital Statistics		Docs	$ 10	paper
Monthly Bibliography:Articles		Docs	$ 12	paper
Current Bibliographical Info		Docs	$ 20	paper

Monthly Bulletin of Statistics	not subscribing
Commodity Trade Statistics	not subscribing
Statistical Indicators...	not subscribing
Industrial Research...	not subscribing
Monthly Bibliography:Books	not subscribing

MICROPRINT (Readex)	Acq	$1200	micro

INTERNATIONAL ORGANIZATIONS

Extensive Collection

International Court of Justice (ICJ)
Organization of American States (OAS)
Council of Europe
International Labour Office (ILO)

Selective Collection

General Agreement on Tarriffs and Trade (GATT)
International Atomic Energy Agency (IAEA)
International Civil Aviation Organization (ICAO)
International Red Cross
International Monetary Fund (IMF)
Organization for Economic Cooperation and Development (OECD)
UNESCO
UNITAR
World Bank
World Intellectual Property Organization (WIPO)
etc.

LOCAL DOCUMENTS

Buffalo

City Court Annual Report
Budget
Report of the Comptroller

Erie County

Budget
Administrative Code
Charter

Other NYS Counties

Charters

ASSOCIATIONS

	Responsibility
American Enterprise Institute	Docs
American Judicature Society	Acq
American Society of Planning Officials	Acq
Council of State Governments	Docs

International Association of Chiefs of Police	Docs?
International Commission of Jurists	Acq + Docs
National Center for State Courts	Acq
National District Attorneys Association	Acq
National Association of Attorneys General	Docs
National Institute of Municipal Law Officers	Acq
National Organization on Legal Problems of Education	Acq
NTIS	Docs
Regional Planning Council	Acq?
Urban Institute	Acq
World Peace Through Law Center	Acq?
Association of Family Conciliation Courts	Docs
Legal Services Corporation	Docs
Merriam Center Library	Docs
Society for the Right to Die	Docs
Vance Bibliographies	Docs

V. SELECTION POLICY FOR GOVERNMENT DOCUMENTS: KEARNEY STATE COLLEGE[1]

Federal Documents

As a selective depository library for Federal Documents it shall be the policy of the Documents Department in the Kearney State College Library to select materials which will: (1) support the curriculum needs of the college; (2) serve the students, faculty, and administrators of the college; and (3) serve the information needs of Nebraskans who desire to utilize Federal documents.

The following areas have been designated by Library Learning Program librarians as needing attention in the selection process:

(1) aging
(2) child abuse
(3) family violence
(4) Geography (Africa, Latin America, and India)
(5) Biology—non technical materials such as guides, surveys, statistics, directories, etc.

(6) Special Education

    (a) mental retardation
    (b) the gifted

(c) education of the handicapped
(d) learning disabilities
(e) speech correction
(f) vocational adjustment
(g) government programs
(h) job opportunities

(7) Speech and Theatre

(a) speech pathology
(b) annual debate topic
(c) politics and government (current events, trends, reports, etc.)

(8) Hearings and Reports
(9) Statistics
(10) Bibliographies
(11) Directories
(12) Periodicals and Abstracts

(13) Literature

American and British Literature
Children's and Adolescent Literature
Creative Writing
Traditional and Transformational Grammar
Development of English Language
Rhetorical Devices
Popular Literature
Literature of Africa and the American Negro

(14) Health and Medicine
(15) Census Materials

In addition to the above designated areas which support the curriculum at Kearney State College, materials must also be selected which will support the information needs of community and area-wide users.

Nebraska Documents

State Documents should be selected which will support the curriculum at Kearney State and serve the information needs of students, faculty, and administrators. Documents should also be selected which will serve the information needs of community and area-wide users.

NOTE

1. Collection development policy for the government document collection at Calvin T. Ryan Library, Kearney State College, Kearney, Nebraska. The statement was supplied by Diana J. Keith, Head, Government Documents Section.

VI. SELECTION AND RETENTION OF U.S. GOVERNMENT DOCUMENTS: UNIVERSITY OF IOWA[1]

The current procedure for selection of depository publications involves the collective opinion of the Documents Librarian, the Technical Services Librarian, the Associate Law Librarian, and the Library Director. Selection criteria are purposefully broad, and publications are chosen whenever they seem to have potential value for our users.

Because the selection policy *is* broad, however, evaluation of documents material is a necessary step in maintaining a viable collection. Further reasons that evaluation is necessary include:

1. Requirements of depository status. As stated in the INSTRUCTIONS TO DEPOSITORY LIBRARIES: "All selections should be reviewed *once a year* to determine whether the library is receiving material which is not being used and to eliminate wasteful use of taxpayers' money and unnecessary costs to the Federal Government in supplying material which is not needed." (Emphasis theirs.)

2. The current system of depository distribution. Often "low priority" publications are received on the same Item number as "high priority" publications.

3. Availability and automatic receipt of free material. Since most governmental publications are free, we are able to acquire materials of an ephemeral nature which have topical or current interest, but which do not have permanent research value.

4. Lack of essential information at the time of selection. It is often very difficult to accurately determine the nature and value of the material before it is received.

Evaluation of publications has a positive and a negative component. The current criteria for retention of publications include:

1. The material could be cited in the legal literature.
2. The subject is of particular interest to our geographic area, or is one which a law professor may wish to research.
3. Tools are available which enable retrieval of the subject matter.

4. The publication is an annual report of a major, regulatory, or judicial agency.

On the negative side, the following will be reasons for not retaining documents material:

1. The publication is a superseded edition of a document and is not likely to be cited; or the material is covered satisfactorily in other publications (e.g., regulations in the *CFR*)
2. The publication is ephemeral in nature (leaflets, flyers, etc.)
3. The material is very technical in a non-law subject.
4. The publication is an isolated issue of a serial which we are not likely to fill in.

Acquiring Non-Depository U.S. Government Documents (Revised 1980)

The Documents Department attempts to acquire publications needed by our collection but not available through the depository distribution system. Particularly, requests from our patrons will be honored and given prompt attention. The following are the means by which we currently acquire non-depository materials:

GPO Sales Department Orders. The Library will maintain a GPO deposit account to facilitate payment for GPO sales materials. The balance of this account will be kept at a minimum of $800. When the Documents Assistant notes that our balance is approaching $800, the Acquisitions Librarian will be notified to transfer funds to the GPO Account. One thousand five hundred dollars ($1500) will be the usual amount transferred. (The above guidelines may vary according to budget considerations.)

Departmental Orders for Monographs. The Documents Department will request publications from the issuing agency when the order information indicates the document is not GPO sales stock. Ordinarily the Documents Department will send the initial request, even if a price is indicated. Special departmental order forms will be used for such requests. If the publication is subsequently received with an invoice, it will be given to Acquisitions for payment. If the issuing agency returns the order with a request for prepayment, the order will be turned over to Acquisitions which will reorder the publication via a purchase order. Information necessary for processing the publication will be transferred to the purchase order from the original order slip (e.g., SUDOCS no., proof slip, routing information, etc.). The purchase order should indicate that the publication be sent to the Documents Department for processing.

NTIS Deposit Account.   The library will maintain an NTIS (National Technical Information Service) deposit account and, as with the GPO accounts, orders will be sent directly from the Government Documents Department to NTIS. The balance of this account will be kept at a minimum of $250. When the Documents Assistant notes that our balance is approaching $250, the Acquisitions Librarian will be notified to transfer funds to the NTIS Account. Two hundred fifty dollars ($250) will be the usual amount transferred. (The above guidelines may vary according to budget considerations.) Document purchases should be recorded as account material. "NTIS" in parentheses should be written after the receiving date.

Departmental Orders for Serials.   Serial publications will be ordered from the issuing agency when there is reason to believe the publication is free. The order will request that the mailing label read: "Attn: Gov. Docs.," and the material thus received will be checked in as any other document. If the issuing agency indicates a charge for the subscription, the following procedure will be used:

The Acquisitions Department will initiate a purchase order.

The agency will be requested to send the material to the Law Library (rather than to the Gov. Docs. Department).

The title will be fully cataloged and entered on serials kardex. Materials subsequently received will be checked in and paid for on kardex as with other library subscriptions.

Examples of serial documents received in the above manner include:

U.S. Court of Claims. Cases decided. Slip opinions.

NOTE

1.   These guidelines for the Law Library, the University of Iowa, Iowa City, were supplied by Sandra B. Lockett, government documents librarian.

VII. COLLECTION DEVELOPMENT POLICY STATEMENT: STANFORD UNIVERSITY[1]

U.S. Government Documents

I. Programmatic Information and Collection Description

The U.S. Federal Collection includes depository and non-depository titles printed by the Government by the Government Printing Office.

Stanford has been a complete depository library since 1895 except for the category "charts;" other categories were "deselected" in 1976 including the monthly periodicals from the military branches (Defense Dept.), the Defense Department's *Cataloging handbook series, Military standards, FIIG series* (loose-leaf), and the Civil Service Commission's *Federal Personnel Manual.* All of the "deselected" material is generally not used by the Stanford community but by the general public using the Government Documents Dept. It is available on interlibrary loan from the Regional Depository Library in Sacramento. Most items offered are selected, including the new area of microfiche representing materials not available in paper.

Since 1953 a private publishing company has made the non-depository items listed in the *Monthly Catalog* available on microprint. Stanford has purchased this set, and the collection has everything listed in the *Monthly Catalog* in paper copy or in microprint.

II. Coordination and Cooperative Information

Berkeley Government Documents Dept.
Africana Curator, Hoover Institution
Law Library
Lane Library (mostly weeding contact to insure that one remains on the Stanford campus)
Lackson Library (" " " " ")
U.S. History, Political Science, and Communication bibliographers
Meyer Library
Central Map Room
Special Collections (some federal documents housed there but others of value in department)
Engineering Library
Branner Earth Sciences
Government Documents Dept., other collections (mostly state/local)

III. Types of Material and Format

The Depository item selection is collection rather than program driven
The Bibliographer actively selects non-depository materials emphasizing
the following areas:

> statistics
> census publications
> guidelines
> bibliographies, lists
> directories, telephone books, government organization guides
> annual report (administrative)
> decisions, reports, opinions
> diplomatic reports
> commercial publications for reference use

The Bibliographer does not collect:

> reports done on contract or grant from the federal government
> (usually NTIS)
> patents (only the abstracts)
> working papers (unless collected in volumes and sent on depository),
> maps, tapes, recordings (spoken, music); film (sound, motion)

IV. Publication Date

Since the basic collection is complete, collecting is of current imprints
unless unpublished material is made available on microform. This would
include the National Archives and Records Service filming of State Department records, and also commercial publishing on microform of previously classified materials.

V. Special Considerations

Four indexes issued for various periods of publishing offer access to
the collection. The index to current publications is the *Monthly Catalog of
U.S. Government Publications.*

The 1895 Printing Act established the Government Printing Office to
centralize government printing, but complete centralization has not been
the course. If anything, the volume printed outside of the G.P.O. had
increased and has become harder to detect. Furthermore, a document
does not have to be printed by the U.S. Government to be considered a
government document. The largest area of non-G.P.O. materials is the
publishing by the National Technical Information Service (NTIS), part
of the Department of Commerce. These publications represent work

done on grant or contract requiring publication of a report. These reports are issued in an overwhelming number with little information as to quality for a library's review. There is no library in the State of California subscribing to the whole output although the State Library does receive three categories in microfiche and makes them available on interlibrary loan.

VI.   Collecting Levels by Agency*

Congress	A
Agriculature Dept.	A
Commerce Dept.	A
Defense Dept.	B
Energy Dept.	B
Health Education and Welfare Dept.	A
Housing and Urban Development Dept.	B
Interior Dept.	A
Justice Dept.	B
Labor Dept.	A
State Dept. (except AID C)	A
Treasury Dept.	A
Transportation Dept.	C
Civil Rights Commission	A
Civil Service Commission	B
Federal Communications Commission	C
Federal Reserve Board	C
Library of Congress	B
NASA	B
National Archives and Records Service	B
Presidential	A
National Academy of Science	D
National Science Foundation	D
Securities and Exchange Commission	C
Small Business Administration	A
Smithsonian Institution	D
Central Intelligence Agency	A

*Shows no breakdown within the executive departments; some subagencies may be strong, others not.

State and Local Documents

I.   Programmatic Information

This collection is both program and collection driven. Because of the depository status for California documents, no attempt is made to restrict acquisition of materials which conform to the subject areas included in academic programs at Stanford. Instead, an attempt at completeness is made, not from the standpoint of subject, but from the standpoint of the available published output of the executive and legislative branches of the State Government. This means, for example, that we attempt to acquire all of the agricultural publications of the State although Stanford has no agricultural program.

Acquisition of documents from city, county, regional, state, and interstate agencies in the United States and Puerto Rico focuses on the demonstrated research and academic program needs. While certain subjects and forms of material are collected from most of the states, e.g., statistical abstracts and the governors' budgets, there is generally a conscious selectivity in the range of documents collected outside the boundaries of the state publications from California. Publications of some state, regional, interstate, and standard metropolitan statistical areas (SMSA's) are of more interest to Stanford than publications of others. See Section III 'Geographical.'

In general, the collection provides research material for the History Department and social sciences departments, and for coursework in the natural sciences and Engineering focussing on planning materials. The School of Law and the Graduate School of Business also depend on this collection.

II.   Coordination and Cooperative Information

Because of the subject range of government publications, they are of interest to many bibliographers, especially the bibliographers for Education, Engineering, Political Science, and U.S. History. The Bibliographer consults with the U.S. Federal Bibliographer over filling gaps in range and frequency of statistical publications at the national and state level, and to sort out categories of publications such as state coastal plans, which are either jointly published by the federal government or state government, or parts of which are published by the state and federal governments separately. The Bibliographer depends upon the Manuscripts Division of the Special Collections Department for a variety of state collections, including farm labor manuscripts and the papers of several important California political figures. The Hoover Institution also collects archival material of interest, such as the papers of Governor Reagan.

Cubberley Education Library receives most first copies of the California Department of Education publications through the State Documents Unit. Other state and local publications which are devoted to important education topics other than curriculum materials are selected by the

State Documents Librarian for review by the Education Bibliographer. Cubberley also depends on State Documents Unit for acquisition of county and state education directories.

Publications on water, energy, planning, and other engineering topics are selected for review by the Engineering Bibliographer. Refinement of subject and geographical areas selected for coverage by Engineering and a policy for coordination of acquisition of planning materials are matters which need to be addressed in the near future.

State Geological Survey publications and Bureau of Mines publications are ordered and claimed through the State Documents Unit by Branner Earth Sciences Library. Publications which list possible survey and mines publications are forwarded to Branner Library by the State Documents Librarian. Gradual reduction of standing orders for Geological Survey publications and demand for pre-payment of each item ordered have necessitated more stringent recordkeeping and more correspondence between the State Documents Unit, Branner, the State geological surveys, and the Business Services Department of the University Libraries in order to adequately serve Branner's needs.

The Law Library and the State Documents Librarian agree that Law collects city charters, state constitutions, constitutional conventions, state laws, and the *California Administrative Code*. In turn, the State Documents Unit collects the California statutes, bills, and other legislative material heavily used to trace legislative history and intent. Law often agrees to share the expense of acquiring retrospective State publications such as California bills and early State publications in microform.

There is informal coordination with the Graduate School of Business. Jackson Library maintains banking, finance, and manufacturers material as well as current annual reports and statistical compilations from selected state agencies. Jackson relies (it appears) upon the State Documents Bibliographer for maintenance of historical runs of annual reports and statistical compilations. The State Documents collection will benefit from a more fully developed cooperative program with the Documents Librarian at Jackson Library.

The Bibliographer contacts State Documents Librarian at Berkeley for borrowing California publications issued prior to 1968 not at Stanford. Berkeley also has a strong collection from other states up to about 1976 when its collections became more selective. Berkeley does not collect local documents, and both Stanford and Berkeley consider the Institute of Governmental Studies a resource for local documents not held at Stanford.

III.   Subject and Language Modifiers

> *Language*: English is the primary language with some publications from California and the Southwestern states in Spanish.

Geographical: The 50 states and Puerto Rico are represented in the collection and the geographical priorities are the following. California is of first importance. Hawaii, Alaska, Washington, Oregon, Arizona, New Mexico, and Texas are next; followed by Idaho, Utah, Wyoming, Montana, Colorado, New York, Nevada, Illinois, and Florida; followed by Pennsylvania, New Jersey, Michigan, Ohio, Puerto Rico, and Massachusetts. All remaining states receive the least emphasis.

Below the state level, first importance is given to Santa Clara County and then the remaining eight Bay Area Counties, major cities within the Bay Area, particularly Oakland, San Francisco, Palo Alto and San Jose, and regional agencies which cross the Bay Area county lines, such as the Association of Bay Area Governments (ABAG). Next, attention is given to other major SMSA's in California, e.g., Los Angeles and San Diego, and areas within California which engage in trendsetting activities, such as the current conflict of planning interest in the tiny Chinese community of Locke by Sacramento County, the State of California, and foreign investment interests.

Government documents are collected from 33 SMSA's of 1 million persons or more. Six of these are in California and are fairly well represented in the collection. It has proven impossible to collect documents consistently and in a representative manner from the remaining 27 SMSA's. In addition, some of the SMSA's are of lesser importance than others to the academic and research needs of Stanford.

Selected interstate agencies are also represented in the State and Local collection. These agencies' publications are usually devoted to specific subject areas such as transportation or energy, and the agencies usually have several important SMSA's under their umbrellas. One interstate organization, the Council of State Governments, is particularly well represented because its publications pull together comparative data from all of the states on the most important contemporary political issues.

IV. Description of Materials Collected

Types of Material and Format: Agencies at the state and local level publish according to their own needs and interests; consequently, a wide range of subjects and audiences are included in these government documents. The bibliographer acquires those publications which trace the evolution of the agency itself, such as minutes of meetings, news releases, annual reports, publication lists, and annual budgets. Next, the Bibliographer tries to acquire statistical compilations which are indicators of a wide variety of historical changes in the human environment. The Bibliographer acquires current directory information from agencies at the state and local level and collects from all states' current blue books and other publications which indicate the organization of government at the state level. Documents which chronicle the passage of legislation in California, election results and demographic studies from all of the states, and substantive documents from states and localities which address issues of national significance are collected. State, regional and city planning materials including general development plans, land use and recreation, housing and urban renewal, and general transportation plans are acquired (see geographic priorities, Section III).

Excluded are agricultural documents from states other than California, and all documents mentioned above collected by the Law and Business libraries. An attempt is made to avoid documents which appear to be more appropriate for Lane Medical Library. University and college publications are not selected unless the topic covered is useful for reference purposes.

The collection includes monographs, monographic series, and serials, printed materials, processed materials, and microforms.

Publication Date: Emphasis is on current materials. Retrospective materials are actively sought to strengthen the California State collection and to cover some categories of early local California publications such as Board of Education and planning documents. Close attention is not given to purchasing individual retrospective items for states other than California (except through cooperative efforts with the History Bibliographer and the Social Sciences Curator).

V.   Special Considerations

Poor bibliographic control and limited publication runs from most agencies are chronic problems. Some documents are never published in sufficient number to be sent to depository libraries or other libraries interested in their acquisition. Consequently, documents must be promptly ordered because they are soon out of print. Few agencies keep a library on a mailing list and standing orders are uncommon. Agencies also tend to change publication titles, alter their frequency, or discontinue them. Furthermore, frequent reorganization of the executive branches of state governments results in frequent changes in agency names and the types of publications they produce.

Cooperative research and publication between state and local agencies and the U.S. federal government necessitates frequent consultation with the U.S. Federal Librarian to cover all possible publication sources for important state and local issues.

VI. Conspectus of Field and Levels of Collecting

California—depository documents	A
California—non-depository documents	B
Alaska	C
Washington	C
Oregon	C
Hawaii	C
Arizona	C
New Mexico	C
Texas	C
Idaho	C/D
Utah	C/D
Nevada	C/D
Colorado	C/D
Wyoming	C/D
Montana	C/D
Illinois	C/D
New York	C/D
Florida	C/D
Pennsylvania	D
Michigan	D
Ohio	D
New Jersey	D
Massachusetts	D
Puerto Rico	D
North Dakota	E
South Dakota	E
Nebraska	E
Kansas	E
Oklahoma	E
Minnesota	E

Iowa	E
Missouri	E
Arkansas	E
Wisconsin	E
Indiana	E
Kentucky	E
Tennessee	E
Maine	E
New Hampshire	E
Vermont	E
Connecticut	E
Rhode Island	E
Delaware	E
Maryland	E
West Virginia	E
Virginia	E
North Carolina	E
South Carolina	E
Georgia	E
Alabama	E
Mississippi	E
Louisiana	E

Interstate, Regional, County, and City Conspectus

	Collecting Level
Bay Area Counties:	
Marin	C
Contra Costa	C
Napa	C
Sonoma	C
Alameda	C
San Francisco	C
San Mateo	C
Santa Clara	B
Santa Cruz	C
Other California Counties:	D
Major Bay Area Cities:	C

California SMSA's of 1 Million Persons or More:

San Francisco-Oakland	C
San Jose	C
San Diego	D
Anaheim-Santa Ana-Garden Grove	D
Los Angeles	D
San Bernardino-Riverside-Ontario	D

Regional Organizations in the Bay Area:	C
Regional Organizations in California Excluding the Bay Area:	E
Counties in States Other Than California:	E
SMSA's of 1 Million Persons or More Outside California:	E
Regional Organizations in States Other Than California:	E
Interstate Organizations:	E

International Documents

I.   Programmatic Information

The Bibliographer for International Documents acquires publications prepared, issued, or sponsored by international governmental organizations that meet the teaching and research needs of Stanford University. A secondary objective is to acquire and maintain as complete collections as possible for major agencies that have designated Stanford as a depository library (e.g., the United Nations) or that supply all publications through blanket standing orders (e.g., UNESCO, the Organization of American States, the Organization for Economic Cooperation and Development). The collection is heavily used by social science departments and, to a lesser degree, by the sciences and School of Engineering, and by the faculty, research staff, and students of the Law School, the Graduate School of Business, the Hoover Institution, and the Food Research Institute.

II.   Coordination and Cooperative Information

The Bibliographer has primary responsibility for those documents issued by international governmental agencies that define and chronicle agency activities or that are of reference or general interest. Non-government publications that describe the agencies or facilitate access to their documents are also acquired. Acquisition is coordinated with the subject and language bibliographers, especially the Social Sciences and

Latin American curators, bibliographers in the General Reference Department, and bibliographers for the sciences, engineering, and education. Because many international documents are acquired as gifts or through exchange agreements, there is ongoing coordination with the Gifts and Exchange Librarian.

International documents are heavily used by the primary clientele of many coordinate libraries, therefore cooperation between the International Documents Bibliographer and bibliographers in those libraries is essential. There is a great deal of interaction with the Food Research Institute librarian, and many international documents (including the primary collection of FAO documents) are housed in the FRI Library. The Hoover Institution maintains the League of Nations collection, the depository collection of European Communities documents, the primary collection of Council of Europe documents, and the economic and political documents of NATO. Over the years, some Hoover documents (e.g., International Labor Organization publications) more appropriate to the University Libraries collection have been transferred to the Government Documents Department from Hoover. There is ongoing coordination with the Hoover Curator for Western Europe and the African Curator. The Government Documents Department collects heavily in areas that are of interest to the Jackson Library, such as development bank publications, economics, trade, and labor. The International Documents Bibliographer and Jackson bibliographers consult on major purchases or on areas in which duplication seems imminent and undesirable. The Lane Library has Stanford's global standing order for World Health Organization documents. The International Documents bibliographer acquires selective publications of the WHO and collects health and nutrition publications of other agencies that are needed to support undergraduate and graduate study.

Outside Stanford, primary coordination is with the international documents librarians at U.C. Berkeley and U.C. Davis. U.C. Berkeley and Stanford consult on expensive items that can be shared by researchers at the two institutions. U.C. Davis has northern California's comprehensive collection of FAO documents.

III. Subject and Language Modifiers

Geographical: There are no geographical limitations.

Chronological: The collection is basically a twentieth century one as most international organizations were established after 1900.

Language: English is the primary language but other Western languages are also collected. When an agency publishes in more than one language, English is preferred. Oriental and Middle Eastern languages are not collected.

IV. Description of Materials Collected

Types of Material and Format: Materials as diverse as the interests of the agencies are collected. Emphases: documents that record the activities of the agency (annual reports, minutes of meetings, resolutions, official statements, agreements, conference proceedings, budgets); bibliographies and publications lists; statistical compilations; substantial publications on a variety of subjects including international relations, economics, demography, science and technology, history, agricultural development, education, art, literature, and music.

V. Special Considerations

International documents are generally published in small editions and bibliographic control is weak. Often publications that are most valuable for researchers are not "published" or included in publications lists but are written for and circulated among individuals working on agency projects. These are difficult to learn about and acquire. Other "documents" are published and distributed by commercial publishers. These pose a challenge to Stanford's definition of "government document" and to a clear assignment of responsibility for collecting them.

There is a growing tendency for more than one international agency or an international agency and one or more national governments to cooperate on research and publications. This complicates both acquisition and the provision of adequate bibliographic access. There is a trend in the United Nations for publications to be issued by regional commissions or sub-committees within the U.N. in order to avoid red tape and budgetary control. These publications are not included in U.N. publications lists, are not assigned U.N. classification numbers, and are not available from or recognized by the Headquarters Sales office. These are not distributed to depository libraries and must be acquired from the office that issued them.

VI. Conspectus of Field and Level of Collecting

Asian Productivity Organization	D	
Commonwealth Agricultural Bureau	D	
Council of Europe	D	(Hoover has primary collectio

European Communities	E	(Hoover is depository)
Food and Agriculture Organization of the United Nations	D	(FRI has primary collection)
Institute for Latin American Integration	C	
Inter-American Development Bank	C	
Inter-Governmental Maritime Consultative Organization	C	
International Atomic Energy Agency	C	
International Bank for Reconstruction and Development	C	
International Civil Aviation Organization	C	
International Labor Organization	C	
International Monetary Fund	C	
International Telecommunication Union	D	
International Union for the Publication of Customs Tariffs	D	
Latin American Free Trade Association	C	
North Atlantic Treaty Organization	D	(SUL collects scientific & technical publications— Hoover, economic & political
Organization for Economic Cooperation and Development	C	
Organization of African Unity	C	
Organization of American States	C	
Organization of the Petroleum Exporting Countries	D	(Publications only in Arabic are not collected)
Pan American Health Organization	C	
Pan American Institute of Geography and History	C	
United Nations	B	(A level for depository items)
United Nations Education, Scientific and Cultural Organization	C	
World Health Organization	D	(Lane has blanket order)
World Intellectual Property Organization	D	
World Meteorological Organization	D	

Foreign Government Documents

I.   Programmatic Information

Foreign government documents are collected for current information and for long-term research needs; the importance of any title is weighed by the significance of the topic covered in relation to the social, cultural, political or economic position of the specific country or jurisdiction and the research interests of Stanford. Three specific programs are primarily supported regardless of selectors: statistics/economics, demography, and history. Within these areas coordination occurs firstly with the faculty of the Departments and secondly with the bibliographers serving these subject fields. Because of the special nature of the British document collections, particularly close ties are maintained with those faculty involved with British studies. The nature of government documents as prime source materials makes them particularly useful to those members of the community doing original research. Selecting them is geared especially with graduate and post graduate needs in mind. Of the three branches of government, executive, legislative, and judicial, primary emphasis is on executive agency publications and secondary emphasis on legislative publications. Legislative documents are collected strongly for Britain, France, Latin America and Australia. Judicial publications are generally excluded, being within the scope of collecting by the Law Library.

II.   Coordination and Cooperative Information

A. Since the collecting of government documents is collecting by provenance, and not by subject or even format, selection responsibilities overlap with the responsibilities of selectors who serve individual programs or formats: in particular, Latin American Studies, Earth Sciences, Economics, Education, History, and Social Sciences. In addition, responsibilities overlap with virtually all other selectors, at one time or another, for governments publish in all fields of endeavor. Collecting by provenance, then, requires a constant coordination with bibliographers, both within the Green Library, including the curatorial staff, and within the coordinate libraries, especially the Western European and African offices of the Hoover Institution, Food Research, and Law. This coordination is needed to insure continuity, rationality, and completeness of resources within larger programs.

B. Coordination with U.C. Berkeley is especially close on expensive purchases and special projects. Stanford assumes the responsibility for major collection of these materials for Great Britain and relies on Berkeley to cover the entire Indian subcontinent and Scandinavia. Stanford purchases only volume 1 (all-union data) of each Indian census, while Berkeley relies on Stanford for Australian state parliamentary materials. Because Berkeley is a partial depository for Canadian federal publications, Stanford collects selectively in that area. Responsibility for collecting Oceania is left with the University of California at Santa Cruz, as well as East/West Center in Hawaii.

II. Subject and Language Modifiers

A. All countries are included except the United States of America. Great Britain, sub-Saharan Africa, and Latin America are the primary countries emphasized. The 'central' European countries (i.e., the central western European countries of Austria, West Germany and Switzerland), and France are the secondary regions emphasized. The English speaking countries of the Irish Isles, Canada, and Australia receive a lesser emphasis but are maintained because of the historic strength of the collections. Slavic countries are collected by the Hoover Institution (except for special needs: Nineteenth century documents, portfolio ministry reports, statistics and archives). Great Britain, sub-Saharan Africa, and Latin America are collected on the national, provincial, regional and municipal levels. Provincial, regional, and municipal documents of all other countries are acquired to meet the requirements of subject areas.

The strongest individual collection is that of Great Britain; *all publications* are collected from the Public Record Office, Historical Manuscripts Commission, Office of Population Census and Surveys, and Parliament. There is strong selective acquisition of other agencies and of microfilm of Public Record Office manuscripts. The latter include primarily the Foreign Office, State Paper Office, Cabinet Office and Prime Minister's Office.

France is collected intensively because its documentation of social and cultural developments is especially thorough and trend-setting. There is in-depth selection of the human and social sciences from La Documentation Francaise; in-depth selection of subjects pertinent to Stanford or the French economy from Institut National de la Statistique et des Etudes Economiques;

in-depth selection of the human sciences from Office de L Recherche Scienteifique et Technique d'Outre Mer; in-dept selection of all titles from Centre National de la Recherch Scientifique; in-depth selection of all publications of Archive Nationales; and selective acquisition of inventories of the dé partments and regions. Regional, departmental, and municipa publications are collected selectively to provide a more loca perspective of developments.

Latin America is collected strongly both for the program an because of the strength of the collection. In addition, the gov ernments of Latin America are the driving publishing force i their countries and government documents are probably th most significant molders of society, thought and direction. Th following categories are collected in-depth: publications of th Offices of the Presidents, Planning Agencies, Foreign Relation Ministeries, Statistical Offices, Economic and Finance Ministries and publications on agricultural reform and on development Annual reports of all agencies are collected. For Brazil, specia attention is also given to collecting congressional debates an proceedings, and, to monographic titles generally, especiall from the Instituto de Planjameto Economico e Social. Particu lar emphasis is also placed on titles from Mexico, Argentina and Chile although the general emphasis for all of Latin Amer ica is strong.

Sub-Saharan Africa is especially strong in serial holdings an this collection is actively maintained. Annual reports of all min istries except Justice, which is within the purview of the Law Library, and specific health boards are included. Monographic works are selected when available. Nigerian state publication are emphasized and serve as a cross-section providing a loca perspective. Other countries' state publications are collected with less intensity. Because of the difficulty in securing title from French-speaking sub-Saharan Africa, virtually any item available is selected in order to provide an insight into tha region.

'Central Europe' is collected with concentration on mono graphic works, including voting statistics for the national par liaments, and in West Germany also for the *land* parliaments. This pattern follows generally: national publications for Aus tria, Switzerland and West Germany; state publications for West Germany.

Spain and Italy are collected predominantly for the governments' research agency publications: the Consejo Superior de Investigaciones Cientificas and the Istituto Nazionale di Ricerche. These two countries as well as Portugal will be receiving new emphasis and selecting will be extending to monographic titles which reflect the changing nature of society and government. Serial publications will be emphasized somewhat less.

Australia is collected to maintain a historically strong collection, particularly parliamentary materials, serials, and, to a lesser degree, monographs. The states with historic strength in the library are maintained at a mid level of selection: New South Wales, South Australia, and Queensland.

Hong Kong and Japan are collected as major trade areas of the Pacific. Virtually all publications in the Government Information Services catalog of Hong Kong are acquired, except laws and regulations. All white papers of Japan are collected if in a western language.

East European countries are collected selectively with input from the Slavic and East European curator's office because of the difficult official bibliography. Government archives are of especial importance.

For all countries the prime area of collecting is statistical office publications. There is in-depth selection of all subjects pertinent to Stanford or to a specific country's economy.

B. Publications of governmental jurisdictions fall within the scope of the foreign documents collection for the period beginning with the emergence of the modern nation/states at the time of the Enlightenment. The exception to this are the publications of England, France, Spain, and Portugal, which are collected back to the eleventh century.

C. Publications are collected when in a West European or Slavic language. Oriental languages, which are collected by Hoover, and Arabic script documents, which are collected by the University of California at Berkeley, are excluded. Multi-lingual documents are collected when one of the languages is West European or Slavic.

IV.   Description of Materials Collected

A. *Bellas artes* publications from Latin America are excluded when these titles are not from a Ministry of Culture, but merely printed by the official printer. Current official gazettes are excluded except for Brazil; occasionally a short run will be established for particular information, such as Chile during the Allende years. General compilations of law are collected by the Law Library; individual laws are collected as relevant to a particular aspect of a subject.

B. All types and formats of material are collected since governments publish in all areas. These include journals, monographs microform, technical reports, etc.

C. Great Britain, Latin America and sub-Saharan Africa are collected on the current and retrospective levels, particularly but not exclusively with regard to annual reports and other serial titles. Desiderata lists are prepared for out-of-print materials and routed to dealers. 'Central Europe' and France are collected on the current and retrospective levels with regard to statistics, planning and annual reports of government departments. Other subjects are collected on the current level only except as inventories indicate substantial gaps which can be filled with titles still in print. For all other countries, collecting is primarily at the current level.

In all countries except Great Britain, sub-Saharan Africa, and Latin America, publications issued more frequently than annually are not collected if the material has an annual compilation.

V.   Special Considerations

A. Publications of academies; universities; museums; national and public libraries; financial banks; chambers of commerce and industry; communication bodies; operating arms of publicly owned transportation systems; and East European publications other than reports directly from portfolio ministries, from statistical offices, and from archives are excluded. These enumerated bodies are considered non-governmental and are covered by the other selectors.

B. Foreign government documents have perhaps the worst bibliographic control of any type of publication. This varies from region to region, with parts of Europe, Australia, and Canada among the better, and Latin America and Africa among the worst. This lack of control impedes systematic selection. With countries such as Chad, Niger and Mali any item is selected in order to place in the collection primary source material. That the particular government decides to publish and distribute a title, in itself, makes the title significant as an indicator of an official position. Obtaining large runs of serials, especially retrospectively, is not a significant factor in opting for acquisition. On the historic level, an issue per decade can give a sample of development; of course, the fuller the run the better the ability to provide a fuller view.

COUNTRY CONSPECTUS
AFRICA

Algeria	D
Angola	B
Benin	B
Botswana	B
Burundi	B
Cameroon	B
Cape Verde	C
Central African Republic	B
Chad	B
Comoros	C
Congo	B
Djibouti	B
Egypt	D
Equatorial Guinea	B
Ethiopia	B
Gabon	B
The Gambia	B
Ghana	B
Guinea	B
Guinea-Bissau	B
Ivory Coast	B
Kenya	B
Lesotho	B
Liberia	B
Libyan Arab Republic	D
Madagascar	B
Malawi	B

Mali	B
Mauritania	B
Mauritius	B
Morocco	D
Mozambique	B
Namibia	B
Niger	B
Nigeria	B
Rwanda	B
St. Helena	D
Sao Tome	B
Senegal	B
Seychelles	B
Sierra Leone	B
Somalia	B
South Africa	B
Sudan	B
Swaziland	B
Togo	B
Tunesia	D
Uganda	B
Cameroon	B
Tanzania	B
Upper Volta	B
Western Sahara	C
Zaire	B
Zambia	B
Zimbabwe	B

NORTH AMERICA

Antigua	D
Bahamas	D
Barbados	D
Belize	C
Bermuda	D
Canada	C
Cayman Islands	D
Costa Rica	C
Cuba	C
Dominica	D
Dominican Republic	C
El Salvador	C

Greenland	E
Grenada	D
Guatemala	B
Haiti	D
Honduras	C
Jamaica	D
Mexico	B
Montserrat	D
Netherlands Antilles	C
Nicaragua	C
Panama	C
St. Kitts-Nevis-Anguilla	D
St. Lucia	D
St. Vincent	D
Trinidad and Tobago	D
Turks and Caicos Islands	D

SOUTH AMERICA

Argentina	B
Bolivia	C
Brazil	B
Chile	B
Columbia	B
Ecuador	C
Falkland Islands	E
Guyana	C
Paraguay	C
Peru	B
Surinam	D
Uruguay	C
Venezuela	B

ASIA

Afghanistan	D
Bahrain	D
Bangladesh	D
Bhutan	E
Brunei	D
Burma	D
China	D
Cyprus	D
Cambodia	D

Hong Kong	C
India	D
Indonesia	D
Iran	D
Iraq	D
Israel	D
Japan	C
Jordan	D
Democratic People's Republic of Korea	D
Republic of Korea	D
Kuwait	D
Laos	D
Lebanon	D
Macau	D
Malaysia	D
Maldives	D
Mongolia	E
Nepal	E
Oman	E
Pakistan	D
Philippines	D
Qatar	E
Saudi Arabia	D
Singapore	D
Viet Nam	D
Sri Lanka	D
Syrian Arab Republic	D
Taiwan	D
Thailand	D
Turkey	D
United Arab Emirates	D
Yemen	E
Democratic Yemen	E

EUROPE

Albania	D
Andorra	E
Austria	B
Belgium	C
Bulgaria	C
Guernsey	E
Jersey	E

Czechoslovakia	C
Denmark	C
Finland	C
France	B
German Democratic Republic	C
Federal Republic of Germany	B
Gilbraltar	C
Great Britain	A
Greece	D
Hungary	C
Iceland	C
Ireland	B
Isle of Man	C
Italy	B
Liechtenstein	C
Luxembourg	C
Malta	C
Monaco	C
Netherlands	C
Northern Ireland	C
Norway	C
Poland	C
Portugal	B
Romania	C
San Marino	D
Spain	B
Sweden	C
Switzerland	B
USSR	C
Vatican City	D
Yugoslavia	C

OCEANIA

Australia and New Zealand	C
All other countries	E

SUBJECT CONSPECTUS

Censuses	A
General national statistical abstracts	A
Statistical compendia	B
Bibliographies	B

Annual reports of government	(level of intensity
departments and commissions	of country)
Government directories	A
Official yearbooks	A
National budgets and budget speeches	A
Economics	B
Planning	B
Energy	B
Environmental problems	B
Transportation	B
Trade	B
Voting	B
Education	B
Earth Sciences	B
Art	B
History	B
Political movements	B
Agrarian reform	B
Foreign relations	B
Demography	B
Women, youth, and minorities	B
Urbanization	B
Non-roman script	F
Official gazettes (except Brazil)	F
General compilations of law	F

NOTE

1. The collection development policy statements for government documents at Stanford University cover the publications of the U.S. government, state and local governments, international organizations, and foreign governments. These statements comprise one section of *The Libraries of Stanford University, Collection Development Policy Statement, 1980*, edited by Paul H. Mosher and John Rawlings (Stanford, CA: Stanford University Libraries, 1981).

Appendix B

The 200 Item Numbers Chosen Most Frequently by Selective Depositories
N = 1295

Rank	Series Title	Number Libraries Selecting	Percent Libraries Selecting
1	Monthly Catalog	1281	98.9
2	Statistical Abstract	1274	98.4
3	U.S. Government Manual	1269	98.0
4	Congressional Directory	1255	96.9
5	Statistical Abstract Supplement	1241	95.8
6	Zip Code Directory	1207	93.2
7	Monthly Labor Review	1205	93.1
8	Department of State Bulletin	1192	92.0
9	U.S. Code and Supplement	1183	91.4
10	Federal Register	1166	90.0
11	L.C. Subject Headings and Supplement	1165	90.0
12	Educational Directory	1163	90.0
13	Catalog of Federal Domestic Assistance	1154	89.1
14	Public Papers of the President	1147	88.6
15	Statutes at Large	1147	88.6
16	Uniform Crime Reports	1136	87.7
17	Congressional Record	1129	87.2
18	Weekley Compilation of Presidential Papers	1119	86.4
19	Agriculture Department Yearbook	1115	86.1
20	Monthly Checklist of State Publications	1113	85.9

Rank	Series Title	Number Libraries Selecting	Percent Libraries Selecting
21	Survey of Current Businesss Statistics	1112	85.9
22	Your Federal Income Tax	1103	85.2
23	Congressional District Atlas	1102	85.1
24	Budget of the United States	1099	84.9
25	Publications Reference File	1098	84.8
26	Economic Report of the President	1098	84.8
27	United States Reports	1094	84.5
28	Digest of Public General Bills	1093	84.4
29	Treaties in Force	1092	84.3
30	Occupational Outlook Handbook	1088	84.0
31	Budget in Brief	1087	83.9
32	Price List (#36 only one still published)	1081	83.5
33	American Education	1078	83.2
34	Occupational Outlook Quarterly	1078	83.2
35	Code of Federal Regulations	1076	83.1
36	Pocket Data Book	1065	82.2
37	Background Notes on Various Countries	1055	81.5
38	Handbook of Labor Statistics	1052	81.2
39	Social Security Bulletin	1050	81.1
40	Selected U.S. Government Publications	1050	81.1
41	Vital Statistics	1047	80.8
42	U.S. Government Purchasing and Specification Directory	1040	80.3
43	Reports and Publications- National Commission on Libraries and Information Science	1039	80.2
44	FDA Consumer	1038	80.2
45	Subject Bibliographies	1038	80.2
46	L.C. Classification Schedules	1037	80.1
47	U.S. Treaties and Other International Agreements	1036	80.0
48	Consumer Price Index	1033	79.8
49	Bureau of Census, Catalog of Publications	1031	79.6
50	Aging	1026	79.2
51	Conservation Yearbooks	1022	78.9
52	Quarterly Journal of Library of Congress	1022	78.9
53	Minerals Yearbook	1019	78.7
54	Library of Congress Classification, Additions and Changes	1019	78.7

Rank	Series Title	Number Libraries Selecting	Percent Libraries Selecting
55	Children Today	1017	78.6
56	Annual Report—Library of Congress	1016	78.5
57	Reports and Publication—Civil Rights Commission	1015	78.4
58	Numerical List and Schedule of Volumes...	1013	78.2
59	Economic Indicators	1008	77.8
60	Slip Laws	998	77.1
61	Special Commissions and Committees— President of the U.S.	998	77.1
62	Area Handbooks—Dept. of the Army	994	76.8
63	National Register of Historic Places	994	76.8
64	Annual Report of the Attorney General	993	76.7
65	U.S. Industrial Outlook	982	75.8
66	Bibliographies and List of Publications— Library of Congress	975	75.3
67	Annual Report—Federal Bureau of Investigation	968	74.7
68	Problems of Communism	967	74.7
69	Reports and Publications—White House Conferences	964	74.4
70	Business Conditions Digest	963	74.4
71	Foreign Relations of the United States	961	74.2
72	Current Population Reports	960	74.1
73	Census of Population. Final Volumes (Other than by States and Areas)	960	74.1
74	Business Americas	959	74.1
75	Special Analyses—Office of Management and Budget	957	73.9
76	Library Statistics at Colleges and Universities	956	73.8
77	Smithsonian Year	956	73.8
78	Crime and Delinquency Issues (Monograph series)	952	73.6
79	Annual Report—Labor Department	952	73.6
80	General Publications—Subject Cataloging Division, LC	949	73.3
81	Annual Reports—Council on Environmental Quality	949	73.3
82	HUD Statistics Yearbook	942	72.8
83	Women-Owned Business	938	72.4
84	Census of Manufactures—Final Volumes	937	72.4

Rank	Series Title	Number Libraries Selecting	Percent Libraries Selecting
85	Code of Federal Regulations— Hardcopy	936	72.3
86	Library of Congress Information Bulletin	935	72.2
87	Annual Report—Environmental Protection Agency	934	72.1
88	General Foreign Policy Series—State Department	932	72.0
89	Resources in Education	931	71.9
90	EPA Journal	930	71.8
91	Marihuana and Health	929	71.7
92	Condition of Education	925	71.4
93	General Publications—Library of Congress	924	71.4
94	CIA Publications	923	71.3
95	General Publications—General Reference and Bibliography Division, L.C.	921	71.1
96	Census of Population: Preliminary Reports (by States)	914	70.6
97	National Park Service Handbooks	914	70.6
98	Health United States	908	70.1
99	Letters of Delegates to Congress, 1774-1789	908	70.1
100	Annual Report—Commerce Department	907	70.0
101	National Conference on Child Abuse and Neglect: Publications...	907	70.0
102	Employment & Earnings	907	70.0
103	Catalog of Federal Education Assistance Programs	906	70.0
104	Annual Report—Federal Communications Commission	903	69.8
105	Agricultural Statistics	900	69.5
106	Supreme Court Decisions	899	69.4
107	Major Legislation of Congress	898	69.3
108	Digest of Education Statistics	896	69.2
109	Children's Books	894	69.0
110	Indians of:	891	68.8
111	Annual Report—American Historical Association	889	68.6
112	Annual Report—National Science Foundation	880	68.0
113	CIA Maps and Atlases	878	67.8

Rank	Series Title	Number Libraries Selecting	Percent Libraries Selecting
114	United States Army in World War II	876	67.6
115	General Publications—Government Printing Office	876	67.6
116	International Economic Indicators	875	67.6
117	Digest of International Law	873	67.4
118	Postage Stamps of United States	872	67.3
119	Annual Report on State of Finances, Annual Report Revenue Sharing	871	67.3
120	Annual Report—Federal Trade Commission	870	67.2
121	Astronomical Almanac	869	67.1
122	Our Public Lands	869	67.1
123	Diplomatic List—State Department	868	67.0
124	Annual Report—Interstate Commerce Commission	867	66.9
125	Annual Report—Transportation Department	864	66.7
126	Congressional District Data	862	66.6
127	Census of Governments	862	66.6
128	United States Court Directory	858	66.3
129	Annual Report—Housing and Urban Development	856	66.1
130	General Publications—National Gallery of Art	856	66.1
131	Dictionary of American Fighting Ships	855	66.0
132	Annual Report—Securities and Exchange Commission	854	65.9
133	General Publications—National Portrait Gallery	853	65.9
134	Federal Statistical Directory	852	65.8
135	Annual Report—Energy Department	847	65.4
136	Annual Report—Internal Revenue Service	847	65.4
137	Statistics of Income—Internal Revenue Service	847	65.4
138	Annual Report—Consumer Product Safety Commission	845	65.3
139	Census of Population: General Publications	844	65.2
140	General Publications—General Reference and Bibliography Division, L.C.	842	65.0
141	Historic American Buildings	840	64.9

Rank	Series Title	Number Libraries Selecting	Percent Libraries Selecting
142	Reports and Publications—Equal Employment Opportunity Commission	840	64.9
143	General Publications—Descriptive Division, L.C.	839	64.8
144	Annual Report—Human Development Services Office	838	64.7
145	Annual Report—Law Enforcement Assistance Administration; Annual Report of the National Institute of Juvenile Justice and Delinquency Prevention	838	64.7
146	Employment and Training Report of the President	838	64.7
147	FBI Uniform Crime Reports	834	64.4
148	Small Business Management Series	834	64.4
149	Bulletin—Labor Statistics Bureau	833	64.3
150	Annual Reports—National Labor Relations Board	833	64.3
151	General Publications—President of the United States	832	64.2
152	Mental Health Directory	831	64.2
153	Annual Survey of Manufacturers	830	64.1
154	Monthly Energy Review	830	64.1
155	Higher Education Statistics	829	64.0
156	General Publications—National Collection of Fine Arts	829	64.0
157	Drug Use Among American High School Students	828	63.9
158	Smithsonian Studies in History and Technology	828	63.9
159	Drug Enforcement	828	63.9
160	Occupational and Career Information Series	827	63.9
161	General Publications—Council on Environmental Quality	827	63.9
162	Publications (List) National Archives and Records Service	827	63.9
163	Information Circulars—National Park Park Service	821	63.4
164	Preservation Leaflets—Library of Congress	821	63.4
165	Annual Report—Immigration and Naturalization Service	820	63.3

Rank	Series Title	Number Libraries Selecting	Percent Libraries Selecting
166	Department of State News Letter	819	63.2
167	Reports and Publications—Commissions, Committees, Boards	818	63.2
168	Annual Report—Education Department	817	63.1
169	Weekly Business Statistics	816	63.0
170	Mosaic	816	63.0
171	East Asian and Pacific Series—State Department	816	63.0
172	General Publications—Law Enforcement Assistance Administration	815	62.9
173	General Publications—Union Catalog Division, L.C.	813	62.8
174	Public Health Reports	812	62.7
175	President's Papers	811	62.6
176	Bulletins—Women's Bureau, Department of Labor	810	62.5
177	List of Publications (Miscellaneous)—Assistant Public Printer	809	62.5
178	Federal Probation	807	62.3
179	National Parks and Landmarks	806	62.2
180	Handbooks, Manuals, Guides—Library of Congress	806	62.2
181	African Series—State Department	806	62.2
182	Department and Foreign Service Series—Department of State	803	62.0
183	Highway Statistics	802	61.9
184	Camping National Park System	801	61.9
185	Reports and Publications—Interdepartmental Committee on Status of Women	801	61.9
186	General Publications—Reader's Services, L.C	800	61.8
187	Bibliographies and Lists of Publications —Health and Human Services Department	798	61.6
188	Near and Middle Eastern Series—State Department	797	61.5
189	Annual Report—Personnel Management Office	794	61.3
190	Reports and Publications—National Endowment for the Humanities	794	61.3
191	Near East and South Asian Series—State Department	794	61.3

Rank	Series Title	Number Libraries Selecting	Percent Libraries Selecting
192	General Publications—Smithsonian Institution	792	61.2
193	Report and Publications—National Academy of Sciences	791	61.1
194	Inter-American Series—State Department	791	61.1
195	Annual Report to Congress—Nuclear Regulatory Commission	791	61.1
196	Home and Gardens Bulletin	790	61.0
197	Federal Textbook on Citizenship	789	60.9
198	National Referral Center for Science and Technology Publications	788	60.8
199	Starting and Managing Series—Small Business Administration	788	60.8
200	National Criminal Justice Information and Statistics Service, Statistics Center Reports...	787	60.8

Appendix C

List of Items for Selection by Depository Libraries

Office of the Assistant Public Printer (Superintendent of Documents), U.S. Government Printing Office, Washington, D.C., 20401

Note: This list includes all item numbers, titles, and SuDoc classifications through Survey 81-14, July 1981. Only part of the list, however, has been reprinted

Item Number	
1	Agricultural Statistics A 1.47: (Agriculture Department)
2	Agriculture Decisions (monthly) A 1.58/a: (Agriculture Department)
	Rural Telephone Bank Publications A 1.116: (Agriculture Department)
3	Agriculture Handbooks A 1.76: (Agriculture Department)
4	Agriculture Information Bulletin A 1.75: (Agriculture Department)
6	Annual Report A 1.1: (Agriculture Department)

Item Number	
6-B	Information and Technical Assistance Delivered by the Department of Agriculture in Fiscal Year, Annual Report to Congress A 1.1/2: (Agriculture Department)
6-C	Outlook for U.S. Agriculture Exports A 1.80/2: (Agriculture Department)
6-D	Rural Development Goals, Annual Report of Secretary of Agriculture to the Congress A 1.85/2: (Agriculture Department)
6-E	Location of New Federal Offices and Other Facilities, Annual Report A 1.111: (Agriculture Department)

24-N   Institutional Meat Purchase
      Specificaitons
      A 103.15:
      (Food Safety and Quality
      Service)

24-O   Laws
      A 88.5:
      (Agricultural Marketing
      Service)

24-P   Handbooks, Manuals Guides
      A 88.6/4:
      (Agricultural Marketing
      Service)
      United States Standards for
      (Various Foods)
      A 103.6/2:
      (Food Safety and Quality
      Service)
      Official United States Standards
      for Grain
      A 104.6/2:
      (Federal Grain Inspection
      Service)

24-P-1   Cotton Varieties Planted
      (annual)
      A 88.11/13:
      (Agricultural Marketing
      Service)

24-R   Sugar and Sweetner Report
      (quarterly)
      A 1.115:
      (Agriculture Department)
      Sugar Market Statistics
      (monthly)
      A 105.53:
      (Economics, Statistics Service)

24-S   Quik-Quiz (series)
      A 1.118:
      (Agriculture Department)

24-T   Food for Peace, Annual Report
      on Public Law 480
      A 1.119:
      (Agriculture Department)

24-V   Horse Protection Enforcement,
      Annual Report to the Secre-
      tary of Agriculture
      A 1.120:
      (Agriculture Department)

25-A   Agricultural Research (monthly)
      A 106.9:

      (Science and Education
      Administration)

25-A-1   Addresses
      A 77.10:
      (Agriculture Research
      Service)

25-A-2   Dairy Herd Improvement
      Letters (irregular)
      A 106.34:
      (Science and Education
      Administration)

25-A-3   Livestock and Veternary
      Sciences, Annual Report of
      the National Research
      Program
      A 106.33:
      (Science and Education
      Administration)

25-B   Advances in Agricultural Tech-
      nology, ATT (series)
      A 106.24:
      (Science and Education
      Administration)

25-D   Conservation Research Reports
      (numbered)
      A 1.114:
      (Agriculture Department)

26-C-1   Eastern Regional Research
      Center: Publications and
      Patents (list)
      A 77.17/4:
      (Agriculture Research
      Service)

30-A-1   APHIS (series)
      A 101.10/2:
      (Animal and Plant Health
      Inspection Service)

30-A-2   ACTION Pamphlets (numbered)
      AA 1.11:
      (ACTION)

30-A-3   Handbooks, Manuals, Guides
      A 101.8:
      (Animal and Plant Inspection
      Service)
      Meat and Poultry Inspection
      Manual
      A 103.8/3:
      (Animal and Plant Inspection
      Service)

30-A-5   General Publications

Item Number		Item Number	
	A 101.2:		Equipment
	(Animal and Plant Inspection Service)		A 103.6/3: (Food Safety and Quality Service)
30-A-06	Plant Quarantine Import Requirements of (various countries)	32-A-3	Handbooks, Manuals, Guides A 103.8:
	A 101.11: (Animal and Plant Inspection Service)		(Food Safety and Quality Service)
31	Index-Catalogue of Medical and Veterinary Zoology, By Subject	32-A-4	Bibliographies and Lists of Publications
	A 77.219/3: (Agricultural Research Service)		A 101.19: (Animal and Plant Health Inspection Service)
	Index-Catalogue of Medical and Veterinary Zoology, Special Publications (numbered)	34	Annual Report A 82.301: (Commodity Credit Corporation)
	A 106.15: (Science and Education Administration)	34-A	Charts Providing Graphic Summary of Operations A 82.311:
31-A-1	Handbooks, Manuals, Guides A 102.8:		(Commodity Credit Corporation)
	(Rural Development Service)	35	General Publications
31-B-1	Regulations, Rules, Instructions A 104.6:		A 82.302: (Commodity Credit Corporation)
	(Federal Grain Inspection Service)	36	Laws A 82.305:
31-B-2	Handbooks, Manuals, and Guides		(Commodity Credit Corporation)
	A 104.8: (Federal Grain Inspection Service)	37	Regulations, Rules, Instructions A 82.306:
31-B-3	General Publications A 104:2:		(Commodity Credit Corporation)
	(Federal Grain Inspection Service)	39	General Publications Y 3.C73/5:2
31-C	General Publications A 103.2:		(Commodity Futures Trading Commission)
	(Food Safety and Quality Service)	39-B	Annual Report Y 3.C 73/5:1
31-E	Information Guidance Series D 2.17:		(Commodity Futures Trading Commission)
	(Armed Forces Information Service)	39-C	Economic Bulletins (numbered) Y 3.C 73/5:3-2/
32-A	Meat and Poultry Inspection Directory (semi-annual)		(Commodity Futures Trading Commission)
	A 103.9: (Food Safety and Quality Service)	40-A-2	General Publications A 94.2: (Cooperative State Research Service)
32-A-2	Accepted Meat and Poultry		

40-A-3 Handbooks, Manuals, Guides
A 94.8:
(Cooperative State Research
Service)
40-B-1 List of Plants Operating Under
USDA and Egg Grading and
Egg Products Inspection Pro-
grams
A 103.10:
(Food Safety and Quality
Service)
42-A Farm Real Estate Taxes, Recent
Trends and Developments
(annual)
A 93.9/6:
(Economic Research Service)
Farm Mortgage Debt (annual)
A 93.9/12:
(Economic Research Service)
Farm Real Estate Market
Developments
A 105.19/2:
(Economics, Statistics Service)
42-B Foreign Agricultural Economic
Reports (numbered)
A 105.22:
(Economics, Statistics Service)
42-C Agricultural Economic Reports
A 1.107:
(Agriculture Department)
42-D Wheat Outlook and Situation
(annual)
A 105.19/3:
(Economics, Statistics Service)
42-E Foreign Agricultural Trade of
United States (monthly)
A 105.14:
(Economics, Statistics Service)
U.S. Foreign Agricultural
Report
Fiscal and Claendar Year
A 105.14/2:
(Economics, Statistics Service)
42-J World Economic Conditions in
Relation to Agricultural
Trade
A 105.22/2:
(Economics, Statistics Service)
42-M Agriculture Outlook (issued 11
times a year)

A 105.27:
(Economics, Statistics Service)
42-N AGERS (series)
A 93.21/3:
(Economic Research Service)
42-P Agricultural-Food Policy
Review (Irregular)
A 105.50:
(Economics, Statistics Service)
42-R Fertilizer Situation, FS (series)
(annual)
A 93.36:
(Economic Research Service)
59-A Circulars (numbered)
A 43.4:
(Extension Service)
60 Extension Review (Quarterly)
A 106.10:
(Science and Education
Administration)
61-A Regulations, Rules, Instructions
A 43.16:
(Extension Service)
61-B Handbooks, Manuals, Guides
A 43.16/2:
(Extension Service)
64-A Cooperative Research Reports
A 109.10:
(Agricultural Cooperative
Service)
64-B Special Reports (series)
A 89.20:
Farmer Cooperative Service
64-C ACS Service Reports (series)
A 109.9:
(Agricultural Cooperative
Service)
65-B Cooperative Information Reports
A 109.10/2:
(Agriculture Cooperative
Service)
66 Farmer Cooperatives (monthly)
A 105.19:
(Economics, Statistics Service)
68 General Publications
A 84.2:
(Farmers Home Administra-
tion)
68-A Handbooks, Manuals, Guides
A 84.6/2:

Item Number

A 67.40/4:
(Foreign Agriculture Service)

76-L   Weekly Roundup of World Production and Trade WR
(series)
A 67.42:
(Foreign Agriculture Service)

77   General Publications
A 67.2:
(Foreign Agriculture Service)

77-A-3   Quarterly Report of the General
Sales Manager
A 67.43:
(Foreign Agriculture Service)

78-A   World Agricultural Situation
(irregular)
A 105.10/3:
(Economics, Statistics Service)
World Agricultural Situation
Supplements
A 105.10/3-2:

80   Annual Report
A 13.1:
(Forest Service)
Report of (Forest Service) (FY)
A 13.1/3:
(Forest Service)
Pacific NW Experiment Station
Annual Report
A 13.66/i:
(Forest Service)

80-A   American Woods (Pamphlets)
A 13.31:
(Forest Service)

80-A-1   Proceedings of the Annual
Western International Forest
Disease Work Conference
A 13.69/13:
(Forest Service)

80-D   Current Information Reports
A 13.91:
(Forest Service)

80-E   Telephone Directory
A 1.89:
(Agriculture Department)
Telephone Directory, Alpha-
betical Listing (semiannual)
A 1.89/4:
(Agriculture Department)

80-F   Final Environmental Statements

Item Number

A 13.92:
(Forest Service)
Draft Environmental Statement
A 13.92/2:
(Forest Service)

80-G   Maps and Charts
A 13.28:
(Forest Service)
Shawnee Sportsmans Maps
(various countries)
A 13.28/3:
(Forest Service)
Maps
A 13.65/16:
(Forest Service)

80-H   Posters and Maps
A 1.32:
(Agriculture Department)
Posters
A 13.104:
(Forest Service)

80-J   Forest Insect and Disease Conditions, Intermountain Re-
gion (annual)
A 13.52/12:
(Forest Service)

81-B   TT (Training Text) (series)
A 13.36/4:
(Forest Service)

82   Fire Management Notes
(quarterly)
A 13.32:
(Forest Service)

82-A   Forest Insect & Disease Leaflets
(numbered)
A 13.52:
(Forest Service)

82-A-1   Alaska Region Reports
(numbered) (irregular)
A 13.103:
(Forest Service)

82-A-2   General Report SA-GR (series)
A 13.105:
(Forest Service)

82-B   Forest Insect Conditions in the
U.S.
A 13.52/2:
(Forest Service)
Forest Insect Conditions in
NE U.S.

Item Number

A 13.52/9:
(Forest Service)
Forest Insect and Disease
Management Evaluation
Reports
A 13.93:
(Forest Service)
Forest Insect and Disease
Management Survey Reports
A 13.93/2:
(Forest Service)
Forest Insect and Disease
Management
A 13.93/3:
(Forest Service)

82-B-1 Forest Insect and Disease
Conditions in the Southwest
(annual)
A 13.52/11:
(Forest Service)

82-B-2 National Wildfire Coordination
Group NWCG Handbook
(series)
A 13.99:
(Forest Service)

82-B-3 Field Identification Cards
A 13.100:
(Forest Service)

82-C Forest Service Comments on
Resolutions Relating to the
National Forest System
A 13.86:
(Forest Service)

82-D-1 Equipment Development and
Test Program, Fiscal Year
A 13.49/5:
(Forest Service)

82-D-2 Wildfire Statistics (annual)
A 13.32/2:
(Forest Service)

82-D-3 Equipment Development and
Test Reports (numbered)
A 13.49/4:
(Forest Service)

82-D-4 Publications of Southern Forest
Experiment Station (list)
A 13.40/8-3:
(Forest Service)

82-D-5 Southern Forest Experiment Station: Research Accomplished

Item Number

A 13.32/3:
(Forest Service)

82-D-7 Forest Insect and Disease
Conditions in the Northern
Region (annual)
A 13.52/7:
(Forest Service)

82-D-8 Southern Forest Experiment Sta-
tion: Technical Publication
SA-TP (series)
A 13.40/12:
(Forest Service)

82-G Pacific Southwest Forest and
Range Experiment Station
Publications (List) (annual)
A 13.62/11:
(Forest Service)

83 Forest Resource Reports
(numbered monographs)
A 13.50:
(Forest Service)

83-A Forest Service Films Available
on Loan for Educational
Purposes (annual)
A 13.55:
(Forest Service)

83-B Research Papers (numbered)
A 13.78:
(Forest Service)
Research Notes (numbered)
A 13.79:
(Forest Service)
Resource Bulletins (numbered)
A 13.80:
(Forest Service)
General Technical Reports
(numbered)
A 13.88:
(Forest Service)
Forest Products Utilization
Technical Reports
A 13.96:
(Forest Service)

83-C Engineering Technical Informa-
tion System EM (series)
A 13.84/2:
(Forest Service)

83-C-2 Annual Grazing Statistical
Report
A 13.83:
(Forest Service)

Item Number		Item Number	
	A 88.6: (Agricultural Marketing Service) Regulations, Rules, Instructions A 101.6: (Animal and Plant Health Inspection Service)		(Rural Electrification Ad- ministration) Telecommunications Engineer ing & Construction Manual A 68.6/4: (Rural Electrification Ad- ministration)
110	Regulation, Rules, and Instruc- tions A 82.6: (Agricultural Stabilization and Conservation Service)		List of Materials Acceptable fo₁ Use on Telephone Systems o₁ REA Borrowers A 68.6/5: (Rural Electrification Ad-
110-A	ASCS Background Information BI-(series— A 82.82: (Agricultural Stabilizaiton and Conservation Service)		ministration) Handbooks, Manuals, Guides A 68.6/6: (Rural Electrification Ad- ministration)
110-B- (nos.)	Annual Reports by States A 82.1/2: (Agricultural Stabilization and Conservation Service)	116-B	Laws A 68.5: (Rural Electrification Ad- ministration)
115	Annual Report A 68.1: (Rural Electrification Ad- ministration) Annual Statistical Report, Rural Electric Borrowers A 68.1/2: (Rural Electrification Ad- ministration) Annual Statistical Report, Rural Telephone Borrowers A 68.1/3: (Rural Electrification Ad- ministration)	117-A 117-B 119-A	Environmental Impact State- ments A 68.22: (Rural Electrification Ad- ministration) Environmental Impact State- ments (nos.) A 68.22: (Rural Electrification Ad- ministration) Conservation Information, SCS- CI-(series) (Soil Conservation Service) A 57.44:
116	General Publications (Rural Electrification Ad- ministration) A 68.2: Bulletins A 68.3: (Rural Electrification Ad- ministration)	119-B 120	Conservation Highlights, Digest of Progress Report of Soil Conservation Service A 57.1/2: (Soil Conservation Service) General Publications A 57.2:
116-A	List of Materials Acceptable for Use on Systems of REA Elec- trification Borrowers A 68.6/2: REA Telephone Operstions Manual A 68.6/3:	120-A 121-A	(Soil Conservation Service) Handbooks, Manuals, Guides A 57.6/2: (Soil Conservation Service) Soil Survey Investigations Reports A 57.52: (Soil Conservation Service)

Item Number		Item Number	
121-B	Technical Releases (numbered) A 57.51: (Soil Conservation Service)	125-A-8	World Military Expenditures (annual) AC 1.16: (Arms Control & Disarmament Agency)
121-B-1	Annual Technical Report of the National Plant Materials Center A 57.54: (Soil Conservation Service)	125-A-9	Annual Report AC 1.1: (Arms Control & Disarmament Agency)
121-C	Final Environmental Impact Statements A 57.65/2: (Soil Conservation Service)	126	Annual Report C 1.1: (Commerce Department)
121-D	Technical Publications SCS-TP (series) A 57.15: (Soil Conservation Service)	126-A	Bibliographies and Lists of Publications C 1.54: (Commerce Department) Publications Catalog (annual) C 1.54/2-2: (Commerce Department)
122	Soil and Water Conservation News (monthly) A 57.9/2: (Soil Conservation Service)	126-C	Access, U.S. Dept. of Commerce Publication form Office of Minority Business Enterprise, Incorporating Outlook C 1.57/4: (Commerce Department)
122-A-2	Commercial Fertilizers: Consumption in the United States (annual) A 105.41/2: (Economics, Statistics Service)		
122-A-3	Stocks of Grains in all Positions (quarterly) A 105.20: (Economics, Statistics Service)	126-D	Telephone Directory C 1.37: (Commerce Department)
122-A-4	Noncitrus Fruits & Nuts (annual) A 105.11:	126-D-2	Interagency Auditor Training Center Bulletin for Fiscal Year C 1.61: (Commerce Department)
122-A-6	Small Grains, Annual Summary and Crop Winter Wheat and Rye Seedings A 105.20/6: (Economics, Statistics Service)	126-D-3	OT Bulletin C 1.60/4: (Commerce Department) NTIA-SP (series) C 60.9: (National Telecommunications and Information Administration)
125-A-3	General Publications AC 1.2: (Arms Control & Disarmament Agency)		
125-A-5	Addresses AC 1.12: (Arms Control & Disarmament Agency)		NTIA Reports (numbered) C 60.10: (National Telecommunications and Information Administration)
125-A-6	Bibliographies and Lists of Publications AC 1.13: (Arms Control & Disarmament Agency)	126-D-5	NTIA Contractor Reports C 60.12: (National Telecommunications and Information Administration)

Item Number

126-D-6   Interagency Task Force Product Liability, ITFPL-(series)
C 1.66:
(Commerce Department)

126-D-7   Statistical Policy Working Papers
C 1.70:
(Commerce Department)

126-D-8   Annual Report, National Voluntary Laboratory Accreditation
C 1.71:
(Commerce Department)

126-D-9   Footwear Industry Revitalization Program, Annual Progress Report
C 1.72:
(Commerce Department)

126-D-10   NTIA Technical Memorandum Series, NTIA-TM (nos.)
C 60.11:
(National Telecommunications and Information Administration)

126-D-11   Semi-Annual Report of the Inspector General to the Congress
C 1.1/2:
(Commerce Department)

126-D-12   Office of Federal Statistical Policy and Standards: Technical Papers
C 1.73:
(Commerce Department)

126-D-13   Franchising in the Economy (annual)
C 62.16:
(Industrial Economics Bureau)

126-E-1   Bibliographies and Lists of Publications
C 60.13:
(National Telecommunications and Information Administration)

126-E-2   Handbooks, Manuals, Guides
C 60.8:
(National Telecommunications and Information Administration)

Item Number

126-E-3   Institute for Telecommunication Sciences: Annual Technical Progress Report
C 60.14:
(National Telecommunications and Information Administration)

127   Commerce Publications Update (biweekly)
C 1.24/3:
(Commerce Department)

127-A   Business Americas (biweekly)
C 61.18:
(International Trade Administration)

128   General Publications
C 1.2:
(Commerce Department)

128-A   Handbooks, Manuals, Guides
C 1.8/3:
(Commerce Department)
Federal Meteorological Handbooks (numbered)
C 1.8/4:
(Commerce Department)

130-C   Handbooks, Manuals, Guides
C 46.8:
(Commerce Department)

130-D   General Publications
C 46.2:
(Economic Development Administration)

130-D-1   General Publications
C 59.2:
(Economic Analysis Bureau)

130-D-2   Handbooks, Manuals, Guides
C 59.8:
(Economic Analysis Bureau)

130-F   Annual Report
C 46.1:
(Economic Development Administration)

130-J   Directory of Approved Projects
C 46.19/2:
(Economic Development Administration)
Qualified Areas Under Public Works & Economic Development Act of 1965, Public Law 89-136 Reports (annual)

Item Number

P-(nos.)
C 5k9.13:
(Census Bureau)

140-A-1 Construction Reports:
Housing Starts, C20-(series)
C 3.215/2:
(Census Bureau)

140-A-2 Construction Reports:
Value of New Construction
Put in Place, C 30-(series)
C 3.215/3:
(Census Bureau)

140-A-3 Construction Reports: Housing
Authorized by Building Per-
mits and Public Contracts,
C40-(series)
C 3.215/4:
(Census Bureau)

140-A-5 Construction Reports: Residen-
tial Alterations and Repairs,
Expenditures on Residential
Additions, Alterations, Main-
tenance and Repairs, and Re-
placements, C50-(series)
C 3.215/8:
(Census Bureau)

140-A-6 Construction Reports: New One-
Family Homes Sold and For
Sale, C25(series)
C 3.215/9:
(Census Bureau)

140-A-7 Construction Reports: Price
Index of New One-Family
Houses Sold, C27-(series)
C 3.215/9-2:
(Census Bureau)

140-A-8 Construction Reports: Housing
Completions, C22-(series)
C-3.215/13:
(Census Bureau)

140-A-9 Construction Reports: New
Residential Construction in
Selected Standard Metropoli-
tan Statistical Areas,
C21(series)

140-B Congressional District Atlas
C 3.62/5:
(Census Bureau)

140-B-1 Congressional District Data
(series)

Item Number

C 3.134/4:
(Census Bureau)

140-B-2 State County Subdivision Maps
C 3.62/6:
(Census Bureau)

141 Cotton Ginning Series, A-10
C 3.20:
(Census Bureau)
Cotton Ginnings, Report on
Cotton Ginnings by Countries,
A-20 (series)
C 3.20/3:
Report on Cotton Ginnings
(NON-GPO)
C 3.32:
(Census Bureau)

141-A Current Housing Reports
C 3.215:
(Census Bureau)
Annual Housing Survey Studies
HH 1.78:
(Housing and Urban Devel-
opment Department)

141-C Current Selected Service Reports: Monthly Selected Services Receipts (NON-GPO)
C 3.239:
(Census Bureau)

142-A Current Industrial Reports:
C 3.158:
(Census Bureau)
Advance Report on Durable
Goods, Manufacturers, Ship-
ments and Orders, M3-1
(series)
C 3.158/2:
(Census Bureau)

142-B Enterprise Statistics (ES series)
C 3.230:
(Census Bureau)

142-B-1 Small-Area Statistics Papers,
Series GE-41
C 3.238/2:
(Census Bureau)

142-C Current Population Reports
C 3.186:
(Census Bureau)

142-D Data Access Descriptions:
-Computer Tape Series CT
C 3.240/3: ˙

eral Imports, Shipping Weight and Value, FT-986 (annual)
C 3.164:
(Census Bureau)

44-A-16   Highlights of U.S. Export and Import Trade, FT-990 (monthly)
C 3.164:
(Census Bureau)

44-A-17   Bunker Fuels, FT-810, (monthly)
C 3.164:
(Census Bureau)

44-A-18   U.S. Exports, Schedule B, Commodity by Country, FT 446 (annual)
C 3.164:446/
(Census Bureau)

45-A   Special Domographic Analyses, CDS (series)
C 3.261:
(Census Bureau)

General Publications
C 3.2:
(Census Bureau)

146-A   Handbooks, Manuals, Guides
C 3.6/2:
(Census Bureau)

146-D   Current Business Reports, Imports: Green Coffee Inventories, Imports, Roastings, (BG series)
C 3.236:
(Census Bureau)

146-E   Quarterly Summary of State and Local Tax Revenue (GT series)
C 3.145/6:
(Census Bureau)

Government Finances (GF series)
C 3.191/2:
(Census Bureau)

146-F   ISP (series)
C 3.205/3:
(Census Bureau)

ISP Supplemental Course (series)
C 3.205/4:
(Census Bureau)

146-F-1   International Research Documents (numbered)
C 3.205/6:
(Census Bureau)

146-K   United States Maps, GE-50 (series)
C 3.62/4:
(Census Bureau)

Urban Atlas, tract data for Standard Metropolitan Statistical Areas, GE 80 series
C 3.62/7:
(Census Bureau)

United States Maps, GE 70 Series (numbered)
C 3.62/8:
(Census Bureau)

146-L   Governmental Finances and Employment at a Glance
C 3.191/3:
(Census Bureau)

147-A-1   Economic Censuses of Outlying Areas OAC (series)
C 3.253/2:
(Census Bureau)

147-B   Current Business Reports:
-Monthly Retail Trade
C 3.138/3
(Census Bureau)
-Annual Retail Trade
C 3.138/3-2:
(Census Bureau)
-Advance Monthly Retail Sales
C 3.138/4:
(Census Bureau)
-Weekly Retail Sates
C 3.138/5:
(Census Bureau)
-Monthly Retail Sales
C 3.138/3-3:
(Census Bureau)

147-C   Current Business Reports:
Monthly Wholesale Trade
C 3.133:
(Census Bureau)
Monthly Wholesale Trade, Sales and Inventories
C 3.133/2:
(Census Bureau)

Item Number

Wholesale Trade, Annual Sales and Year-End Inventories of Merchant Wholesalers
C 3.133/3:
(Census Bureau)

148 U.S. Foreign Trade Schedules
C 3.150:
(Census Bureau)

148-A Census of Governments
C 3.145/4:
(Census Bureau)
Government Employment, GE (series)
C 3.140/2:
(Census Bureau)
State & Local Government Special Studies
C 3.145:
(Census Bureau)
Preliminary Reports
C 3.145/5:
(Census Bureau)

148-B Current Business Reports:
Monthly Department Store Sales in Selected Areas BD (series)
C 3.211/5:
(Census Bureau)

148-C Data User News (monthly)
C 3.238:
Census Update, Supplement To Data User News
C 3.238/3:
Summary Tape Processing Centers and State Data Centers Address List
C 3.238/4:

148-D Boundary and Annexation Survey
C 3.260:
(Census Bureau)

148-E Finances of Selected Public Employee Retirement Systems, Government Quarterly Report, GR (series)
C 3.242:
(Census Bureau)

148-A Census of Government : State & Local Government Special Studies

Item Number

C 3.145:
(Census Bureau)

148-F Directory of Data Files
C 3.262:
(Census Bureau)

148-G Retail Sales and Inventories of Fuel Oil (monthly)
C 3.263:
(Census Bureau)
Wholesale Fuel Oil Distributors (monthly)
C 3.263/2:
(Census Bureau)
Inventories and Sales of Fuel Oil and Motor Gasoline: Wholesale Distributors, SBR-2 (series) (monthly)
C 3.263/3:
(Census Bureau)

150 Statistical Abstracts of U.S. (annual)
C 3.134:
(Census Bureau)

150-A Pocket Data Book
C 3.134/3:
(Census Bureau)

151 Statistical Abstracts of U.S. Supplement
C 3.134/2:
(Census Bureau)

151-A Technical Papers
C 3.212:
(Census Bureau)

151-B Working Papers (numbered)
C 3.214:
(Census Bureau)

151-C Technical Notes (numbered)
C 3.212/2:
(Census Bureau)

152 Census of Agriculture:
Final Volumes (other that area, general and special reports)
C 3.31/12:
(Census Bureau)
Special Reports
C 3.31/5:
(Census Bureau)

152-A to Census of Agriculture

Item Number

C 55.25:
(National Oceanic and At-
mospheric Adminstration)

108-B-10 Collected Reprints:
Atlantic Oceanograhic and
Meteorological Laboratories
C 55.612:
(Environmental Research
Laboratories)
Wave Propagation Laboratory
C 55.612/2:
(Environmental Research
Laboaratories)
Atmospheric Physics and Chemis-
try Laboratory
C 55.612/3:
(Environmental Research
Laboratories)

208-C-1 NOAA Technical Reports: EDIS
(series)
C 55.13:
(National Oceanic and At-
mospheric Administration)
NOAA Technical Memoran-
dums: EDIS (series)
C 55.13/2:
(National Oceanic and At-
mospheric Administration)

208-C-2 NOAA Technical Reports ERL
(series)
C 55.13:
(National Oceanic and At-
mospheric Administration)
NOAA Technical Memoran-
dums: ERL (series)
C 55.13/2:
(National Oceanic and At-
mospheric Administration)

208-C-3 NOAA Technical Reports:
NESS (series)
C 55.13:
(National Oceanic and At-
mospheric Administration)
NOAA Technical Memoran-
dums: NESS (series)
C 55.13/2:
(National Oceanic and At-
mospheric Administration)

208-C-4 NOAA Technical Reports:
NMFS (series)
C 55.13:

Item Number

(National Oceanic and At-
mospheric Administration)
NOAA Technical Memoran-
dums: NMFS (series)
C 55.13/2:
(National Oceanic and At-
mospheric Administration)

208-C-5 NOAA Technical Reports:
NOS (series)
C 55.13:
(National Oceanic and At-
mospheric Administration)
NOAA Technical Memoran-
dums: NOS (series)
C 55.13/2:
(National Oceanic and At-
mospheric Administration)

208-C-6 NOAA Technical Reports:
NSW (series)
C 55.13:
(National Oceanic and At-
mospheric Administration
NOAA Technical Memoran-
dums: NWS (series)
C 55.13/2:
(National Oceanic and At-
mospheric Administration)

208-C-7 Environmental Assessment of the
Alaskan Continental Shelf,
Principal Investigators
Reports
C 55.622:
(Environmental Research
Laboratory)
Environmental Assessment of the
Alaskan Continental Shelf,
Annual Reports of Principal
Investigators (Microfiche
Reduction Ratio 24x)
C 55.622/2:
(Environmental Research
Laboratory)
Environmental Assessment of the
Alaskan Continental Shelf,
Annual Reports of Principal
Investigators (Microfiche)
Reduction Ratio 24x)
C 55.622/2:
(Environmental Research
Laboratory)
Environmental Assessment of the

Item Number

Alaskan Continental Shelf
(various publications)
C 55.622/3:
(Environmental Research
Laboratory)

208-C-8 NOAA Technical Report OEE
(series)
C 55.13:
(National Oceanic and At-
mospheric Administration)

208-D BAO Reports (numbered)
C 55.623:
(Environmental Research
Laboratories)

211 Export Administration Regu-
lations
C 61.23:
(International Trade
Administration)

212 Export Control Bulletin Sup-
plement to Export Control
Regulations
C 61.23/2:
(International Trade
Administration)

212-A-1 General Publications
C 57.402:
(East-West Trade Bureau)

212-A-2 Market Assessments for (various
countries)
C 57.412:
(East-West Trade Bureau)

212-A-3 Handbooks, Manuals, Guides
C 57.408:
(East-West Trade Bureau)

215 General Publications
C 62.2:
(Industrial Economics Bureau)

215-D Confectionary Manufacturers'
Sales Distribution (annual)
C 57.13:
(Industry and Trade Admin-
istration)

215-G Handbooks, Manuals, Guides
C 57.508:
(Domestic Commerce Bureau)

215-H Printing and Publishing, Quar-
terly Industry Report
C 62.9:
Industrial Economics Bureau)

Item Number

215-L U.S. Industrial Outlook
C 57.18:
(Industry and Trade Admin-
istration)
U.S. Industrial Outlook
C 62.17:
(Industrial Economics Bureau)

215-L-2 Fire Technology Abstracts
(bi-monthly)
FEM 1.109:
(U.S. Fire Administration)

215-L-3 Catalog of Grants, Contracts,
and Interagency Transfers
(annual)
C 58.12:
(U.S. Fire Administration)

215-L-4 Resource Exchange Bulletin
(irregular)
FEM 1.110;
(U.S. Fire Administration)
Arson Resource Bulletin
(irregular)
FEM 1.110/2:
U.S. Fire Administration)

215-L-5 Fully Involved (biweekly)
FEM 1.111:
(U.S. Fire Administration)
Fully Involved (special issues)
FEM 1.111/2:
(U.S. Fire Administration)

215-Q World Motor Vehicle and Trailer
Production and Registration
C 57.21:
(Industry and Trade Admin-
istration)

215-U U.S. Lumber Exports, (annual)
C 57.24:
(Industry and Trade Admin-
istration)

216-A-1 General Publications
FEM 1.109:
(U.S. Fire Administration)

216-A-2 Fire in the United States, Deaths,
Injuries, Dollar Loss, and
Incidents at the National,
States, Local Levels (annual)
C 58.13:
(U.S. Fire Administration)

216-A-3 Handbooks, Manuals, Guides
FEM 1.108:

Item Number			*Item Number*	

Item Number		Item Number	
	(U.S. Fire Administration)		Report
216-A-4	Disaster Information (irregular)		C 62.12:
	FEM 1.9:		(Industrial Economics
	(Federal Emergency Agency)		Bureau)
216-A-5	Annual Report	223	Forest Products Review
	FEM 1.1:		(quarterly)
	(Federal Emergency Manage-		C 62.11:
	ment Agency)		(Domestic Commerce Bureau)
	General Publications	227-B	Manufactures' Shipments,
	FEM 1.2:		Inventories and Orders, M 3
	(Federal Emergency Manage-		C 3.231:
	ment Agency)		(Census Bureau)
216-A-6	Telephone Directory	228	Survey of Current Business
	FEM 1.14:		(monthly)
	(Federal Emergency Manage-		C 59.11:
	ment Agency)		(Economic Analysis Bureau)
216-A-8	Annual Report		Business Statistics, Biennial
	FEM 1.1:		Supplement to Survey of Cur-
	(Federal Emergency Manage-		rent Business
	ment Agency)		C 59.11/3:
216-A-9	Addresses		(Economic Analysis Bureau)
	FEM 1.15:		Supplement (special to Survey of
	(Federal Emergency Manage-		Current Business)
	ment Agency)		C 59.11/4:
216-A-10	Emergency Management		(Economic Analysis Bureau)
	(quarterly)	229	Weekly Business Statistics
	FEM 1.16:		C 59.11/2:
	(Federal Emergency Manage-		(Economic Analysis Bureau)
	ment Agency)	231-A	General Publications
219	Construction Review (monthly)		C 57.109:
	C 62.10:		(Export Development Bureau)
	(Industrial Economics Bureau)	231-B	Overseas Business Reports
219-B	Consumer Goods Research		C 61.12:
	C 57.118:		(Industry and Trade Admin-
	(Export Development Bureau)		istration)
219-C	Commercial News USA	231-B-1	General Publications
	(bimonthly)		C 61.2:
	C 61.10:		(International Trade Admin-
	(International Trade Admin-		istration)
	istration)	231-B-2	Overseas Export Promotion
	Commercial News USA: New		Calendar
	Products Annual Directory		C 61.19:
	C 61.102:		(International Trade Admin-
	(International Trade Admin-		istration)
	istration)	231-B-3	Bibliographies and Lists of
220-A	Copper Industry Report		Publications
	(annual)		C 61.15:
	C 57.512/2:		(Industry and Trade Admin-
	(Domestic Commerce Bureau)		istration)
	Copper Quarterly Industry	231-B-4	Franchise Opportunities

Item Number

(National Bureau of
Standards)

247-A-1 Letter Circulars (numbered)
C 13.16:
(National Bureau of
Standards)

247-B NBS Consumer Information
Series (numbered)
C 13.53:
(National Bureau of
Standards)

247-C Model Weights and Measures
Ordinance, Provisions as
Adopted by National Con-
ference on Weights and
Measures
C 13.55:
(National Bureau of
Standards)

Model State Regulations (on
various subjects)
C 13.55/3:
(National Bureau of
Standards)

247-D NBSIR (series)
C 13.58:
(National Bureau of
Standards)

247-G NBS Time & Frequency Broad-
cast Services
C 13.60:
(National Bureau of
Standards)

247-H NBS-GCR Grantee-Contractor
Report (series)
C 13.57/2:
(National Bureau of
Standards)

248-B National Standard Reference
Data Series, NSRDS-NBS
C 13.48:
(National Bureau of
Standards)

248-D Federal Information Processing
Standards Publication Series
(numbered)
C 13.52:
(National Bureau of
Standards)

249-A Technical Notes (numbered)

Item Number

C 13.46:
(National Bureau of
Standards)

250 Dimensions, NBA
C 13.13:
(National Bureau of
Standards)

250-E Federal Coordinator for Meteorological Services and Supporting Research FCM (series)
C 55.10:

250-E-1 NOAA (bimonthly)
C 55:14:
(National Oceanic and At-
mospheric Administration)

250-E-2 General Publications
C 55.2:
(National Oceanic and At-
mospheric Administration)

250-E-3 NOAA Program Plans,
(numbered)
C 55.15:
(National Oceanic and At-
mospheric)

250-E-4 Federal Plan for Marine En-
vironmental Prediction,
Fiscal Year
C 55.16:
(National Oceanic and At-
mospheric Administration)

250-E-6 Regulations, Rules, Instructions
C 55.6:
(National Oceanic and At-
mospheric Administration)

250-E-7 NOAa Photoessays (numbered)
C 55.19:
(National Oceanic and At-
mospheric Administration)

250-E-8 Natural Disaster Survey Reports
(numbered)
C 55.20:
(National Oceanic and At-
mospheric Administration)

250-E-9 Atlases
C 55.22:
(National Oceanic and At-
mospheric Administration)

250-E-10 International Field Year for the
Great Lakes: IFYGL Bulletin
C 55.21:

Item Number

(National Oceanic and Atmospheric Administration)
250-E-11 Bibliographies and Lists of Publications
C 55.26:
(National Oceanic and Atmospheric Administration)
250-E-12 Manned Underseas Science and Technology Program, Fiscal Year Reports
C 55.29:
(National Oceanic and Atmospheric Administration)
250-E-13 Report to the Congress on Ocean Dumping Research (annual)
C 55.31:
(National Oceanic and Atmospheric Administration)
Report to Congress on Ocean Pollution, Overfishing and Offshore Developments
C 55.31/2:
(National Oceanic and Atmospheric Administration)
250-E-14 State Coastal Zone Management Activities (annual)
C 55.32/3:
(National Oceanic and Atmospheric Administration)
Coastal Zone Management: Annual Report
C 55.32:
(National Oceanic and Atmospheric Administration)
250-E-15 Handbooks, Manuals, Guides
C 55.8:
(National Oceanic and Atmospheric Administration)
NOAA Manuals
C 55.8/3:
(National Oceanic and Atmospheric Administration)
250-E-17 International Field Year for the Great Lakes: Technical Manual Series
C 55.21/4:
(National Oceanic and Atmospheric Administration)
250-E-18 Draft Environmental Impact Statements

Item Number

C 55.34:
(National Oceanic and Atmospheric Administration)
250-E-19 NOAA Dumpsite Evaluation Reports (numbered)
C 55.35:
(National Oceanic and Atmospheric Administration)
250-E-20 Coastal Zone Management: Technical Assistance) Documents
C 55.32/2:
(National Oceanic and Atmospheric Administration)
250-E-21 Sea Grant (biennial)
C 55.38:
(National Oceanic and Atmospheric Administration)
250-E-22 Office of Coastal Zone Management: Management Plans
C 55.32/6:
(National Oceanic and Atmospheric Administration)
250-E-23 Aquatic Sciences and Fisheries Information System: AFSIS Reference Series
C 55.39:
(National Oceanic and Atmospheric Administration)
250-E-24 Universities and their Relations with the National Oceanic and Atmospheric Administration (annual)
C 55.40:
(National Oceanic and Atmospheric Administration)
250-E-25 NOAA Data Reports
C 55.36:
(National Oceanic and Atmospheric Administration)
250-F Maps
C 55.22/2:
(National Oceanic and Atmospheric Administration)
250-P-1 Personnel Research and Development Center Personnel Reports (numbered)
PM 1.43:
(Personnel Management Office)

Item Number

(Personnel Management Office)

290-Q Issues in State and Local Governments Labor Management Relations (irregular)
CS 1.80/2:
(Civil Service Commission)

290-R Fiscal Year (report)
CS 1.71/5:
(Civil Service Commission)

291 Position Classification Standards (Irregular)
CS 1.39:
(Civil Service Commission)

291-C Spotlight (bimonthly)
PM 1.18:
(Personnel Management Office)

291-D Interagency Training Calendar of Courses (quarterly)
PM 1.19/2:
(Personnel Management Office)

291-E Technical Memorandums (numbered)
CS 171/4:
(Civil Service Commission)

291-F Personnel Management Training Center, Course Catalogue
CS 1.65/10:

291-G Catalogs of Training Courses, (various subjects)
PM 1.19/4:
(Personnel Management Office)

292 Announcement of Examinations
PM 1.21/2:
(Personnel Management Office)
Current Federal Exam Announcements (bimonthly)
PM 1.21:
(Personnel Management Office)

292-A Presidential Management Intern Program, IP Series (numbered)
PM 1.36:
(Personnel Management Office)

Item Number

292-A-1 Exemplary Practices in Federal Productivity
PM 1.37:
(Personnel Management Office)

292-A-2 Productivity Research Program, Fiscal Year
PM 1.38:
(Personnel Management Office)

293-A Federal Facts (numbered)
PM 1.25:
(Personnel Management Office)

293-B Federal News Clip Sheet (monthly)
PM 1.12:
(Personnel Management Office)

293-D Federal Labor-Management Consultant (biweekly)
PM 1.13:
(Personnel Management Office)

293-D-1 Index of Federal Labor Relations Cases
PM 1.39:
(Personnel Management Office)

293-E Monthly Release, Federal Civilian Workforce Statistics
PM 1.15:
(Personnel Management Office)

294 Federal Personnel Manual: Transmittal Sheets
PM 1.14:
(Personnel Management Office)
Bulls, Inst. & Letters
PM 1.14/2:
(Personnel Management Office)
Supplements
PM 1.14/3:
(Personnel Management Office)

295 General Publications
MS 1.2:
(Merit Systems Protection Board)

Appendix D

Faculty Questionnaire

USE AND NON-USE OF GOVERNMENT PUBLICATIONS
BACKGROUND INFORMATION

1. Select, from among the following categories, the areas of specialty reflected in your teaching.

a. comparative economic systems____
b. demography____
c. econometrics and statistics____
d. economic theory____
e. history____
f. industrial organization____
g. international economics____

h. labor and human resource development____
i. planning____
j. public finance____
k. public utility____
l. urban economics____
m. other (please specify)
_____

2. Do you use publications of: (check as many options as apply)[1]

a. federal government____
b. state government____
c. municipal government____
d. foreign governments____

e. United Nations and other international agencies____
f. do not use government publications____

3. If you use government publications, is it for: (check as many options as apply)

a. teaching____
b. research or scholarly writing____
c. consulting____

d. recreational reading material____
e. other (please specify)
_____

LIBRARY USE

4. Estimate how many times you used the resources at the college or university library last year.

a. more than 50___
b. 31-50___
c. 26-30___
d. 21-25___
e. 16-20___

f. 11-15___
g. 6-10___
h. 1-5___
i. 0___

5. Estimate how many times last year you used U.S. government publications located in the college or university library.

a. more than 50___
b. 31-50___
c. 26-30___
d. 21-25___
e. 16-20___

f. 11-15___
g. 6-10___
h. 1-5___
i. 0___

6. If you answered "h" or "i" to question 5, please indicate why your use is infrequent. Check as many as apply. (If you responded to the other items, move to the next question.)

a. government publishes little or nothing of value in my particular field___
b. unaware of the existence of such materials at the library___
c. unfamiliar with arrangement of the government publications collection___
d. obtain personal copies of government publications___
e. do not need government publications on a regular basis___
f. the amount of time expended in trying to find relevant information in government publications is out of proportion to what I find___
g. the library staff members provide minimal assistance in use of government publications___
h. government publications provide more detailed information than I need___
i. rely on secretary, student or research assistants to gather any needed government publications___
j. the desired government publication is available in the library only on microform___
k. government publications on microform are separated from the rest of the government publications collection___
l. was not a member of this faculty last year___
m. other (please specify)_____

IF GOVERNMENT PUBLICATIONS ARE NOT USED AT ALL,
PLEASE STOP; OTHERWISE COMPLETE THE REST OF THE
QUESTIONNAIRE

UNITED STATES GOVERNMENT

7. Do you consult government publications in your field to obtain:
(check as many options as apply)

a. current events and issues of interest＿＿
b. general interest reading＿＿
c. grant information＿＿
d. information of historical value＿＿
e. legal material＿＿
f. research and technical reports＿＿
g. resources that may be of value to students＿＿
h. statistical data＿＿
i. other (please specify)

8. Indicate the type(s) of government publications you are most likely
to use. (check as many options as apply)

a. annual reports＿＿
b. bibliographies or lists of
   publications＿＿
c. bills and resolutions＿＿
d. committee and commission
   reports＿＿
e. decisions and opinions (e.g.,
   from the Supreme Court)＿＿
f. directories＿＿
g. films and other audio-visual aids＿＿
h. general information pamphlets＿＿
i. hearings＿＿
j. journals and proceedings (e.g.,
   Congressional Record)＿＿
k. laws and statutes＿＿
l. periodicals＿＿
m. press releases and newsletters＿＿
n. reports of investigation and
   research＿＿
o. rules and regulations＿＿

p. statistical reports (e.g., census publications)——
q. treaty texts——
r. other (please specify)

_____

s. no pattern; use varies——

9. Indicate which title(s) you are most likely to use. (check as many options as apply)

a. Business Conditions Digest——
b. Code of Federal Regulations——
c. Consumer Price Index (CPI Detailed Report)——
d. County and City Data Book——
e. Current Population Reports——
f. Economic Indicators——
g. Economic Report of the President——
h. Employment & Earnings——
i. Federal Register——
j. Federal Reserve Bulletin——
k. Historical Statistics of the United States: Colonial Times to 1970——
l. Monthly Labor Review——
m. Statistical Abstract of the United States——
n. Survey of Current Business——
o. Treasury Bulletin——
p. Other (please specify)

_____

10. Please check those government departments, agencies, and bodies which you are most likely to consult.

AGRICULTURE DEPARTMENT——
Forest Service——
Soil Conservation Service——
Federal Crop Insurance Corporation——
Foreign Agricultural Service——
Rural Electrification Administration——
Agricultural Research Service——
Agricultural Statilization and Conservation Service——
Commodity Credit Corporation——
Farmers Home Administration——
Agricultural Marketing Service——
Farmer Cooperative Service——
Statistical Reporting Service——

Economic Research Service——
Rural Development Service——
Federal Grain Inspection Service——
Economics, Statistics, and Cooperatives Service——
Other (please specify)——

_____

ACTION——

ARMS CONTROL AND DISARMAMENT AGENCY——

COMMERCE DEPARTMENT——
Census Bureau——
National Bureau of Standards——
Patent and Trademark Office——

Civil Aeronautics Board———
Maritime Administration———
Economic Development
  Administration———
National Technical Information
  Service———
Environmental Data and
  Information Service———
Industry and Trade
  Administration———
Export Development Bureau———
Resources and Trade
  Assistance Bureau———
East-West Trade Bureau———
Domestic Commerce Bureau———
Economic Analysis Bureau———
International Trade
  Administration———
Industrial Economics
  Bureau———
Other (please specify)———
————————————

CIVIL AERONAUTICS BOARD———

FEDERAL COMMUNICATIONS
COMMISSION———

CIVIL RIGHTS COMMISSION———

CIVIL SERVICE COMMISSION———

COMMUNITY SERVICES
ADMINISTRATION———

DEFENSE DEPARTMENT———
Defense Intelligence
  Agency———
Defense Mapping Agency———
Defense Logistics Agency———
Defense Documentation
  Center———
Army Department———
Navy Department———
Marine Corps———
Air Force Department———
Other (please specify)
————————————

ENERGY DEPARTMENT———
Federal Energy Regulatory
  Commission———
Energy Information
  Administration———
Economic Regulatory
  Administration———
Other (please specify)
————————————

EDUCATION DEPARTMENT———

ENVIRONMENTAL PROTEC-
TION AGENCY———

FARM CREDIT
ADMINISTRATION———

FEDERAL EMERGENCY
MANAGEMENT AGENCY———

FEDERAL HOME LOAN BANK
BOARD———

FEDERAL MEDIATION AND
CONCILIATION SERVICE———

FEDERAL MARITIME
COMMISSION———

FEDERAL POWER COMMISSION———

FEDERAL RESERVE SYSTEM
BOARD OF GOVERNORS———

FEDERAL TRADE COMMISSION———

FOREIGN-TRADE ZONES
BOARD———

GENERAL SERVICES
ADMINISTRATION———
National Archives and Records
  Service———
Federal Register Office———
Consumer Information Center———
Other (please specify)———
————————————

HEALTH AND HUMAN
SERVICES DEPARTMENT———
Aging Administration———
Youth Development Office———

Child Development Office____
Children's Bureau____
Consumer Affairs Office____
Social Security Administration____
Assistance Payments
  Administration____
National Center for Social
  Statistics____
Education Division____
Education Office____
National Institute of
  Education____
National Center for
  Education Statistics____
Public Health Service____
National Institutes of
  Health____
National Library of
  Medicine____
National Institute on
  Aging____
Food and Drug
  Administration____
Health Services
  Administration____
Health Resources
  Administration____
National Center for
  Health Statistics____
National Center for
  Health Services
  Research____
Center for Disease
  Control____
National Institute of
  Mental Health____
National Institute on
  Drug Abuse____
National Institute on
  Alcohol Abuse and
  Alcoholism____
Health Care Financing
  Administration____
Medicaid Bureau____
Public Services
  Administration____
National Clearinghouse
  on Aging____

Other (please specify)
_____

HOUSING AND URBAN DEVEL
OPMENT DEPARTMENT____
Federal Housing
  Administration____
Federal National Mortgage
  Association____
Federal Insurance
  Administration____
New Communities Administration____
Federal Disaster Assistance
  Administration____
Other (please specify)_____

INTERIOR DEPARTMENT____
Geological Survey____
Mines Bureau____
National Park Service____
Land Management Bureau____
Outdoor Recreation Bureau____
Other (please specify)_____

INTERSTATE COMMERCE
COMMISSION____

INTERNATIONAL COMMUNI-
CATION AGENCY____

JUSTICE DEPARTMENT____
Federal Bureau of Investigation____
Immigration and Naturalization
  Service____
Drug Enforcement
  Administration____
Law Enforcement Assistance
  Administration____
National Institute of Justice____
Other (please specify)_____

JUDICIARY____
Court of Claims____
Supreme Court____
Administrative Office of U.S.
  Courts____
Tax Court____
Other (please specify)_____

LABOR DEPARTMENT____
Labor Statistics Bureau____

Veterans' Reemployment Rights
Office____
Employees Compensation
Appeals Board____
International Labor Affairs
Bureau____
Occupational Safety and Health
Administration____
Employment Standards
Administration____
Women's Bureau____
Wage and Hour Division____
Worker's Compensation
Programs Office____
Employment and Training
Administration____
Unemployment Insurance
Service____
United States Employment
Service____
Mine Safety and Health
Administration____
Other (please specify)
_____

LIBRARY OF CONGRESS____
Copyright Office____
Congressional Research
Service____
Other (please specify)
_____

NATIONAL LABOR RELATIONS
BOARD____

NATIONAL ACADEMY OF
SCIENCES____

NATIONAL AERONAUTICS AND
SPACE ADMINISTRATION____

NATIONAL CREDIT UNION
ADMINISTRATION____

NATIONAL FOUNDATION ON
THE ARTS AND
THE HUMANITIES____

NATIONAL MEDIATION
BOARD____

NATIONAL SCIENCE
FOUNDATION____

OVERSEAS PRIVATE
INVESTMENT
CORPORATION____

UNITED STATES POSTAL
SERVICE____

PERSONNEL MANAGEMENT
OFFICE____

PRESIDENT OF THE UNITED
STATES____

EXECUTIVE OFFICE OF THE
PRESIDENT____
Management and Budget
Office____
Central Intelligence
Agency____
Economic Advisors Council____
Foreign Broadcast Information
Service____
Office of Special Representative
for Trade Negotiations____
Council on Environmental
Quality____
Domestic Council____
Council on Wage and Price
Stability____
Other (please specify)____

RAILROAD RETIREMENT
BOARD____

STATE DEPARTMENT____
Agency for International
Development____
Other (please specify)____

SMALL BUSINESS
ADMINISTRATION____

SECURITIES AND EXCHANGE
COMMISSION____

SMITHSONIAN INSTITUTION____

TREASURY DEPARTMENT____
Internal Revenue Service____

Public Debt Bureau——
Savings Bonds Division——
Alcohol, Tobacco and Firearms
  Bureau——
Other (please specify)————

INTERNATIONAL TRADE
COMMISSION——

TRANSPORTATION
DEPARTMENT——
National Transportation Safety
  Board——
Federal Highway Administration——
Motor Carrier Safety Bureau——
Federal Railroad
  Administration——
Federal Aviation
  Administration——
Civil Aviation Security Service——
Urban Mass Transportation
  Administration——
National Highway Traffic Safety
  Administration——
Other (please specify)————

VETERANS ADMINISTRATION——

CONGRESS——
Advisory Council on
  Social Security——
Advisory Commission on
  Intergovernmental
  Relations——
Commodity Futures Trading
  Commission——
National Advisory Council
  on Economic
  Opportunity——
Equal Employment
  Opportunity Commission——
Export-Import Bank of
  United States——
Federal Labor Relations
  Authority——
Foreign Claims Settlement
  Commission——
General Accounting Office——
Government Printing Office——

National Advisory Council
  on International Monetary
  and Financial Policies——
Nuclear Regulatory
  Commission——
Federal Paperwork
  Commission——
Pension Benefit Guaranty
  Corporation——
East-West Foreign Trade
  Board——
Congressional Budget
  Office——
Other (please specify)———— ————

  Committees:
Agriculture (House)——
Agriculture (Senate)——
Appropriations (House)——
Appropriations (Senate)——
Armed Services (House)——
Armed Services (Senate)——
Banking... (House)——
Banking... (Senate)——
Budget (House)——
Budget (Senate)——
Commerce, Science and
  Transportation
  (Senate)——
Finance (Senate)——
Governmental Affairs (Senate)——
Interstate and Foreign Com-
  merce (House)——
Judiciary (House)——
Judiciary (Senate)——
Labor and Human Resources
  (Senate)——
Post Office and Civil Service
  (House)——
Public Works and Transportation
  (House)——
Small Business (House)——
Ways and Means (House)——
Joint Economic Committee——
Joint Committee on Taxation——
Energy and Natural Resources
  Committee (Senate)——

Select Committee on Congressional Operations (House)——
Select Committee on Small Business (Senate)——
Other (please specify)——————

OTHER (PLEASE SPECIFY)——

———————————

11. Generally how old are the government publications you most frequently consult? (mark only *one* response)

    a. less than a year old——
    b. 1-3 years old——
    c. 4-5 years old——
    d. 6-10 years old——
    e. over ten years old——
    f. no set pattern; age varies——

12. Are you currently engaged in, or have you recently completed within
the past year, a scholarly activity intended for publication, which
cites a government publication(s) in the bibliography or footnotes?

    a. yes——
    b. no——

13. If you answered "yes" to the preceding question and if the government publication(s) was not specified in your answer to question 9,
please supply the complete citation.

PLEASE RETURN COMPLETED QUESTIONNAIRE TO:

Peter Hernon
Graduate School of Library and
Information Science
Simmons College
300 The Fenway
Boston, Massachusetts 02115

NOTE

1. A government publication means informational matter that has been published as an
individual document at government expense, or as required by law. For example, it
could be published by the U.S. Government Printing Office, National Technical Information Service, Congress, or an agency.

Government Bodies Consulted by Highest Degree Offered

	Highest Degree Offered			
Government Bodies	Baccalaureate (Number)	Master's (Number)	Doctorate (Number)	Total
Department of Agriculture	3	15	26	44
Arms Control and Disarmament Agency	—	2	4	6
Department of Commerce	10	33	63	106
Civil Aeronautics Board	—	3	3	6
Federal Communications Commission	—	—	7	7
Civil Rights Commission	—	—	1	1
Community Services Administration	—	—	1	1
Department of Defense	—	3	2	5
Department of Energy	—	9	17	26

	Highest Degree Offered			
Government Bodies	*Baccalaureate* *(Number)*	*Master's* *(Number)*	*Doctorate* *(Number)*	*Total*
Department of Education	—	3	3	6
Environmental Protection Agency	—	2	13	15
Farm Credit Administration	—	1	1	2
Federal Home Loan Bank Board	—	2	7	9
Federal Mediation and Conciliation Service	1	—	1	2
Federal Maritime Commission	—	1	2	3
Federal Power Commission	—	5	6	11
Federal Reserve System Board of Governors	8	24	41	73
Federal Trade Commission	3	11	13	27
Foreign-Trade Zones Board	—	1	1	2
General Services Administration	—	1	7	8
Department of Health and Human Services	2	14	22	38
Department of Housing and Human Development	—	5	9	14
Department of the Interior	—	7	11	18

	Highest Degree Offered			
Government Bodies	*Baccalaureate (Number)*	*Master's (Number)*	*Doctorate (Number)*	*Total*
Interstate Commerce Commission	—	6	13	19
International Communication Agency	—	2	1	3
Department of Justice	—	6	6	12
Judiciary	—	4	9	13
Department of Labor	6	26	45	77
Library of Congress	—	2	10	12
National Labor Relations Board	2	4	6	12
National Academy of of Sciences	1	4	7	12
National Aeronautics and Space Administration	—	1	1	2
National Credit Union Administration	—	—	3	3
National Foundation on the Arts and the Humanities	—	1	1	2
National Mediation Board	—	—	2	2
National Science Foundation	—	2	16	18
Overseas Private Investment Corporation	—	2	2	4
Personnel Management Office	—	—	1	1

	Highest Degree Offered			
Government Bodies	Baccalaureate (Number)	Master's (Number)	Doctorate (Number)	Total
President of the United States	1	2	5	8
Executive Office of the President	2	20	45	67
Department of State	1	8	11	20
Small Business Administration	—	5	5	10
Securities and Exchange Commission	1	4	3	8
Smithsonian Institution	—	—	1	1
Department of Treasury	1	5	13	19
International Trade Commission	1	7	6	14
Department of Transportation	—	4	5	9
Veterans Administration	—	—	1	1
Congress	2	26	46	74
Other	—	—	2	2

Bibliography

Articles

Baughman, James C. (1977), "Toward a Structural Approach to Collection Development," *College and Research Libraries* 38: 241-248.

"Collection Development for Government Publications," *Government Publications Review* 8A (1981), Numbers 1 and 2.

Cuadra, Carlos and Robert V. Katter (1967), "Opening the Black Box of 'Relevance'," *Journal of Documentation* 23: 291-303.

Dobbyn, Margaret (1972), "Approval Plan Purchasing in Perspective," *College and Research Libraries* 33: 480-484.

Fossum, Paul (1931), "Government Documents in Liberal Arts Colleges," *Bulletin of the American Library Association* 25: 581-585.

Fry, Bernard M. (1977), "Government Publications and the Library: Implications for Change," *Government Publications Review* 4: 111-117.

Goehlert, Robert (1979), "A Citation Analysis of International Organization: The Use of Government Documents," *Government Publications Review* 6: 185-193.

Gordon, Catherine C. (1979), "Administrative Reorganization: An Attempt to Control Government Documents in the Library," *Government Publications Review* 6: 241-248.

Hajnal, Peter I. (1981), "Collection Development: United Nations," *Government Publications Review* 8A: 89-109.

Haro, Robert (1967), "Book Selection in Academic Libraries," *College and Research Libraries* 28(March): 104-106.

Hernon, Peter (1980), "Functional Documents Collections," *Microform Review* 9: 209-219.

———(1980), "Use of GPO Bookstores," *Government Publications Review* 7A: 283-299.

———(1976), "State 'Documents to the People'," *Government Publications Review* 3:255-266.

Hernon, Peter and George W. Whitbeck (1977), "Government Publications and Commercial Microform Publishers: A Survey of Federal Depository Libraries," *Microform Review* 6 (September): 272-284.

Lane, David O. (1968), "The Selection of Academic Library Materials: A Literature Survey," *College and Research Libraries* 29(September): 364-372.

Larson, Kathleen T. (1979), "Establishing a New GPO Depository Documents Department in an Academic Law Library," *Law Library Journal* 72 (Summer): 484-496.

Magrill, Rose Mary and ʻMona East (1978), "Collection Development in Large University Libraries." Pp. 2-54 in Michael H. Harris (ed.), *Advances in Librarianship*. New York: Academic Press.

McClure, Charles R. (1977), "Administrative Integration of Microformatted Government Publications: A Framework for Analysis," *Microform Review* 6 (September): 259-271.

——(1978), Indexing U.S. Government Periodicals: Analysis and Implications," *Government Publications Review* 5: 409-421.

——(1978), "Microformatted Government Publications," *Government Publications Review* 5: 511-515.

——(1979), "Microformatted Government Publications: Space and Facilities," *Government Publications Review* 6: 405-412.

——(1981), "An Integrated Approach to Government Publication Collection Development," *Government Publications Review* 8A:5-15.

——(1981), "Online Government Documents Data Base Searching and Use of Microfiche Documents Online by Academic and Public Depository Librarians," *Microform Review* 10(Fall): 245-259.

Morton, Bruce (1980), "Toward a Comprehensive Collection Development Policy for Partial U.S. Depository Libraries," *Government Publications Review* 7A: 41-46.

Newman, Wilda B. and Michlean J. Amir (1978), "Report Literature: Selecting Versus Collecting," *Special Libraries* 69 (November): 415-424.

Osburn, Charles B. (1979), "Some Practical Observations on the Writing, Implementation, and Revision of Collection Development Policy," *Library Resources and Technical Services* 23(Winter): 7-15.

Phillips, Vicki W. and John B., (1981), "Microformatted Government Publications: Selection and Acquisitions," *Government Publications Review* 8A: 127-133.

Purcell, Gary R. (1980), "The Use of Tennessee State Government Publications," *Tennessee Librarian* 32(Spring): 20-31.

"Resolutions Approved by the Depository Library Council to the Public Printer," *Documents to the People* 9 (July 1981): 160-163.

Richardson, John V., Dennis C.W. Frisch, and Catherine M. Hall (1980), "Bibliographic Organization of U.S. Federal Depository Collections," *Government Publications Review* 7A: 463-480.

Rips, Rae Elizabeth (1965), "Reference Use of Government Publications," *Drexel Library Quarterly* 1 (October): 3-18.

Robinson, William C. (1981), "Evaluation of the Government Documents Collection: An Introduction and Overview," *Government Publications Review* 8A: 111-125.

——(1982), "Evaluation of the Government Documents Collection: A Step by Step Process," *Government Publications Review* 9:131-141.

Roper, Fred W. (1974), "Selecting Federal Publications," *Special Libraries* 65 (August): 326-331.

Saracevic, Tefco (1975), "Relevance: A Review of and a Framework for the Thinking on the Notion in Information Science," *Journal of the* American Society for Information Science 26 (November-December): 321-343.

Schlueter, Kay (1978), "Selection of Government Documents in Law School Libraries," *Law Library Journal* 71 (August): 477-480.

Soper, Mary Ellen (1976), "Characteristics and Use of Personal Collections," *The Library Quarterly* 46 (October): 397-415.

Trueswell, Richard W. (1965), "A Quantitative Measure of User Circulation Requirements and Its Possible Effect on Stack Thinning and Multiple Copy Determination," *American Documentation* 16 (January): 20-25.

Weech, Terry L. (1971), "Weeding of U.S. Government Publications in Illinois Depository Libraries," *Illinois Libraries* 53 (June): 394-399.

———(1978), "The Use of Government Publications: A Selected Review of the Literature," *Government Publications Review* 5: 177-184.

Whitbeck, George W., Peter Hernon, and John Richardson Jr. (1978), "The Federal Depository Library System: A Descriptive Analysis," *Government Publications Review* 5: 253-267.

White, Herb (1980), "Library Effectiveness—The Elusive Target," *American Libraries* 11 (December): 282-283.

Books

Berdie, Douglas R. and John F. Anderson (1974), *Questionnaires: Design and Use*. Metuchen, N.J.: Scarecrow.

The Bowker Annual, 1981. New York: Bowker.

Boyd, Anne Morris and Rae Elizabeth Rips (1949), *United States Government Publications*. New York: H.W. Wilson.

Bradford, Samuel C. (1948), *Documentation*. London: Crosby Lockwood.

Buckland, Michael K. (1975), *Book Availability and the Library User*. Elmsford, N.Y.: Pergamon Press.

Crowley, Terence and Thomas Childers (1971), *Information Service in Public Libraries*. Metuchen, N.J.: Scarecrow.

Ellsworth, Ralph (1969), *The Economics of Book Storage in College and Research Libraries*. Washington: Association of Research Libraries.

Evans, G. Edward (1979), *Developing Library Collections*. Littleton, Col.: Libraries Unlimited.

Futas, Elizabeth (1977), *Library Acquisition Policies and Procedures*. Phoenix, Ariz.: Oryx Press.

Gardner, Richard K. (1981), *Library Collections: Their Origin, Selection, and Development*. New York: McGraw-Hill.

Grieder, Ted (1978), *Acquisitions: Where, What, and How: A Guide to Orientation and Procedure for Students in Librarianship, Libraries, and Academic Faculty*. Westport, Conn.: Greenwood Press.

Hernon, Peter (1979), *Use of Government Publications by Social Scientists*. Norwood, N.J.: Ablex Publishing Corp.

———(1981), *Microforms and Government Information*. Westport, Conn.: Microform Review, Inc.

———(1982), *Collection Development and Public Access of Government Information. Proceedings of the First Annual Library and Government Documents Conference*. Westport, Conn.: Meckler Books.

Investigation into Information Requirements of the Social Sciences. Research Report No. 1, Volume 1. Text by Maurice B. Line, Project Head. Bath, England: Bath University of Technology, University Library, May 1971.

Jackson, Ellen P. (1953), *The Administration of the Government Documents Collection*. ACRL Monographs No. 5. Chicago: Publications Committee of the Association of College and Reference Libraries.

Johnson, Richard D. (1977), *Libraries for Teaching, Libraries for Research*. Chicago: American Library Association.

Katz, William A. (1980), *Collection Development: The Selection of Materials for Libraries*. New York: Holt, Rinehart and Winston.

Kent, Allen and Thomas J. Galvin (1977), *Library Resource Sharing*. New York: Marcell Dekker.

Kent, Allen, et. al. (1979), *Use of Library Materials: The University of Pittsburgh Study.* New York: Marcel Dekker.

Lancaster, F.W. (1977), *The Measurement and Evaluation of Library Services.* Washington: Information Resources Press.

Leidy, W. Philip (1976), *A Popular Guide to Government Publications.* New York: Columbia University Press.

Marulli, Luciana (1979), *Documentation of the United Nations System.* Metuchen, N.J.: Scarecrow.

Miller, Kathryn Naomi (1937), *The Selection of United States Serial Documents for Liberal Arts Colleges.* New York: H.W. Wilson.

Nakata, Yuri (1979), *From Press to People.* Chicago: American Library Association.

Newsome, Walter L. (1978), *New Guide to Popular Government Publications.* Littleton, Col.: Libraries Unlimited.

Perkins, David L. (1979), *Guidelines for Collection Development.* Chicago: American Library Association.

Peterson, Richard J. and Geneva C. Davis (1980), *Education Directory, Colleges and Universities 1979-80.* Washington: National Center for Education Statistics.

Slote, Stanley J. (1975), *Weeding Library Collections.* Littleton, Col.: Libraries Unlimited.

Spyers-Duran, Peter and Thomas Mann, Jr. (1980), *Shaping Library Collections for the 1980's.* Phoenix, Ariz.: Oryx Press.

SSCI Journal Citation Reports (Social Sciences Citation Index). 1978-1980 Annual. Volume 6. Philadelphia, Penn.: Institute for Scientific Information.

Stueart, Robert D. and George B. Miller (1980), *Collection Development in Libraries: A Treatise.* Greenwich, Conn.: JAI Press.

Van Zant, Nancy P. (1978), *Selected U.S. Government Series.* Chicago: American Library Association.

Wilson, Louis R. (1940), *The Practice of Book Selection.* Chicago: University of Chicago Press.

Wittig, Alice J. (1979), *Government Publication for the School Media Center.* Littleton, Col.: Libraries Unlimited.

ERIC Publications

Edsall, Shirley, "A Study of the Administration, Utilization and Collection Development Policies of Government Document Collections In Community College Libraries Which Have Been Designated as Depositories." ED 146 954.

Government Publications

Biennal Report of Depository Libraries. October 1979. Washington: GPO.

Fry, Bernard M. (1978), *Government Publications: Their Role in the National Program for Library and Information Services.* Prepared for the National Commission on Libraries and Information Science. Washington: GPO.

Guidelines for the Depository Library System. (As Adopted by the Depository Library Council to the Public Printer). October 18, 1977.

"List of Classes of United States Government Publications Available for Selection by Depository Libraries." Washington, GPO.

"List of Items for Selection by Depository Libraries." July 1981. Washington: GPO.

Potter, Dale R., et. al. (1972), *Questionnaires for Research.* USDA Forest Service Research Paper. Portland, Oreg.: U.S. Department of Agriculture, Forest Service, Pacific Northwest Forest and Range Experiment Station.

U.S. Congress, House (1981), *Legislative Branch Appropriations for 1982*. Hearings before a Subcommittee of the Committee on Appropriations. Part 2. Washington: GPO.

Unpublished Materials

McAninch, Sandra, "Memorandum: Position Paper on Proposed Solutions to the Problems of Regional Depositories for U.S. Government Publications." Unpublished report prepared for the Depository Library Council and dated March 30, 1981.

University of California, Berkeley. General Library. *Report of the Documents Department Study Group*. Prepared by Suzanne Gold, et. al., November 1976.

Author Index

Selective Title Index

Subject Index